INFRASTRUCT RING URBAN FUT ES

The Politics of Remaking Cities

Edited by
Alan Wiig, Kevin Ward, Theresa Enright,
Mike Hodson, Hamil Pearsall and Jonathan Silver

BRISTOL
UNIVERSITY
PRESS

First published in Great Britain in 2023 by

Bristol University Press
University of Bristol
1–9 Old Park Hill
Bristol
BS2 8BB
UK
t: +44 (0)117 374 6645
e: bup-info@bristol.ac.uk

Details of international sales and distribution partners are available at bristoluniversitypress.co.uk

British Library Cataloguing in Publication Data
A catalogue record for this book is available from the British Library

ISBN 978-1-5292-2562-4 paperback
ISBN 978-1-5292-2563-1 ePub
ISBN 978-1-5292-2564-8 OA Pdf

Cover design: Lyn Davies
Front cover image: Stocksy/MEM Studio
Bristol University Press use environmentally responsible print partners.
Printed in Great Britain by CMP, Poole

Contents

List of Figures and Tables

Figures

v

Tables

Notes on Contributors

Jean-Paul Addie is Associate Professor at the Urban Studies Institute of Georgia State University. He is a critical urban geographer working on urban and regional governance, urban political economy and socio-spatial theory, with a specific focus on the politics of infrastructure. He has published widely with recent research on infrastructural regionalism, urban universities, and comparative urban studies appearing in journals including *Cambridge Journal of Regions, Economy and Society*, *CITY*, *Journal of Urban Technology*, *Regional Studies* and *Urban Geography*.

Kafui Attoh is Associate Professor at the CUNY School of Labor and Urban Studies. His research focuses on three areas: (1) urban transit's role within the political economy of cities; (2) the struggles and livelihoods of the transportation disadvantaged and (3) the role of urban social movements in shaping mass transit policy. He has published widely, including in *ACME: An International E-Journal for Critical Geographies*, *Antipode*, *Progress in Human Geography* and *Urban Studies* and his book *Rights in Transit: Public Transportation and the Right to the City in California's East Bay* was published in 2019 (University of Georgia Press).

Patrick Bigger researches how capitalism tries to manage its socioecological contradictions by making nature investable or governable in new ways. He has written on carbon markets, green bonds, for-profit biodiversity conservation and multilateral development bank programmes to explain the operations of state/finance for decarbonization, climate adaptation and landscape restoration. His secondary research programme is on the geopolitical ecology of the US military, melding critical geopolitics with political ecology to explore how US military action operates on and through nature. Formerly based at Lancaster University in the UK, he is currently the Research Director at the Climate and Community Project.

Theresa Enright is Associate Professor in the Department of Political Science at the University of Toronto. Her primary research interests are in the fields of urban and regional studies, critical theory and comparative political economy. Recent publications on global cities, transit-oriented development, megaprojects and urban–suburban relations have appeared in the journals *Environment and Planning A*, *Antipode*, *Urban Geography* and *Cambridge Journal of Regions, Economy and Society*. Her first book, *The Making of Grand Paris: Metropolitan Urbanism in the Twenty-First Century*, was published in 2016 by MIT Press.

Michael Glass is an urbanist who works at the intersection of geography and planning. He primarily researches city-region governance and planning, housing and urban infrastructure, with regional expertize in South-East Asia, North America and Australasia. He is the co-editor of *Performativity, Politics, and the Production of Social Space* (Routledge, 2014) and co-author of *Priced Out: Stuyvesant Town and the Loss of Middle-Class Neighborhoods* (NYU Press, 2016). He is on the editorial boards of the *Journal of Urban Affairs* and *Regional Studies, Regional Science*. Winner of the 2015 Bellet Award for Teaching Excellence, he is Director of the Urban Studies Program, University of Pittsburgh.

Prince Guma is Post-Doctoral Research Associate at the Urban Institute, University of Sheffield. His research work focuses on infrastructural vulnerabilities in the cities of sub-Saharan Africa. His recent work draws on the intersection of science and technology studies, urban studies and postcolonial studies to examine the contingent and place-based articulations of cities, and how these are mediated through the diffusion and uptake of information and communications technology–based plans and infrastructures. His findings are hoped to enhance our understanding of urban, digital and infrastructural possibilities in the Global South and elsewhere.

Mike Hodson is Professor at the University of Manchester, where he is based in the Sustainable Consumption Institute, and formerly Senior Research Fellow at Salford University in the Centre for Sustainable Urban and Regional Futures working on urban and regional governance, urban infrastructure and urban sustainability transitions. His developing research interests are at the interface of systemic transitions and territorial transitions and the ways in which relationships between the two are, are not, and might be organized. As part of this he researches relationships between digital platforms and urban transformation. Mike has published and presented widely.

Andrés Luque-Ayala is Associate Professor in the Department of Geography at Durham University. His research focuses on the politics of urban infrastructures and sociotechnical examination of 'smart' forms of urbanization and the coupling of digital and material infrastructures as a new security apparatus in the city. He has published widely in leading journals and is the co-editor of three recent collections for Routledge on *Rethinking Urban Transitions* (2018), *Energy, Power and Protest on the Urban Grid* (2016) and *Smart Urbanism* (2015).

Nate Millington is Lecturer in the Department of Geography at the University of Manchester. His research is focused on the politics of the urban environment in an era of climate crisis, with particular interests in the governance of water and waste. He has published his work in *Environment and Planning A*, *International Journal of Urban and Regional Research*, *Political Geography* and *Progress in Human Geography*.

Jen Nelles is Senior Research Fellow with the Innovation Caucus and co-director of the Oxford Regions, Innovation, and Enterprise Lab (ORIEL) at Oxford Brookes Business School. She specializes in innovation and productivity policy, urban and metropolitan governance, regional economic development, infrastructure, and system dynamics. Recent books include *Discovering American Regionalism: An Introduction to Regional Intergovernmental Organizations* (Routledge, 2019) and *Mobilizing the Metropolis* (University of Michigan Press, 2023). She is an editor for *Regional Studies, Regional Science*, a co-convenor of the RSA Network on Infrastructural Regionalism and co-director of Project RIGO, a network of scholars studying regional intergovernmental organizations.

Hamil Pearsall is Associate Professor in the Geography and Urban Studies Department at Temple University in Philadelphia, USA. Her research bridges several themes in human-environment and urban geography: the social dimension of sustainability; environmental justice and health; and community resilience to environmental and economic stressors. Her recent work has focused on environmental gentrification, the role of vacant land in urban greening efforts, and the impact of environmental justice on urban sustainability planning. She is currently working on a new project on the future of urban public spaces in Philadelphia, which has been funded by the William Penn Foundation.

Jonathan Rutherford is a senior researcher at LATTS (Laboratoire Techniques, Territoires et Sociétés), at Paris Est University and Ecole des Ponts ParisTech (France). His research focuses on the processes and politics of urban sociotechnical change through a focus on the shifting relations between infrastructure and cities. He has co-edited special issues of *Urban Studies* and *Energy Policy* and the Routledge collection *Beyond the Networked City* (2016) and is the author of *Redeploying Urban Infrastructure: The Politics of Urban Socio-Technical Futures* (Palgrave Macmillan, 2020).

Mimi Sheller is the inaugural Dean of the Global School at Worcester Polytechnic Institute. Her research has focused on various types of mobility, studies of the Caribbean and urban theory. She has published her work in the *Annals of the American Association of Geographers*, *Current Sociology*, *Geoforum* and *Mobilities*. Author and editor of numerous books, including *Mobility Justice: The Politics of Movement in an Age of Extremes* (Verso, 2018) and *Island Futures: Caribbean Survival in the Anthropocene* (Duke, 2020).

Jonathan Silver is Senior Research Fellow at The Urban Institute at the University of Sheffield. His research centres on three themes, first, in thinking about the infrastructural geographies of everyday urbanisms across popular neighbourhoods in Global Norths and Souths; second, in examining the political ecologies of urban infrastructural transformation and third, in considering the urban politics of infrastructure in relation to race and capitalism. Jon has published in many of the major geography and planning journals, including *Environment and Planning A*, *International Journal of Urban and Regional Research*, *Transactions of the Institute of British Geographers* and *Urban Geography*.

Mark Usher is Lecturer in Environmental Geography at the University of Manchester and a member of the Manchester Urban Institute (MUI). Drawing on environmental, political and urban geography, his research explores how urban ecological management, planning and design impacts on collective public life, reconfiguring relations between citizens, the state and the city. His current project is investigating how green infrastructure and natural capital accounting is redefining local environmental governance under conditions of austerity in England. Previously, Mark explored how water infrastructure – reservoirs, canals and desalination – facilitated state-building in Singapore in a literal, physical register.

Kevin Ward is Professor of Human Geography at the University of Manchester, and Editor in Chief at *Urban Geography*. His research interests centre on comparative urbanism, municipal finance, policy mobility studies and urban governance. He is author and editor of 11 books and author of over 80 book chapters and journal articles, including publications in *Antipode*, *Environment and Planning A*, *International Journal of Urban and Regional Research*, *Urban Geography* and *Urban Studies*.

Meredith Whitten is Fellow in Environment in the Department of Geography and Environment at the London School of Economics. Her research focuses on the urban environment, particularly the intricate, evolving and often contested relationship between cities and nature, and how this relationship is mediated through planning to address urban sustainability. Meredith's current project examines how a socio-culturally constructed priority for enclosing green spaces affects implementation of active – or green – travel policies aiming to shift to more physically active and environmentally sustainable modes of transport.

Alan Wiig is Associate Professor in the Department of Urban Planning and Community Development at the University of Massachusetts, Boston. His research critiques the new digital divides emerging alongside smart city projects, the anti-democratic politics of large-scale urban revitalization efforts, and the spatial strategies through which transnational logistics corridors are remaking city-regions. Alan's work has been published in journals including: *Cambridge Journal of Regions, Economy, and Society, City: Analysis of Urban Trends, Theory, Policy, Action, Environment and Planning C, Journal of Urban Technology, Regional Studies* and *Urban Geography*.

Acknowledgements

Editing an academic book is never easy. Doing it during a global pandemic makes a hard task even harder. In 2018 when we secured funding from the Urban Studies Foundation to organize two events over the course of 2019 and 2020, we thought much of the hard work was done. We were wrong. After our first workshop, in Manchester, England in September 2019, the six of us set about organizing its follow-up in Philadelphia for May 2020. While the Manchester workshop was a largely academic affair, comprising plenaries and academic paper sessions, its US successor was to be a more outward-facing event. The focus was on drawing upon the city's policy makers and practitioners to explore the theme of infrastructural futures in the reindustrializing cities of the Global North as experienced by some of those who are involved in the making of these futures. Unfortunately, as the dates for the event neared, so it became clear that life, as we had understood it was changing, and changing quickly. In Canada, the UK and the US, the countries in which we live and work, the emergence of COVID-19 in March 2020 led us initially to postpone the Philadelphia workshop. We continued to envisage a second event until in early 2021 it became apparent that the COVID-19 global pandemic was going to outlast our extension from the Urban Studies Foundation. Instead, we turned towards generating an edited book, drawing in part upon some of those who presented at the Manchester workshop, and in part from among others whose work we drew on in the initial seminar series proposal.

Fast forward to early 2022 and we have an edited book. Like many others over the last two years, we have become accustomed to seeing each other through a computer screen. Meetings were organized across time zones, often connecting us at our homes, as life went on around us. The centrality of Zoom in the production of this book almost makes us inclined to add it as a seventh editor! We have missed the social relations of book editing and writing that has accompanied our previous works. Nevertheless, editing this book has been fun, as it should be, as each of us has drawn upon our own past work on infrastructure and urbanization in contributing to the overall focus of the volume.

To some acknowledgements. We thank the Urban Studies Foundation for funding the seminar and this book's production. A special mention to Joe Shaw, the Foundation's Director of Operations, for his support in administering (and spending) this award. At Bristol University Press, Emily Watt, Senior Commissioning Editor, has been helpful and supportive. Thank you to the reviewers of the book proposal – whoever you are – and we hope you enjoy the volume. To those who presented at the Manchester workshop in September 2019, when the sun shone brightly and we enjoyed face-to-face, in-person debate and interaction, never again shall we take this for granted! Finally, we thank the authors of the chapters, and in particular, of the two afterwords. All involved met the various deadlines along the way (or only missed them by a matter of days), and the result is a volume of which we are proud.

Closer to home, each of us has our own personal debts.

Alan thanks Renee Tapp for her support through the writing and editing of this volume, and he wants to recognize his nieces and nephews, who will dwell in our urban and infrastructural future: Rowan, Isaiah, Samuel, Rosie, Audrina, and Freddie. In memory of Lisa Tapp (1955–2022).

Kevin thanks his family and friends for their continued encouragement and support.

Theresa would like to thank her colleagues and students at the University of Toronto for ongoing conversations about urban infrastructure.

Mike is grateful for the friendship and intellectual environment provided by his colleagues in the Sustainable Consumption Institute over the course of this book project and beyond. He would also like to thank Dan and James for their love and ongoing support.

Hamil thanks her colleagues and students at Temple University and beyond for their commitment to advancing sustainable and equitable infrastructure.

Jonathan would like to thank Uma and Phil for their kind support.

1

Introduction

Alan Wiig, Kevin Ward, Theresa Enright, Mike Hodson,
Hamil Pearsall and Jonathan Silver

Infrastructuring Urban Futures considers the 'lively' (Amin, 2014: 137) relationship between infrastructure and the ongoing production of urban worlds. It traces how infrastructure engages those who call cities their home and the conditions under which they live, and in turn how these subjects make, remake and even un-make something that they and others label 'infrastructure', and the political nature of these bounding, demarcating and labelling acts (Larkin, 2013).

From the ordinary to the extraordinary, all of us experience infrastructure in its various forms over the course of the day, from when we wake to when we go to sleep – and much in between. In some cases, this is the presence of infrastructure – for example, the digital infrastructures that support performing paid work from home, or the transport infrastructure that facilitates the dropping off and collecting of children from school. In other cases, it is the absence of infrastructure that shapes and structures the lives of some who live in cities, for example, blue infrastructure to ensure drinkable water, or libraries as social infrastructure to support the education and learning among a population. Infrastructure shapes lives, and in turn, these lives are shaped by it (Star, 1999; Venkatesan et al, 2018). This edited collection argues that an attention to the pasts, presents and futures of infrastructure allows for an understanding of the current urban condition as it is relationally constituted and experienced in and across cities of the Global North and South. It is the anticipation and prefiguring now about infrastructural futures – and the various temporalities embodied in these acts and practices – that is our focus, building upon and coming after, in a linear sense, infrastructural pasts (Anderson, 2010; Appel et al, 2018). This is an argument given extra urgency in the context of the fragility and uncertainty generated by ongoing and interwoven ecological, political and public health crises facing cities around the world.

Recent years have underscored the role of infrastructure in structuring how cities and their place-based communities are experiencing the climate emergency, housing inequalities, racialized injustices and, most recently, the COVID-19 pandemic, and how these will continue to be experienced in the medium and longer term. And, of course, these are not being experienced evenly. Massive public investments in cutting-edge infrastructures in East Asia demonstrate how far the US and much of the West has fallen behind (Heathcote, 2017). While promises about retrofitting decaying cities in the US are regularly announced, from Kenya to Kazakhstan, entire new cities and high-tech enclaves are being constructed with Chinese finance. When US President Biden promises an electric vehicle revolution in the coming years, China is adding 10,000 new electric buses to its network every month and cities like Shenzhen run entire fleets without petrol. Moreover, growing international investment flows are now circulating from China – as well as other places in Asia and the Middle East – back into the cities of the Global North, seeking capital accumulation opportunities while also restructuring global financial geographies. The downtowns of cities such as Manchester, London, New York, San Francisco and Vancouver have skylines dominated by new real estate developments financed from the East. The US, the UK and many other of the industrialized nations of the Global North are involved in the politics of catch-up. These efforts to catch up infrastructurally are at least in part funded by China, the country that they are seeking to catch. Recognizing this interweaving of infrastructure and urban futures, for example, the European Investment Bank (2022) is restructuring its infrastructural investment portfolio, establishing two streams, one of which is 'sustainable cities and regions'.

It is in this context of some evaporating futures (and some emerging futures), conditioned by decades of geoeconomic and geopolitical reconfigurations that the Global North emerges as a renewed site of infrastructuring. This edited collection makes sense of this politics of catch-up and the remaking of urban infrastructure in the Global North by drawing on concepts of infrastructure emerging from the Global South. This approach reveals the ways that urban infrastructure – and its conceptualization – is ever-shifting. We illustrate how infrastructuring urbanization is a dynamic process produced through complex relationships that are simultaneously reorganized and reconfigured through infrastructure. It is a process that reflects power dynamics, with direct implications for everyday life. In this introductory chapter we present the central ideas of this edited collection, setting the scene for the chapters that follow. We begin with four stories drawn from popular news media about the interrelations between infrastructure and urbanization.

'Toronto launching first pothole repair blitz of the fall on Saturday'

Toronto, on Lake Ontario's north-western shore in Canada, is subject to a long, cold and often snowy winter. Potholes on its roads, caused by patterns of freezing and thawing, are a chronic issue. It is not alone. Many cities around the world are challenged with how to maintain and repair their roads, in the context of increasingly volatile weather. The holes are the scourge of those cycling and driving cars. Each spring and autumn, the city launches a blitz pothole repair scheme (Chong, 2021). In 2021, this saw teams of city government staff spend 12-hour shifts on four separate days repairing holes on expressways and neighbourhood streets. The first three blitzes saw 13,000 holes repaired. These are part of Toronto's wider strategy to proactively seek out and repair potholes, which led to over 95,000 being fixed over the course of 2021. The city government hopes that these relatively minor or ordinary interventions will proactively delay the need for major work. Maintaining Toronto's infrastructural inheritance – and the everyday life of the city – against weather and other forces of decline and breakdown is a constant battle. And Toronto is not alone in this regard, of course. Retrofitting and repairing older infrastructures is a challenge facing governments in many nations of the Global North. Infrastructure is an active dynamic in the modern urban system, as we argue in this edited collection. Those that govern cities today and plan the future of cities often work with infrastructure produced under earlier eras of urbanization. Efforts to support human and non-human lives through the 21st century's planetary challenges will rest on a foundation of infrastructure designed and built to address the needs of 19th and 20th century cities. In this vignette, seeking infrastructural solutions to maintain everyday life demands city governments think creatively and incrementally. It is an issue explored in some of the edited collection's chapters.

'"Connecting Copenhagen" is the world's best smart city project'

Copenhagen has a reputation of being a city ahead of others when it comes to anticipating the infrastructural requirements of future generations. This has tended to centre on the use of grey, hard infrastructure, such as segregated bike lanes, as part of the city's wider strategies to reduce its carbon emissions and promote active, healthy lifestyles of residents. Most recently and like many other cities, Copenhagen has turned towards digital infrastructure to augment or enhance the grey. In 2014, Copenhagen won the World Smart Cities Award for its Copenhagen Connecting plan (Jakobsen, 2014). This used an Internet-of-Things approach, joining up smartphone apps, Global

Positioning Systems (GPS) and environmental sensors to collect and use data in an effort to reduce air pollution. The data – often collected in real time and displayed in dashboard form – is to be used to design and deliver public services in a more energy-efficient manner. Beyond responding to real or perceived needs, this infrastructure is built to shape urban values and lifestyles in years to come. It is about anticipating the infrastructural needs of a particular urban future, which in turn, we might also think about as an infrastructural future (Hetherington, 2017; Coletta and Kitchen, 2017). This point – about infrastructuring urbanization – is one we make across the edited collection. The turn to digital infrastructure in managing urban lives in this way weaves together the existing material organization of urban infrastructure with new digital modes of control and governance, and in so doing, forming new spatialities and temporalities, whether that be working remotely from home or connecting to city government via a smartphone app. This often generates novel forms of infrastructural citizenships, a point highlighted in a number of chapters in this edited collection.

'Grand Paris Express, the largest transport project in Europe'

A renewed interest in public transport as a mode of moving people in and around large metropolitan areas has the potential for integrating long-divided populations. The Grand Paris Express is argued to be the largest project of its kind in Europe (Société du Grand Paris, 2017). Work on it started in 2016 and it will not be complete until the early 2030s. It involves the laying of 200 km of new railway lines, much of it underground, along which will be 68 new stations on four additional lines. The Express will consist of a route around the outskirts of Paris as well as through some of the city's most disadvantaged suburbs. The Express also serves as a material expression of Paris's continued reassertion of its global city status. Governed by the Société du Grand Paris – a 100 per cent state-owned public agency established in 2010 – the Express is being financed by a range of public and private sources, including from central government, various local governments and a range of bond issues through international capital markets. If infrastructural investments of the past have created enduring urban challenges, a new round of innovative, global *grand projects* is being rolled out to overcome them. New governance mechanisms have been proposed as a means of overseeing the production of infrastructure, often embodying new spatialities and temporalities. Such are the infrastructural challenges facing cities of the Global North that recently we have seen new financial vehicles emerge, often involving the establishment of riskier and more speculative funding mechanisms. This has led to new ways of the state involving itself in the work of global financial markets, as evidenced by the example of the Grand Paris Express, and in some of the chapters in this edited collection.

'The Blackest city in the US is facing an environmental justice nightmare'

The US is replete with examples that remind us how decisions over where and where not to introduce infrastructure is a racialized one (Miller, 2018; Fitzgerald and Agyeman, 2021). Perhaps nowhere is this clearer than in Detroit (Costley, 2020). The city continues to face a series of related crises stemming from past infrastructural planning decisions around the location of roads, factories and refineries. Redlining and White flight from the late 1950s onwards segregated this city, and many others. This trend of White flight and suburbanization left Detroit with less funding to support basic urban services and its metropolitan infrastructure. Additionally, those living in Detroit's neighbourhoods with the highest population concentration of African Americans were exposed to dangerously high levels of pollution when compared to those in nearby, majority White suburbs. A particular kind of racialized, infrastructural citizen or subject was produced. As a result, those in Boynton or Oakwood Heights neighbourhoods live 15 years less on average that those living in the more affluent, White neighbourhoods. And as this industrial-era infrastructure disintegrates or is rendered obsolete, what to do with it and the polluted land on which it is built remains a challenge, one to which some locals have risen through a variety of 'bottom up' and incremental interventions. Some residents of Detroit have sought to re-envision their city through do-it-yourself urbanism such as urban agriculture on land that formerly held homes or factories or even roadways, as a way to realize food sovereignty, contribute positive public health outcomes, and reuse land and infrastructure that the city cannot afford to maintain. In this way, infrastructure is generated from the bottom up, here and in other examples in the collection.

What do we get from these four vignettes? Perhaps most obvious is the diversity of ways cities and infrastructure are intertwined, how they have been, how they are and how they will continue to be as expectations, decisions and imaginaries, as projections of the future of infrastructure are made in the present (Appel et al, 2018). The vignettes are a small subset of those we might have told. In them are examples of 'big' and 'small' infrastructure, of 'top-down' and 'bottom-up' infrastructure, of older and newer infrastructure, of digital and hard infrastructure, of networked and territorialized infrastructure, of the role of infrastructure in segmenting and structuring cities, of how infrastructure embodies wider social systems, of the petroleum-centric economy associated with industrialization and the digital economy associated with smart cities, of the public and private partnerships that are governing infrastructure, and of the mechanisms for financing new infrastructure and for retrofitting and repairing existing infrastructure. While some of these developments are relatively recent in cities, some of them have much longer sets of histories. The 'infrastructural turn' witnessed across many local, national and supranational government agencies in the industrialized nations of the Global North, in some cases responding to the recent developments in China and Asia more generally, has given longer-standing debates an extra economic and political urgency.

Whether or not you subscribe to the view that what we are currently witnessing in some parts of the world amounts to a 'global infrastructure arms race' (Heathcote, 2017), it is probably less contentious to claim that we are in the third decade of a century that constitutes both an infrastructural age *and* an urban age (Burdett and Sudjic, 2010; Khan and Becker, 2020). Yet, and despite this heightened policy expediency, as Steele and Legacy (2017: 1) argue '[u]rban infrastructure ... is an under-explored area of critical urban research, policy and practice'. There is a growing academic literature that has turned its attention to the particular ways in which cities and infrastructure have emerged and evolved co-constitutively, and it is to setting this out that the chapter now turns.

Why study infrastructure to understand cities?

Urban infrastructure is manifold: it is blue, green and grey, digital and material, fixed and fluid, networked and self-sufficient, systemic and subverting of systems, inclusive of some uses (and users) of the city while also cutting off others. Grey refers to that infrastructure that has often been central in the organization of North American and Western European cities, such as the road, sewerage and train networks, while blue and green are reference to the emergence and valuing (at least among policy makers and practitioners) of more nature-based infrastructures, such as rivers, canals, gardens and parks. Much has been made in recent years of the increasing use of green infrastructure as one element of how cities seek to reduce the future consequences of the climate emergency (Gill et al, 2007; Norton et al, 2015). Under COVID-19 these debates took on extra urgency, as the inequalities in the distribution of access to green infrastructure were exposed. In addition, recent scholarship has highlighted the growing role of digital infrastructures in various aspects of urban policy and politics (Karvonen et al, 2018). The liveliness of debates across disciplines within the social sciences, such as anthropology, geography, planning, political science and sociology, suggest that if studying of infrastructure was once 'mundane, to the point of boring' (Star 1999: 377), then that time has passed. Indeed, there might be an argument to be made that in the last couple of years we have approached what might be termed peak infrastructure studies!

While acknowledging and valuing the relatively long history of infrastructural studies in anthropology and sociology (for an overview see Larkin, 2013), one might argue that the last decade or so has seen an 'infrastructural turn' (Dodson, 2017: 87) across architecture, geography, planning and urban studies, where an 'infrastructure age is upon us' (Steele and Legacy, 2017: 1). This scholarly 'turn' has placed cities at the centre of infrastructural debates across many disciplines (Wiig and Silver, 2019). Given the series of parallel claims that we are also living under 'planetary urbanization' (Brenner and Schmid, 2015: 151) or in 'the urban age' or 'urban century' (Burdett and Sudjic, 2010: 151), a generative way of conceiving of these aligned aspects of the planet's sociopolitical, economic and climatic futures is to think through them together, as both infrastructural *and* urban challenges. For, as cities are increasingly understood as sites – in a both territorial and networked sense – through which planetary futures are being made and remade, so there appears some utility in using infrastructure as a lens onto the dynamic, open-ended, relationally constituted and variegated process of urbanization. On the one hand, as part of this turn to examining infrastructure, we have witnessed a growth in studies of the different kinds of infrastructure that maintains, nourishes, supports, sustains and underwrites the global urban system while, of course, also being constitutive of it. This is scholarship both about the material infrastructure (and its uneven presence/absence in and between cities) such as that around energy, transport, waste and water (Bouzarovski et al, 2015), as well as the less material, or tangible, social infrastructures such as that which gives coherence and shape to care and social reproduction (Lopes et al, 2018; Power and Mee, 2020; Wiesel and Liu, 2021) along with finance, expertize and master-planning (Simone, 2004; McCann, 2008; McCann and Ward, 2010; Silver, 2014; Mattern, 2018; Latham and Layton, 2019). This is about infrastructure as an element to wider strategies of worlding, understood as the ways in which those charged with governing and promoting cities and their economies engage in 'the art of being global' (Ong, 2011: 1).

On the other hand, there has also emerged a parallel discussion on infrastructure qua infrastructure, specifically on the ways in which the term infrastructure might itself be used most productively (Berlant, 2016). So, for Appel et al (2015) infrastructure is, 'a productive metaphor – for critical theory and the analysis of social life more broadly', for Carse (2016: 28) it is a collective noun that, 'refers to the subordinate parts of many projects, from the built systems that move water, sewa[er]ge, people, and power to components assembled under the rubrics of security, information, health, finance, political mobilization, and environmental management', while for Wiig and Silver (2019) they understand it as verb, incorporating the making, maintaining and use of infrastructure in the reordering of the world economy and city-regions.

This edited collection draws upon notions of infrastructure – as noun and verb – generated out of work on cities across both the Global North and the Global South. Epistemologically, chapters use understandings of infrastructure emerging out of cities such as Accra, Cape Town, Jakarta, Luanda and Nairobi that have been effective in articulating a sense of flux, incrementalism and incompleteness. These challenge those conceptions of urban infrastructure that have emerged out of studies of cities of the Global North (Simone, 2004; Silver, 2014, 2015; Lemanski, 2020) and attend to infrastructure's more ad hoc, informal and produced nature. While *Infrastructuring Urban Futures* primarily draws upon examples in the Global North, it does so using an understanding of infrastructure that emerges out of studies in and across both the Global North and Global South. In making this manoeuvre we are learning from Roy's (2007: 147) arguments over urban informality and theory-building out of this Southern 'state of exception'. In the Global North, notions of the future are rooted in a particular past, one in which infrastructure emerged under a particular form of industrial capitalism, versus the Southern understanding that emerged out of colonial and postcolonial relations. And, of course, these emergences are interconnected, as the absence and presence of infrastructure in the urban South stems from its place under colonial rule. Infrastructures of North America and Europe unfold in more global relations. This Southern way of seeing infrastructure provides a lens through which to understand some of the more indeterminate, open-ended and processual ways in which infrastructural futures are produced.

Infrastructuring Urban Futures takes stock of these debates and advances new directions for urban infrastructure research based on three arguments. First, with an eye to the networked disposition of urban infrastructure, it argues for the necessity of a grounded, material and geographic analysis for infrastructure research. We claim that a critical urban perspective (building on Graham and Marvin, 2001) is well poised to account for infrastructure's unruly capacity to cross territorial, sectoral, ecological and ideological boundaries, but must do so with awareness of the way infrastructure networks and systems are technologies of control that produce space under conditions of constraint and flux. In accounting for different ways in which infrastructure comes to be present in cities as well as the nature of its co-constitutive relationship between urban dwellers and wider process of urbanization, this volume rethinks what a grounded approach to infrastructure studies might entail. Given the contingencies and complexities of infrastructure–urbanization dynamics, infrastructure is destiny, *sort of*.

Second, it situates infrastructure within the uneven and contradictory logics of contemporary capitalist accumulation. Infrastructure, we stress, is at one and the same time a necessity for daily life and social reproduction, as is clear in the current and ongoing COVID-19 global pandemic, and an essential institution of the exploitation and expropriation constitutive of global, racial capitalism (Laster Pirtle, 2020). We contend that foregrounding the legacies of capitalist inequity literally built into cities and their infrastructural foundations is a key step in identifying and building a more just future. This edited collection thus seeks to highlight the unjust infrastructural inheritances found in cities, such as the legacies of colonialism and empire that continue in various guises (Cowen, 2020) or the gendered infrastructures of the 'man-made' city (Kern, 2020), but it does so with an eye to the future. This overarching focus on the future foregrounds how reparations and repair might also be constructive projects to build new worlds (Táíwò, 2022), and indeed new cities, within and against incumbent ones.

Third, we see a key contribution of the edited collection being its ability to expand scholarly understanding of the form, function and everyday urban politics through the focus on infrastructure's inherently uneven capacity to connect and to provide for some people, certain goods and particular flows information while at the same time disenfranchising and/or disconnecting other residents and other elements of the urban condition. Articulating a more just urban future inherently necessitates understanding the role of and place of infrastructure within and between cities.

In treating infrastructure as both a verb and a noun, the edited collection highlights the duality of infrastructure as both a sociotechnical process and a constructed object, and as both a lived practice and a built, material form. Infrastructure, we argue, not only reflects, but also projects the many discrete and interwoven struggles over the production and reproduction of the city. Thus, the overarching aim of this volume is to contribute to critically synthesizing hitherto fragmented debates on urban infrastructure. In so doing, we advance a more holistic understanding of how precarious futures are being made through the process of infrastructuring. Considering infrastructure as constitutive of 'the urban', the edited collection is organized around the three themes: *infrastructuring urbanization*, *producing infrastructure* and *living infrastructure*.

Infrastructuring urbanization

Infrastructure is not static. It is designed, produced, maintained and lived through complex and dynamic relationships between nature, society and technology. Applying the verbiage of infrastructuring – to infrastructure the city, to infrastructure urbanism – is a means of thinking about infrastructure as an active dynamic in the production and reproduction of the urban form, its social and economic function, and its politics, even as infrastructure is materialized in, for instance, concrete and steel.

Infrastructuring urbanization then is not a simple subject–object relation; rather, it invokes an ongoing co-evolutionary process that dialectically defines infrastructure and the urban. This process is multivalent, multiscalar and non-linear. Infrastructuring urbanization, for example, demands attention to how global transformations of the capitalist economy – including its deepening and extending – are linked to the unfolding of the climate emergency and to the movement of people across borders, processes that are heavily structured by class, gender and race. It also locates these extended connections in discrete geographies, histories and temporalities, the importance of which is underscored by Attoh (Chapter 2) in his examination of the stubborn legacy of past investments in infrastructure that have impeded recent efforts to achieve a more equitable city. In London, Whitten (Chapter 7) argues that recent efforts to frame urban nature as infrastructure, in the form of green space that provides for human and ecological health, requires recognizing the relational, embedded geographies of a multiplicity of local residents, whether human, animal, plant-based or otherwise. As infrastructures move, they propel bodies, neighbourhoods, cities and regions into novel configurations, but ones shaped indelibly by what has come before. Legacies that are inherited, that shape and structure, and that provide the context for prefiguring futures, something that Luque-Ayala and Rutherford (Chapter 4) consider in their examination of how a digital overlay to an industrial-era city was a means of augmenting the urban ecological flows of energy and information, and in so doing lowering domestic energy uses in Bristol, England's under-insulated, brick, terraced residential neighbourhoods. Looking at the reuse of obdurate infrastructural spaces, Silver and Wiig (Chapter 8) detail how London adapted its industrial-era waterfront – an infrastructure of a no longer viable economy – to pivot into speculative economic opportunities that investment in global infrastructure offered to the UK, in the form of connecting to China's Belt and Road Initiative.

Throughout the chapters, the emphasis on infrastructuring recognizes these systems and flows as the foundation of the urban, regardless of location. Of course, considering infrastructure-as-process must also recognize infrastructural, and thus urban, incompleteness, something Guma articulates in Afterword 2. Infrastructures may only ever operate in a patchwork fashion, with haphazard connection or an uneven dispersal throughout a city, raising important questions as to what, how and where does infrastructuring take us? In the moment, infrastructure is typically assumed to be permanent, for connection to be constant, but disruptions happen and systems break down without investment, maintenance and repair. Further, anthropogenic climatic shifts, geopolitical turbulence and/or capitalist transformation can all contribute to infrastructural failure or termination, with attendant urban implications. A focus on the dialectic between infrastructuring and urbanization reveals insights about how change and transformation happen.

Understanding the constituent relationality of cities in this way also calls into question the relationship to time and temporality. On the one hand infrastructures – material, physical objects – are obdurate. They 'offer resistance to change' (Hommels, 2005: 329). Their presence emerges to shape and structure futures, setting paths or parameters beyond any one city and stretching into the wider urban region, as Glass, Nelles and Addie discuss in Afterword 1. Some futures open up and others are closed down, sometimes over relatively short time horizons, an argument reinforced across many of the chapters' diverse understanding of the multiplicity of time and infrastructural rhythms. Multiple temporal frames are woven into thinking infrastructurally: historical legacies, but also anticipatory visions that structure current investment, as Bigger and Millington consider with regard to the ability of water provision networks in Cape Town and New York City to adapt to the climate emergency (Chapter 3). Across all chapters, the future is being made now, in and through infrastructure.

Producing infrastructure

Just as many institutions and systems make infrastructure, infrastructure also creates political, economic, ecological and social capacities. Production is rarely linear and teleological; rather, at its various stages it is stop-start, often incremental, slow and, in some cases, unachievable. Compromises are made, logics questioned, negotiations made, and among it all, infrastructure begins to emerge. Infrastructure can be planned, in a professional sense, involving agendas, frameworks, legislation, regulation and so on, even though as Guma (Afterword 2) argues, this is often the exception and not the norm. The large-scale infrastructural development of the past put the envisioning of certain, modernist societal futures centre stage; more recently this privileged position has been questioned, along with its methodological statism. Those that partner with government to build urban infrastructure are more often than not representatives of capital (the private sector), as the chapter by Wiig and Silver (Chapter 8) details. In other cases, it is civil society, or communities, that get involved in the production of their own hard and soft, digital and material infrastructures. Sheller (Chapter 5), for example, shows that the presence or absence of infrastructure in Caribbean cities can be traced back to the social relations of power of colonialism and slavery. Here the state often does not provide infrastructure and does not allocate resources for maintenance and repair after events like earthquakes or hurricanes, leading her to argue for a politics of infrastructural reparations and reparative justice. Making amends in this way can, potentially, stitch fractured, fragmented cities back together.

Attoh (Chapter 2) examines the long-term effects of state-supported auto-mobility on urban political horizons. His is a historical, geographical account of the emergence of the various arterial highways in Poughkeepsie, New York, over the 1960s and 1970s as part of US post-war planning. It reveals the conflicts and tensions embodied in this mode of infrastructural development. The chapter teases out the different understandings of fairness, justice, progress and even futures, bound up in the construction of these roads. Turning to the finance aspect of the production of infrastructure, again, we see evidence of the changing role of the state in recent years. Bigger and Millington (Chapter 3) highlight one of the most recent ways in which global financial capital has found ways of generating revenue streams off the back of infrastructural challenges. Future proofing, so to speak, has become the language increasingly used by architects, engineers and planners, as well as those in banking and finance; that is, those charged both with producing new urban infrastructures and working within the parameters set by current infrastructure. The use of green debt for the adaptation of existing infrastructure in the name of the climate emergency, of which Bigger and Millington write, comes with some risk calculations that exacerbate, as opposed to address, issues of class, gender and racialized inequalities. This argument about attempts to turn future urban infrastructural uncertainties into predictable and realizable revenue streams is a point picked up by Usher (Chapter 6). His chapter includes a case study of the recent politics around the flow of sewage through the UK's water infrastructure, which was privatized at the end of the 1980s. Private corporations as rentiers have sweated their assets, profits rising as household bills have risen. That these revenues stem in part from the private owners of water infrastructure failing to update and upgrade it has become a dominant narrative, with illegal sewage discharges one high-profile example of increased acceptance of lower standards in the UK water industry. Usher complicates this argument. He puts infrastructure at the centre of his analysis, arguing that the overuse of combined sewer overflows, and the admission of illegal sewage discharges, reflects the longer-term demise of the modern infrastructural ideal (Graham and Marvin, 2001). Sewerage has not received adequate investment during periods of both public and private management, leaving the Victorian-era system buckling under 21st-century pressures.

While the two are often presented as two different modes of planning governance – 'bottom up' and 'top down' – more appropriate might be an understanding that sees both modes involving combinations of unevenly distributed expertize, knowledge and, most importantly, power. Seeing production in this way also reframes questions of the role of the state. An expansive view of (re)production can broaden the horizon of infrastructural actors and enable analyses that go beyond the narrow, expert-driven way that infrastructure is produced and conceived. Usher (Chapter 6) draws attention to the way everyday citizens are involved in practices of repair, management and maintenance of stormwater, culverts and rivers, respectively. Whitten

(Chapter 7) shows how green spaces that have been traditionally viewed as places of leisure and reproduction are becoming green infrastructure, and therefore are suddenly subject to new realties and rationalities. Rather than managing green spaces as isolated islands of local amenity, green space planning and governance should reflect the more strategic, cross-jurisdictional approach used with grey infrastructure, such as transport. Crucially, infrastructure is produced through material hardware and through symbols, affects and imaginaries. Producing infrastructure involves creating a cohesive logic for urbanization: the creation of particular infrastructure for specific uses creates a narrative of what connects, for whom and for what uses, that inherently includes some parts and functions of a city and leaves out other areas.

Living infrastructure

Infrastructures are deeply differentiated technologies that produce citizenship as well as distribute resources, opportunities and power in different and inequitable ways. This occurs through organized lack and abandonment, and organized excesses. The agency, politics and publics of infrastructure in its manifold forms include the building, maintenance, repair and retrofitting of urban infrastructure. As a whole, this entails a particular vision of the function of a network or system that facilitates or constrains certain urban activities and processes; it is focused on the physical and social aspects of infrastructure as it sits in place and/or is reinvented to address emergent urban needs. Within this set of relations is space for things labelled infrastructure to act. Living infrastructure captures the relationship between people and those infrastructures that shape their lives, and that they, in turn, shape. For Lemanski (2020: 590), this interrelationship and interweaving highlights 'how citizens' everyday access to, and use of, public infrastructure in the city affect, and are affected by, their citizenship identity and practices'. This includes not only material infrastructures, but also infrastructures of care, civic life, education and social reproduction (Amin, 2014; Latham and Layton, 2019). It brings into view the role of digital infrastructures in mediating the relationship between municipal service providers and residents' domestic needs. Luque-Ayala and Rutherford (Chapter 4) pick up this point. Through their fieldwork in Bristol, UK, they explore how the digitization of traditional urban infrastructures and associated ecological flows opens the possibility of a novel understanding of the city–nature relationship. Including citizens in self-reflexive practices of managing metabolic flows also transforms their subjective relationships from consumers to prosumers.

When public systems no longer provide – as planned or promised – people may push back, make new claims or self-organize. Bigger and Millington (Chapter 3) highlight how communities on the receiving end of some of the most extreme effects of the climate emergency forged alliances across space in order to contribute to a more just future. Their study of green debt also connects efforts at infrastructural provision to reductions in household indebtedness to the issuance of debt at the municipal level. In this way, households are constituted as subjects in the webs woven in and through the new financial logics that structure bond issuances. Usher (Chapter 6) makes this argument in relation to the UK's urban water infrastructure. In and through this, citizens and subjects are manufactured. Water and sewerage infrastructure connects vast numbers of people and groups that are geographically distributed, unknown to one another, yet intimately connected. Underinvestment in maintaining these piped flows by private operators has led to sewage discharge into rivers and other waterways during rainstorms, bringing to the surface and making visible what is expected to remain underground. As global heating increases the severity of rainstorms, it is likely that this hazardous situation is exacerbated in the coming decades, leading to citizen groups coming together around anti-sewerage campaigns and creating what Usher (Chapter 6) notes is an urban commons brought together by infrastructural concerns. With Sheller's (Chapter 5) examination of infrastructural repair, reconstruction and the politics of infrastructural citizenship – or the absence of said citizenship – is, moreover, a matter of who is considered human. Whereas the subjects of infrastructure are often presumed by planners and policy makers in advance, contributors here show how infrastructural subjectivity is more iterative and emergent, negotiated through dynamic political, ethical and technical assemblages.

Next steps: infrastructural thinking

It is halfway through 2022. Or that is what the calendar tells us. It actually feels earlier, as in it feels like the middle of 2020. This is one of the things with over 24 months of a global pandemic. It challenges how many of us think about time as it is experienced and lived (Cage, 2020). And yet, life in many cities has slowly, incrementally, begun to return to some sort of post-COVID 19 or endemic COVID-19 normal. Infrastructure – its lack and its abundance – has been an essential element in structuring how this set of cities have experienced COVID-19 (Enright and Ward, 2021). So it will be that infrastructure in all its various guises will be important to how cities go about managing the shorter-, medium- and longer-term consequences of COVID-19 (some of which certainly have yet to be revealed). And many will be doing this while also wrestling with how best to deal with other economic and social challenges, some of which have been deepened and extended by COVID-19 such as the lasting classed, gendered and racialized inequalities. Moreover, the experience of the climate emergency, particularly among the poorest urban residents, is a challenge to both today's infrastructure and the infrastructure yet to come.

This edited collection contributes to a wider renewing of interest in infrastructure across the social sciences. Despite once being labelled, perhaps rather ironically, as 'singularly unexciting' (Star, 1999: 377), the last two decades have revealed infrastructure to be anything but. Across disciplines, we have witnessed what some have termed a 'global infrastructure turn' (Amin, 2014; Dodson, 2017). This has seen a range of competing conceptual frameworks emerge, as apparently taken-for-granted understandings of infrastructure have been challenged and questioned. In their place has emerged a more heterogeneous, incomplete, incremental, open-ended, processual and relational ontology of infrastructure. Longer-standing political-economic theorizations have been augmented (and, in many ways, critiqued) by insights from actor network theory, assemblage theories, postcolonial studies and science and technology studies (Graham and Marvin, 2001; Furlong, 2014; Graham and McFarlane, 2015).

The chapters and the afterwords that follow this introduction emerge out of this renewal of interest, while also extending it. They are theorized out of empirical sites in cities across primarily the Global North but also the parts of the South, using a range of qualitative methods and infused with elements of older and newer approaches to understanding infrastructure. They constitute an argument that, given what we think we know about the futures of these cities (and what we probably do not know), there will remain a central role for infrastructure. Automation technologies, the climate emergency, the decarbonization and net zero agendas, the ongoing digitalization of activities and services via apps, dashboards and platforms, are all at play, often combining in unique and not always internally consistent ways. And yet, as some chapter contributors also argue, what will probably appear will be never-to-be-complete infrastructures that are most productively understood as relationally constituted, emerging incrementally through the performance of a range of situated socio-material practices. This is exemplified by studies influenced by what Jackson (2014) terms 'broken world thinking', where attention is turned towards repair and maintenance, of work done by a range of experts and populations with inherited infrastructural legacies, of remaking infrastructure to get by and make do. For the making of the future will occur in the context of the present and the shadow of the past. And, as Urry (2016) asks, what is future? What work does futurity do with respect to infrastructure? And how do infrastructures create different sorts of futures? And for whom? As the contributors to this edited collection make clear, infrastructures are involved in multiple projects to anticipate, plan and visualize a version of the future. From corporate forecasting to financial models, from to state planning to technical regulations, infrastructure as object and as processes relies on projections of what is to come, even while acting to bring those assumptions into being. Populations with different recourse to the axes of politics and power are both fleetingly and lastingly absent and present in the different non-linear phases of infrastructural emergence. Quite what the urban infrastructural end game is remains unclear. Faced with predictable and unpredictable turbulence and uncertainty, the future of today's urban infrastructures remains to be seen, a future being forecast, planned, designed, financed and built, but which has yet to be realized.

References

Amin, A. (2014) 'Lively infrastructure', *Theory, Culture & Society*, 31(7-8): 137-161.

Anderson, B. (2010) 'Preemption, precaution, preparedness: anticipatory action and future geographies', *Progress in Human Geography*, 34(6): 777–98.

Appel, H., Anand, N. and Gupta, A. (2015) 'The infrastructure toolbox', *Theorizing the Contemporary, Fieldsights, Society for Cultural Anthropology*, 24 September. Available from: https://culanth.org/fieldsights/series/the-infrastructure-toolbox [Accessed 30 November 2021].

Appel, H., Anand, N. and Gupta, A. (2018) 'Introduction: temporality, politics, and the promise of infrastructure', in N. Anand, A. Gupta and H. Appel (eds) *The Promise of Infrastructure*, Durham, NC: Duke University Press, pp 1–40.

Berlant, L. (2016) 'The commons: infrastructures for troubling times', *Environment and Planning D: Society and Space*, 34(3): 393–419.

Bouzarovski, S., Bradshaw, M. and Wochnik, A. (2015) 'Making territory through infrastructure: the governance of natural gas transit in Europe', *Geoforum*, 64: 217–28.

Brenner, N. and Schmid, C. (2015) 'Towards a new epistemology of the urban?', *City*, 19(2/3): 151–82.

Burdett, R. and Sudjic, D. (2010) *The Endless City: The Urban Age Project by the London School of Economics and Deutsche Bank's Alfred Herrhausen Society*, reprint, London: Phaidon Press.

Cage, F. (2020) 'Why time feels so weird in 2020', Reuters Graphics, 6 July. Available from: https://graphics.reuters.com/HEALTH-CORONAVIRUS/TIME/gjnvwwjegvw/ [Accessed 28 January 2022].

Carse, A. (2016) 'Keyword: infrastructure: how a humble French engineering term shaped the world', in P. Harvey, C.B. Jensen and A. Morita (eds) *Infrastructures and Social Complexity: A Companion*, Abingdon: Routledge, pp 27–39.

Chong, J. (2021) 'Toronto launching first pothole repair blitz of the fall on Saturday', Toronto Star, 2 October. Available from: https://www.thestar.com/news/gta/2021/10/02/toronto-launching-first-pothole-repair-blitz-of-the-fall-on-saturday.html [Accessed 30 November 2021].

Coletta, C. and Kitchin, R. (2017) 'Algorhythmic governance: regulating the "heartbeat" of a city using the Internet of Things', *Big Data & Society*, 4(2). Available from: https://doi.org/10.1177/2053951717742418 [Accessed 8 November 2022].

Costley, D. (2020) 'The Blackest city in the US is facing an environmental justice nightmare', The Guardian, 9 January, Available from: https://www.theguardian.com/us-news/2020/jan/09/the-blackest-city-in-the-is-us-facing-an-environmental-justice-nightmare [Accessed 30 November 2021].

Cowen, D. (2020) 'Following the infrastructures of empire: notes on cities, settler colonialism, and method', *Urban Geography*, 41(4): 469–86.

Dodson, J. (2017) 'The global infrastructure turn and urban practice', *Urban Policy and Research*, 35(1): 87–92.

Enright, T. and Ward, K. (2022) 'Governing urban infrastructures under pandemic conditions: some thoughts', *Urban Geography*, 42(7): 1023–32.

European Investment Bank (2022) 'Infrastructure and the EIB', European Investment Bank. Available from: https://www.eib.org/en/about/priorities/infrastructure/index.htm [Accessed 14 February 2022].

Fitzgerald, J. and Agyeman, J. (2021) 'It's time to dismantle racist infrastructure: let's start with American highways', Fast Company, 8 September. Available from: https://www.fastcompany.com/90673415/its-time-to-dismantle-racist-infrastructure-lets-start-with-american-highways [Accessed 14 February 2022].

Furlong, K. (2014) 'STS beyond the "modern infrastructure ideal": extending theory by engaging with infrastructure challenges in the South', *Technology in Society*, 38: 139–47.

Gill, S.E., Handley, J.F., Ennos, A.R. and Pauleit, S. (2007) 'Adapting cities for climate change: the role of the green infrastructure', *Built Environment*, 33(1): 115–33.

Graham, S. and Marvin, S. (2001) *Splintering Urbanism: Networked Infrastructures, Technological Mobilities and the Urban Condition*, New York: Routledge.

Graham, S. and McFarlane, C. (eds) (2015) *Infrastructural Lives: Urban Infrastructure in Context*, New York: Routledge.

Heathcote, C. (2017) 'The global infrastructure arms race', Global Infrastructure Hub, 23 October 2017. Available from: https://www.gihub.org/news/the-global-infrastructure-arms-race/ [Accessed: 5 January 2023].

Hommels, A. (2005) 'Studying obduracy in the city: Toward a productive fusion between technology studies and urban studies', *Science, Technology, & Human Values*, 30(3): 323-351.

Jackson, S.J. (2014) 'Rethinking repair', in T. Gillespie, P.J. Boczkowski and K.A. Foot (eds) *Media Technologies: Essays on Communication, Materiality and Society*, Cambridge, MA: MIT Press, pp 221–307.

Jakobsen, K. (2014) '"Connecting Copenhagen" is the World's Best Smart City Project', State of Green. Available from: https://stateofgreen.com/en/partners/city-of-copenhagen/news/connecting-copenhagen-is-the-worlds-best-smart-city-project/ [Accessed 30 November 2021].

Karvonen, A., Cugurullo, F. and Caprotti, F. (eds) (2018) *Inside Smart Cities: Place, Politics and Urban Innovation*, Abingdon: Routledge.

Kern, L. (2020) *Feminist City: Claiming Space in a Man-Made World*, London: Verso.

Khan, A. and Becker, K. (eds) (2020) *US Infrastructure: Challenges and Definitions for the 21s Century*, Abingdon: Routledge.

Larkin, B. (2013) 'The politics and poetics of infrastructure', *Annual Review of Anthropology*, 42(1): 327–43.

Laster Pirtle, W.N. (2020) 'Racial capitalism: a fundamental cause of novel coronavirus (COVID-19) pandemic inequities in the United States', *Health Education & Behavior*, 47(4): 504–8.

Latham, A. and Layton, J. (2019) 'Social infrastructure and the public life of cities: studying urban sociality and public spaces', *Geography Compass*, 13(7): 1–15.

Lemanski, C. (2020) 'Infrastructural citizenship: The everyday citizenships of adapting and/or destroying public infrastructure in Cape Town, South Africa', *Transactions of the Institute of British Geographers*, 45(3): 589-605.

Lopes, A., Healy, S., Power, E., Crabtree, L. and Gibson, K. (2018) 'Infrastructures of care: opening up "home" as commons in a hot city', *Human Ecology Review*, 24(2): 41–59.

Mattern, S. (2018) 'Maintenance and care', Places Journal, November. Available from: https://placesjournal.org/article/maintenance-and-care/ [Accessed 30 November 2021].

McCann, E. (2008) 'Expertise, truth, and urban policy mobilities: global circuits of knowledge in the development of Vancouver, Canada's "four pillar" drug strategy', *Environment and Planning A: Economy and Space*, 40(4): 885–904.

McCann, E. and Ward, K. (2010) 'Relationality/territoriality: toward a conceptualization of cities in the world', *Geoforum*, 41(2): 175–84.

Miller, J. (2018) 'Roads to nowhere: how infrastructure built on American inequality', The Guardian, 21 February. Available from: https://www.theguardian.com/cities/2018/feb/21/roads-nowhere-infrastructure-american-inequality [Accessed 14 February 2022].

Norton, B.A., Coutts, A.M., Livesley, S.J., Harris, R.J., Hunter, A.M. and Williams, N.S.G. (2015) 'Planning for cooler cities: a framework to prioritise green infrastructure to mitigate high temperatures in urban landscapes', *Landscape and Urban Planning*, 134: 127–38.

Ong, A. (2011) 'Introduction: worlding cities, or the art of being global', in A. Roy and A. Ong (eds) *Worlding Cities: Asian Experiments and the Art of Being Global*, Oxford: Wiley-Blackwell, pp 1–26.

Power, E.R. and Mee, K.J. (2020) 'Housing: an infrastructure of care', *Housing Studies*, 35(3): 484–505.

Roy, A. (2007) 'Urban informality: towards an epistemology of planning', *Journal of the American Planning Association*, 71(2): 147–58.

Silver, J. (2014) 'Incremental infrastructures: material improvisation and social collaboration across post-colonial Accra', *Urban Geography*, 35(6): 788–804.

Silver, J. (2015) 'Disrupted infrastructures: an urban political ecology of interrupted electricity in Accra', *International Journal of Urban and Regional Research*, 39(5): 984–1003.

Simone, A. (2004) 'People as infrastructure: intersecting fragments in Johannesburg', *Public Culture*, 16(3): 407–29.

Société du Grand Paris (2017) 'Grand Paris Express, the largest transport project in Europe', Grand Paris Express. Available from: https://www.societedugrandparis.fr/info/grand-paris-express-largest-transport-project-europe-1061 [Accessed 30 November 2021].

Star, S.L. (1999) 'The ethnography of infrastructure', *American Behavioral Scientist*, 43(3): 377–91.

Steele, W. and Legacy, C. (2017) 'Critical urban infrastructure', *Urban Policy and Research*, 35(1): 1–6.

Táíwò, O. (2022) *Reconsidering Reparations*, Oxford: Oxford University Press.

Urry, J. (2016) *What Is the Future?*, Cambridge: Polity Press.

Venkatesan, S., Bear, L., Harvey, P., Lazar, S., Rival, L. and Simone, A. (2018) 'Attention to infrastructure offers a welcome reconfiguration of anthropological approaches to the political', *Critique of Anthropology*, 38(1): 3–52.

Wiesel, I. and Liu, F. (2021) 'Conceptualising modes of redistribution in public urban infrastructure', *Urban Studies*, 58(8): 1561–80.

Wiig, A. and Silver, J. (2019) 'Turbulent presents, precarious futures: urbanization and the deployment of global infrastructure', *Regional Studies*, 53(6): 912–23.

2

Infrastructure and the Tragedy of Development

Kafui Attoh

It is with mounting disgust and final revulsion that I read about
the things which have happened to John R. Lindmark's collection
of books which was one of the finest ... Such utter lack of regard
for finer things is shameful and causes me to ask the same question
one of my Chicago friends asked me when he read the same AP
story: What kind of people live in Poughkeepsie anyway?
Richard Blouin, 5 May 1963, *Poughkeepsie Journal*

Introduction

In early December 1960, *Poughkeepsie Journal* contributor Helen Myers
announced the newspaper's intention to publish a recurring series of
black and white photographs. The photos would document the various
buildings, streets and neighbourhoods to be demolished in order to make
way for the city's new north–south arterial highway. The general idea of
the series, according to Myers, was to capture a set of scenes from a section
of Poughkeepsie – a small municipality 90 miles north of New York City –
before the bulldozers made it 'impossible to remember how that section
of the city looked'. The photographs were understandably melancholic.
To follow the path of the proposed highway, Myers (1960) wrote, was to
'have the impression of going through a series of small villages each with
its own distinct personality'. Densely settled and within a quarter of a mile
of the Hudson River, the neighbourhoods slated for demolition were not
only some of the city's oldest, but they had also served as a home, however
temporarily, to each of the city's various migrant waves – first to the Irish
and Germans and later to the Italians and Polish. The entire area, in short,

was a palimpsest of the city's past – from the austere brick of working-class housing to the remnants of the early mills themselves. Within a year, Myers noted, it would all be gone.

As part of the same series, Myers included a photograph of an old brick schoolhouse owned by John Lindmark – describing it as one of the many 'landmarks which will disappear to make way for the artery'. Below the image, Myers appended a brief caption: 'Mr. Lindmark specializes in rare and old volumes and has one of the largest collections of such books in the country' (Meyers, 1961). In 1960, few if any, including Myers herself, would have predicted that in only three years, Lindmark – who barely merited a footnote in the series – would grab national headlines as the central protagonist of an urban tragedy.

By the beginning of 1963, wrecking companies had already destroyed roughly 400 buildings in the path of the proposed arterial. This number is taken from a *Poughkeepsie Journal* (1962a) article published on 15 August 1962. In an earlier report (1962b) the number was 133. Lindmark's schoolhouse was the last standing. Two years earlier, in 1961, Lindmark had refused the state's initial offer of $16,500 as compensation for the building. The state would later increase the offer to $22,000. For the 74-year-old bookseller, however, the central problem remained the same. While the state was willing to pay for the building, it refused to cover the associated expense of moving his inventory of over 200,000 books – a cost estimated to exceed $10,000 alone (O'Brien, 1961; Poughkeepsie Journal, 1961: 14).

In April 1963, after 18 months of legal wrangling, John Lindmark was finally evicted. The eviction garnered national coverage if for no other reason than the accompanying photographs.

Here readers glimpsed – whether on the pages of the *New York Times* or the *Chicago Tribune* – the image of some 50,000 books, many rare and old, carelessly scattered along a sloping sidewalk (Chicago Tribune, 1963; O'Brien, 1963a; Stevens, 1963). As with many evictions, the scene was a chaotic one. *New York Times* contributor John Stevens (1963) explained that 'after a day of stacking books in neat rows against a plywood fence', workmen of the Poughkeepsie Wrecking Company had returned the following day only to find that 'children and adults, on their way to school or shops, had kicked down the stacks and trampled the books into a conglomeration of torn covers and pages'. As the *Chicago Tribune* (1963) reported 'the scavengers had left the books in such a mess' that on the third day, the workmen had switched from carefully stacking the books into neat piles to simply dumping them as 'if they were rubbish'.

If pictures of crowds carelessly rummaging through a mountain of books and of children flinging them as weapons were not scandalous enough, the coming weeks offered the city little respite (O'Brien, 1963b). In late May of the same year, the city of Poughkeepsie was once again in the news. To quote one headline: 'City burning books owner left on walk' (Journal-News, 1963: 21). On 22 May 1963, the *Poughkeepsie Journal* reported that the same books so carelessly thrown to the pavement only a month prior had – in the interest of clearing 'accumulated material from the street' – ended their life in a city incinerator. Mixed with city rubbish, it took two furnaces operating well into the evening to burn what amounted to '50 tons of books – some heaps of loose leaves, others still tightly bound volumes' (Poughkeepsie Journal, 1963a). As George Pascoe, a superintendent at the city dump explained 'most of the books are wet and that makes them slow to burn'. With all traces of the former bookshop gone, on 4 January 1964 construction on Poughkeepsie's first arterial highway began in earnest (Poughkeepsie Journal, 1964).

Reactions to the Lindmark case varied. Many in Poughkeepsie blamed Lindmark himself – both for refusing multiple offers of assistance, and for allowing his books to sit for weeks on the street unprotected (Poughkeepsie Journal, 1963b). For observers outside of Poughkeepsie, however, the reaction was different. It was captured in letters to the *New York Times* from astonished readers like J.O. Ronall:

> The *Times* of April 27 reported the eviction of John R. Lindmark, a bookseller whose shop will be razed to make way for an arterial highway. A more adequate caption for the photograph which accompanied your story would have been 'The New Barbarians.' *Pravda* may have captioned it 'Only in America.' (Ronall, 1963)

Even more affecting, were the comments of the writer Edgar Ansel Mowrer writing for the *Lowell Sun*:

> Thirty years ago, almost to the day, this writer stood among a group of foreigners in Berlin while fanatical students and Nazi yahoos laughingly hurled books into a huge bonfire before the famous Humboldt University ... Standing before the Nazi bonfire back in 1933, I felt sure of one thing: such an act of blasphemy could never happen in America! Now I am not sure. For up in Poughkeepsie, N.Y., last Friday something of the sort did happen. (Mowrer, 1963)

Books have long occupied a cherished place in the self-conception of civilized society. Quoting Mowrer (1963) from the same op-ed, they represent 'the chief means whereby the learning and insight of one human generation are passed on to successive generations'. The Lindmark case not only gave lie to any assertion of American cultural superiority, but it marked, for many, an affront to civilization itself. One part *Fahrenheit 451*, another part Humboldt University in 1933, the banality of the case made the story even more jarring. Rather than falling victim to a fascist regime bent on ideological conformity, Lindmark's books fell victim to a sanitation department, and collective neglect. For still others, the reaction to the Lindmark case was expressed in the form of a question. Why had Lindmark rejected help? Why had the state refused to provide the money necessary to move his books? Perhaps most importantly: what kind of people lived in Poughkeepsie, and why had 'progress' necessitated that they run a four-lane highway directly through an old schoolhouse store? (Blouin, 1963; Edison, 1966.)

At least with respect to the last question, this chapter presumes that one answer comes from the work of the philosopher and cultural critic Marshall Berman. In his 1982 book, *All that Is Solid Melts into Air*, Berman attempts to both analyse and provide a history of 'the experience of modernity'. In the first third of the book, Berman uses the legend of Faust – as told by the German playwright Goethe – as an allegory for 'the tragedy of development'. As Berman argues, Goethe's fictional Philomena and Baucis – the elderly couple inadvertently killed after Dr Faust demolishes their rural home as part of a massive construction project – marked the first literary representation of a category of people that were 'going to be very large in modern history: people who are in the way – in the way of history, of progress, of development' (1988 [1982]: 67). For communities the world over, Berman argued, the experience of modernity was not unlike that of Philomena and Baucis. In short, it was marked by tragedy. For Berman, however, the tragedy at the heart of Goethe's *Faust* extended well beyond the experience of displacement. The tragedy of development, Berman argued, was the recognition that the Faustian drives for progress, improvement and redevelopment were as noble and as necessary as they were destructive. For Berman, as it was for Goethe, the horrors visited on people like John Lindmark were inseparable from the ambitions of those seeking to build a world worthy of modern people.

Using Poughkeepsie as a case study, this chapter attempts to paint a finer-grained picture of the 'tragedy of development' as well as the challenges that face planners and other seeking to remake cities in more just and equitable ways. The chapter begins with the history of the city's first arterial highway and the debates that erupted in the 1950s and 1960s over its development. These were debates about traffic and economic growth, as well as what to do with the hundreds of people in the path of progress – including, but not limited to, John Lindmark. The chapter explores the tensions that seemed to define those debates. These were tensions between competing notions of value, between the public good and the rights of individuals, and the difference between the abstract citizens that populate planning manuals and the distinct personalities that populate actual cities. The chapter locates the 'tragedy of development' in the irreconcilability of these tensions.

The second section of the chapter jumps forward to the present and the transformation of Poughkeepsie's arterial highways into objects of scorn. For many contemporary planners and city officials, the arterial highways have not only come to represent one of the many disasters of urban renewal and mid-century planning, but a barrier to future economic development. In seeking to promote the city's revival, local planners have focused their attention on reversing the legacy of the arterial highways. In the absence of funding, their efforts have floundered. For contemporary planners and city officials in Poughkeepsie 'the tragedy of development' is not the tragedy of *Faust* – of noble ambitions gone awry – but rather the tragedy of noble ambitions that have little hope of finding expression. The chapter ends by turning to the future and exploring what new federal spending on infrastructure may mean for Poughkeepsie and the evolving meaning of the 'tragedy of development'.

Before going any further, I should say a brief word about where I believe this chapter falls within the larger edited collection. As with others in this volume, this chapter presumes that struggles and debates over urban infrastructure are almost always implicated in broader social and economic struggles. Conflicts over transportation infrastructure, the retrofitting of wastewater systems or the reshaping of cities around new communication technologies are often proxy fights over everything from climate change and economic justice to the future of urban public life (see, for example, Bigger and Millington (Chapter 3), Luque-Ayala and Rutherford (Chapter 4), and Sheller (Chapter 5). As this chapter makes apparent, debates over infrastructure are also debates over the idea of development. A focus on infrastructure offers a window into how ideas of development change, as well as how we make sense of those changes. To return to the Lindmark case, a focus on infrastructure allows us to answer the question posed by Richard Blouin 'what kind of people live in Poughkeepsie anyway?'

The north–south arterial

The plans for the highway that ultimately destroyed Lindmark's bookstore first appeared in 1947 and as part of a larger traffic study conducted by the State Department of Public Works (Sells et al, 1947). That study begins by observing the radical shift in the region's transportation profile. Between 1920 and 1946, the number of cars registered in Dutchess County – where Poughkeepsie is the county seat – increased by 330 per cent. While the region boasted only one vehicle for every 11 people in 1915, by 1940 that ratio was one in three (p 22). Nowhere were the consequences of the region's new mobility regime more visible than in downtown Poughkeepsie. In the years immediately after the war, the city was defined by bumper-to-bumper congestion and endless traffic jams. For the authors of the traffic study, the problem was largely one of infrastructure:

> The moderate flow of traffic in the horse and buggy era has given way to a veritable flood of autos, trucks and buses. Although roads and streets are better paved, and in some cases widened, they remain essentially the same thoroughfares that were designed for earlier modes and volumes of travel. (Sells et al, 1947: 12)

As was clear in the report, the problems of traffic congestion in Poughkeepsie were compounded by the city's geography. In particular, the issue was the location of the Mid-Hudson Bridge. Opened in 1930 and built partially in response to traffic congestion at the city's ferry piers, the bridge emptied directly into the city's downtown. In 1947, it was one of only two Hudson River crossings between New York City and Albany – the state capital 90 miles to the north. As a result of the bridge location, during the summer and autumn months, the city was inundated with cars heading to holiday towns in the Catskill Mountains and with trucks from Ulster County loaded with agricultural produce bound for New York City markets (Sells et al, 1947). For the authors of the study, the solution to Poughkeepsie's traffic woes was a four-lane, grade-separated highway, running north–south and connected to the Mid-Hudson Bridge by a half-cloverleaf exchange. The report also proposed an east–west arterial highway connecting the bridge to points east.

With few departures from the original 1947 plan – for example the preservation of the Holy Comforter Church – Poughkeepsie's first arterial highway was completed and opened in 1966 (Poughkeepsie Journal, 1952, 1966). The state completed construction of a second arterial highway – the east–west arterial – in 1979. Both projects were ultimately part of a much larger transformation to the city's physical plant (Poughkeepsie Journal, 1979). Between 1960 and 1980, this transformation included the construction of a new city hall, a renovated downtown shopping district and hundreds of new public housing units – often built on land cleared as part of the federal urban renewal programme (Flad, 1987; Opdycke, 1990: 63; Flad and Griffen, 2009). While many in the city welcomed the development of new modern facilities, such changes were not without costs. Between 1960 and 1980, well over 400 families in Poughkeepsie found themselves confronted by a reality defined by the same 19 words (Tobin, 1993a): to quote urban renewal critic Martin Anderson (1964: 1): 'The house or apartment you live in is going to be taken by the government and destroyed ... Please move'. Some 247 families were displaced by the north–south arterial (Poughkeepsie Journal, 1960), 193 families were displaced by the Riverview project (Poughkeepsie Journal, 1971) and 41 families were displaced by the construction of Poughkeepsie's new City Hall (Poughkeepsie Journal,

1969). The north–south arterial marked the first and most extensive of those changes as well as the clearest articulation of the priorities that would define the city in the decades following the Second World War.

As evidenced in the 1947 traffic study, one of those priorities was traffic speed. Based on 1946 conditions, the study found that a commuter travelling by car from the northernmost point of the city to its southern extent could expect to complete the trip in just under 16 minutes. Barring improvements to the city's road infrastructure, the study estimated that by 1960, the same trip would take over 21 minutes. The authors based this estimate on the continued growth in private car ownership. With the construction of the proposed north–south arterial, commuters could expect less congestion as well as significant time savings. According to the study, the same north–south trip through the city would now take less than five minutes. For the study's authors, the benefits of a new north–south arterial could be expressed quantitatively: 16 minutes of travel time saved (1947: 79).

By the late 1950s, arguments in support of the north–south arterial were increasingly tied to economic concerns, and especially the future of Poughkeepsie's retail sector. As early as 1958, the city's regional dominance in retail was showing signs of weakness and decline (City Chamberlain, 1958a: 410; Flad, 1987; Flad and Griffen, 2009). Most attributed this decline to the suburban expansion of IBM – the region's largest employer – as well as the concomitant growth of various suburban shopping malls and housing tracts. Local support for the north–south arterial often drew from those eager to stave off further decline. This view was expressed in 1958 by the president of the Mid-Hudson Industrial Association, an organization representing the city's manufacturers.

> [The north–south arterial] will relieve a serious traffic situation in the commercial and shopping districts of the city which is already affecting property values in the areas and will affect them more so in the future. The traffic density in these areas is already making for an exodus of commercial and retail establishments from the city. [The arterial] will ease the distribution and delivery of freight and will tend to enhance the value of the city as a distribution center. (Poughkeepsie Journal, 1958a)

The president of the local chamber of commerce expressed a similar view. Pointing to the costs that traffic congestion was imposing on 'business volume in the city', the president argued that the only solution was 'an entirely new route for through-traffic moving north and south' (Poughkeepsie Journal, 1957a). The president was joined by the editorial page of the *Poughkeepsie Journal*. To quote the editors: not only was the arterial a 'means of rescuing the city from the strictures growing out of the horse and buggy era' but it remained the only viable alternative to 'letting Poughkeepsie drift further into traffic strangulation and economic damage' (Poughkeepsie Journal, 1958a, 1958b). In 1958 the Newark, New Jersey–based planning firm Candeub and Fleissig, which had been tasked in 1957 with developing the city's Master Plan, advanced a similar analysis. If the city wished to retain its dominance in the retail sector, the 'separation of local traffic from through traffic' was essential (Candeub & Fleissig Planning Consultants, 1960: i; City Chamberlain, 1958a: 436). By the end of 1958, not only had the arterial gained the backing of industry, the press and urban planners – all a part of the city's growth machine – but it also counted the support from the general public. In a poll conducted by the *Poughkeepsie Journal*, respondents in support of the arterial outnumbered opponents by a margin of 3 to 1 (City Chamberlain, 1958a: 436).

Poughkeepsie's elected officials cast their support for the north–south arterial in yet more abstract terms. Where the function of government was to 'give citizens services to which they are entitled' the north–south arterial was important for both easing travel through the city, and for securing the tax revenue necessary to improve city services (City Chamberlain, 1957). In 1957, Republican Mayor Thomas Dietz clarified this view.

> The increase in assessed valuation year after year permits this city to grow to be a progressive community, to give the citizens services to which they are entitled, and enables us to provide the money without any appreciable increase in our taxes. I say this: that if you are far-sighted enough to see the benefits which will arise to the city out of this highway then you will vote in favor of the highway and the progress of the city of Poughkeepsie. (City Chamberlain, 1957)

For Dietz, opposition to the arterial highway was akin to opposing progress itself.

> I feel personally that if I were not in favor of the highway I would be like that ostrich sticking my head in the sand. I would be disregarding the future of the City of Poughkeepsie, its expansion and its progress. I am a native of this city. I like this city. I have lived otherwise and chosen to return. I think that the people who have gone before me have handed to me, through their efforts and foresight, a community to live in which I say is second to none. I, too, have a family which I am raising; and it would not surprise me if they remained here. I want to hand down to them and to the next generation a city which has progressed and grown, and which has remained a wonderful place to live. (City Chamberlain, 1957)

As was the case for most proponents, the social costs of the arterial were not unknown to Dietz. Such costs, however, were insufficient to justify blocking the project. For the 247 families forced to relocate, Dietz offered both sympathy and the promise of fair compensation (City Chamberlain, 1957; Poughkeepsie Journal, 1960).

> I have had deep concern and have given grave consideration to those people who either own homes or live in the path of the highway or adjacent thereto. I have faith that the State of New York when it acquires the property or injures any property adjacent to the highway, will pay fair compensation; and when I say fair compensation, I mean just that. What is your house or garage worth or land worth in today's real estate market? And when you answer that question, then I will tell you – that is what the state ought to pay you. I think the state will be fair in giving the people who are living within the area ample time to seek other similar accommodations and we are always hopeful better accommodations. (City Chamberlain, 1957)

Unsurprisingly, for others the idea of fair compensation was altogether offensive. In late March 1960, Emma Maroney, a 60-year-old resident of 41 Tulip Street sent a letter to the Poughkeepsie Common Council at what seemed a pivotal moment. Earlier that month, and after seven years of negotiations between the city, the state bridge authority and elected officials in Albany, the city's request for help in financing the right-of-way costs of the arterial was finally approved. The announcement marked the closest local advocates had come in their attempt to see the highway realized. In her letter, partially quoted here, Maroney articulates what she saw as a betrayal – one committed by her ward representative, Alderman Walter Van Tine, as well as the city more generally.

> This letter is regarding the artery. What I have to say is not only for my benefit, but for everyone who lives in the locality of the artery. Especially those who really love and want to keep their homes, I make this special statement because after talking with [Alderman Van Tine], he told me how some of the people in this locality (Ward 2) wanted to get rid of their homes. He also told me that he felt he had to vote for the artery because he had to represent them as well as myself and many others. I answered his statement by saying, 'you mean to tell me that you did it to help them sell their homes in preference to help keep homes of hundreds of people.' ... I doubt very much that any of you care to realize how serious it is lose your home, but perhaps I should say most of you. Because some of you must have some consideration in your hearts. You all have homes, don't you think we deserve them

too? ... I am only one person but this letter is to help a great many people, who in your opinion are in the way of putting up an Artery for traffic. Don't you think it's rather hard to consider a place for traffic instead of a place for hundreds of human beings? ... I request that this letter be read at the meeting of the Common Council tonight. I believe in living the way God wants us to live. I'm sure taking homes away from people, surely isn't his way. (City Chamberlain, 1960)

The postscript of the letter puts a yet finer point on the same argument:

P.S. The item Mr. Van Tine put in Sunday's paper about the one person from the 2nd Ward, was me, he shouldn't [have] been afraid to mention my name. Because what I said was true. A home is a home and we love it no matter what the address may be, downtown or uptown we are all the same. (City Chamberlain, 1960)

Irrespective of citywide polls, engineering reports or expert testimony, for Maroney, the principal argument against the arterial was never more complicated than the common dictum: a home is a home. Only three years earlier, the former Democratic Mayor Horace Graham – who had led the Democratic Party's initial opposition to the arterial – had made the same argument:

In the case of the proposed arterial highway, in the interest of the public, the duty of the Democratic Party is clear. It must oppose the highway ... The right of the people to live in and enjoy their homes must come first. If Poughkeepsie cannot offer this protection to its citizens then Poughkeepsie has no reason to exist. To take away the homes of the people, therefore, is nothing more than forcible confiscation. A man's home is his castle, but apparently not in Poughkeepsie. It is pretty well agreed now that the location of the Mid-Hudson Bridge at the foot of Church Street was a blunder. Due to traffic congestion and its dangers, especially to their children, our downtown citizens have suffered for many years. Now in addition to that suffering, they are asked to make another sacrifice, this time to give up their very homes. (Poughkeepsie Journal, 1957b)

For Graham, the proposed construction of an arterial highway in Poughkeepsie not only meant asking hundreds of families to sacrifice their homes, but it meant asking them to do so in the interest of remedying a blunder of the city's own making – namely the poor placement of the Mid-Hudson Bridge. Moreover, it meant asking many of the same families that had been most burdened by the effects of that blunder – in the form of congestion and traffic – to now bear the bulk of the costs. As Graham might have added, there was yet another irony. Only 35 years earlier, and as already noted, it had been problems of traffic congestion at the city's piers that had prompted Poughkeepsie's 'Bridge Movement' to demand a vehicular crossing at Poughkeepsie (Poughkeepsie Eagle, 1922). To quote a prominent bridge booster from 1922, 'the lack of a bridge has placed the residents of the region, automobilist and produce growers at the mercy of antiquated ferry lines … the congestion at each of these ferries on any summer day or holiday has become an annoyance' (Elmira Star Gazette, 1922). Once a solution to the city's traffic congestion, now the bridge was being blamed for it. In either case, the burden of change fell on the same residents, many of whom were among the poorest in the city.

In addition to critics like Graham and Maroney, there were others who sought to challenge the construction of the north–south arterial. For residents like Murray Brown, the former head of Poughkeepsie's Tax and Ratepayer Association, the problem with the arterial highway was that it would further accelerate the outmigration of business from the city's downtown. Citing the example of Wappingers Falls, a village 20 miles to the south, Brown noted that few of the downtown merchants in Wappingers Falls had recovered after the village had been bypassed by Route 9. The city had become an economically depressed ghost town. The arterial, Brown argued, would have the same effect on Poughkeepsie (City Chamberlain, 1958b: 410).

Murray's critiques would ultimately find support in the writings of urbanists like Lewis Mumford (1955), Harrison Salisbury (1959) and Jane Jacobs (1961). The idea of solving congestion by building more highways, to paraphrase Mumford, was like trying to solve obesity by letting out one's belt (Mumford, 1955). Counter to the idea that a highway might stem the city's decline, one needed only read about Los Angeles, a city that *New York Times* contributor Harrison Salisbury termed 'gasopolis'. According to Salisbury, the explosions of 'freeways, parking lots, concrete strips, and weird interchanges' had all functioned to eviscerate the city's core (Salisbury, 1959). Of course, for Maroney and Graham, Brown's critique missed the more fundamental problem. For many, the central argument against the north–south arterial rested on a moral objection. Whether the arterial might assuage traffic congestion or worsen it, encourage growth or condemn the city to ruin, whether it would turn Poughkeepsie into a gasopolis or something else, such questions avoided the central issue: the construction of the highway meant breaching of a fundamental principle: 'the right of people to live and enjoy their homes' (Poughkeepsie Journal, 1957b).

For Marshall Berman the 'tragedy of modern development' was the recognition that the drives for progress, development and modernization are as noble as they are destructive. For him, that tragedy was captured in the story of *Faust* as well as in the story of hundreds of thousands of others cast aside in the name of human betterment. While the motivations and intentions behind the north–south arterial were hardly monolithic, in many instances, those intentions were noble and were in line with the predominant view of how to address traffic congestion. Beyond the question of intentions, in Poughkeepsie, the tragedy of modern development is most apparent in the disconnect between the comments of Emma Maroney and the arguments advanced by city planners and engineers as well as city officials and, arguably, the public at large.

As a rule, large-scale and regional infrastructure projects require that planners abstract from local particularities and 'standardize the subjects of development' (Scott, 1998: 365). In measuring 'throughput', designing interchanges or assessing the value of a property, planners and city officials are invariably forced to rely on abstractions. Unfortunately, people do not live in abstractions. Rather they live in homes, in neighbourhoods and in communities that are distinctive precisely because such places have concrete histories. The tragedy of modern development – and especially when that development takes the form of large-scale or regional infrastructure projects – is that it requires those tasked with realizing such projects to not only bracket that history but to abstract away from the very distinctions that give places meaning. Rather than seeing a bookstore as a bookstore, in the mind of the transportation engineer, a bookstore simply becomes 16 minutes of travel time saved. The history of the north–south arterial (as well as the later history of the east–west arterial finished in 1979) also suggests that the 'tragedy of development' is not simply the tendency to reduce people and places to abstractions but the tendency to apply that process unevenly – namely to place the burden of Faustian development on the poorest in society and those least capable of resisting.

The legacy of the arterials

In 1998, and following a series of high-profile criminal cases, *New York Times* contributor Joseph Berger published an extended profile of what he described as Poughkeepsie's 'long tailspin'. That tailspin, he argued, began in the late 1950s after the city started losing jobs, industry and taxpayers to the suburban developments that had mushroomed immediately to the city's south. By the early 1990s, what had once been a 'storied place to raise a family' had, according to Berger, become a community 'accustomed to violent crime, drugs, prostitution' and racial friction. The effects of downsizing at IBM in 1993 hardly helped. For Berger, however, the city's problems were also connected to the 'cascade of policy debacles' that had defined the decades following the Second World War. As one of the highest per capita recipients of federal aid, Poughkeepsie was, as Berger argued, a 'poster child for all the government and commercial schemes of the 1960s and 1970s that produced unintended and often damaging consequences' (Berger, 1998). Between 1960 and 1980, federal aid transformed the physical structure of the city (New York Department of Transportation, 1973). Beyond the construction of the two major arterial highways (the north–south opened in 1966 and the east–west arterial opened in 1979), this included new municipal buildings and hundreds of new affordable housing units (Flad and Griffen, 2009). The aftermath of these investments was disappointing. While the city had more parking lots and more office buildings, it had fewer jobs, fewer shoppers and fewer retail options. In 1993, and reflecting on the city's post-war efforts at development, *Poughkeepsie Journal* contributor Thomas Tobin expressed a common sentiment:

> The two arterials cannot be returned to city streets with casually lumbering traffic. The caustic effects of urban renewal on lower Main are too great to be reversed. The disappointments of waterfront development are imbedded in the city's psyche. The best thing about downtown's history is that the worst is over. (Tobin, 1993b)

For Tobin and Berger, of all the 'magic potions concocted for downtown Poughkeepsie', the construction of the city's arterial highways was the most poisonous (1993b). In addition to chopping the city into quarters and wounding vibrant neighbourhoods, the highways 'made it easier for manufacturers to locate outside town' and for retailers and shoppers to bypass the city in favour of suburban shopping malls (Berger, 1998). While few go as far to blame Poughkeepsie's arterials for 'all that has gone wrong' in the city, rarely do their impact on the city's economic trajectory go unremarked (Opdycke, 1990: 76). The reasons are clear enough. Where the realities of deindustrialization, uneven development, suburbanization and car dependency remain abstract, the sheer prominence of Poughkeepsie's arterial highways, to borrow from the historian Sandra Opdycke, have made them an easy symbol for those seeking a compelling explanation for the city's failures (Opdycke, 1990: 76). To quote former Poughkeepsie Mayor Colette Lafuente: 'the city of Poughkeepsie was sacrificed to highways' (Berzon, 2000: 10).

For as much as the city's arterial highways are framed as a cause of the city's decline, they are also increasingly understood as barriers to revitalization. In 2013, the City of Poughkeepsie contracted with Kevin Dwarka, a planning consultant associated with the Pace Land Use Law Center based in White Plains, New York. Dwarka was asked to produce a report laying out a strategy to revitalize the city's downtown core and to 'reassert Poughkeepsie as the economic and cultural center of the Hudson Valley' (Dwarka, 2014: 4). Published and released in 2014, the bulk of the report focuses on transportation. The existing street layout, the report concluded, was having an 'immeasurable negative impact on the city's economic development' (Dwarka, 2014: 5). The east–west arterial constructed in the 1970s had created a 'barricade effect' that cut off the city centre from surrounding areas. The city's downtown had become an island unwelcoming to foot traffic. To revitalize the city, the report advocated transforming the arterials into boulevards, adding more frequent transit service and returning many of the city's one-way streets to two-way traffic (Dwarka, 2014: 5).

The ideas and proposals laid out in the Dwarka plan were hardly new. Indeed, they could have been taken directly from the pages of Jane Jacobs (1961) or William Whyte (1980). By 2014, however, they had come to reflect a growing consensus among planners and leaders in Poughkeepsie. Local urban designer Peter Barnard captured one element of that consensus in an article published in 2015. As he argued: 'Poughkeepsie's greatest urban design challenge is reversing the legacy of urban renewal' (Barnard, 2015). Where 'the arterials [had] disconnected city neighborhoods', good urban design, he added, required that the city work to reconnect them. In a 2017 interview with a journalism student from a local college, Poughkeepsie Mayor Rob Rolison expressed a similar view. Elected in 2015, Rolison had entered office with a goal of stabilizing the city's cratered bond rating and pushing Poughkeepsie to match the economic revival of other post-industrial cities in the region. For Rolison, the arterials posed a barrier to that goal and especially given the shifting priorities of young professionals: "People are moving back to cities for all the cool reasons. They want to go to things, they want to walk to things, they want to take a bus to things, they want to ride a bike to things. You can't do that on the arterials' (Nasso, 2017).'

Where some in Poughkeepsie have focused their efforts on reversing the legacy of the arterial highways, for others, just as important is learning how to avoid the mistakes of the past. In 2019, the city of Poughkeepsie was featured prominently in an exhibition hosted by the Center for Architecture in New York City. The exhibition, entitled *Fringe Cities: Legacies of Renewal in the Small American City* was curated by the MASS Design Group – a Boston-based design firm with a satellite office in Poughkeepsie. The exhibition used photography, maps and testimonials to document the experience of urban renewal in small cities across the country. As part of the exhibition, the curators included a quote from an anonymous Poughkeepsie resident who bemoaned what they saw the bipartisan effort in the 1960s and 1970s to destroy the city. The quote ends with a question: 'How do we not repeat the same mistake?' In a separate interview, Michael Murphy, the executive director of MASS Design and a Poughkeepsie native, raises the same issue: 'Fifty years [after urban renewal] ... we face the problem of the same mistakes unless we recalibrate, unless we think about what was happening with good intentions and terrible outcomes' (Budds, 2019).

The invocation against repeating the mistakes of the past has become a common refrain among planners and city officials in Poughkeepsie. What this invocation means in practical terms, however, is often less clear. At the general level, and to quote a review of *Fringe Cities* by the writer Justin Davidson, the exhortation is simply about recognizing 'the dangers of wanting city life to snap to an ideological grid' and of acknowledging the perils of 'imposing a utopian protocol' on complex urban systems (Davidson, 2020). Rather than the 'one size-fits-all, top down planning process', that defined the mid-century planning profession, what cities like Poughkeepsie need, to quote a designer at MASS Design, are, 'location- specific solutions developed in partnership with the people that inhabit them' (Larson, 2022). The invocation against repeating the mistakes of the past is understandable – and especially given the lasting impact of the city's arterials. At the same time, it is a plea that seems strange in the context of more than three decades of fiscal austerity. In cities like Poughkeepsie, the prospect of reversing the legacy of the arterial highways has been unlikely given a lack resources. Similarly, fears of repeating the mistakes of the past are belied by limited capacity.

In Poughkeepsie this fact finds no better illustration than in initiatives like the Poughkeepsie City Center Connectivity Project. Launched in 2016, and in partnership with both transportation consultant Sam Schwartz and the Miami-based Street Plans Collaborative the city organized a series of workshops, demonstration projects and public meetings aimed at gauging support and interest in redesigning the city's many one-way streets. Perceived as both 'ambitious in scope and range' as well as expensive, the initiative focused on a single demonstration project (City of Poughkeepsie, 2017). In early October 2016, the project team used a combination of hay bales, traffic cones, chalk paint and planters to temporarily transform Market Street – a busy one-way thoroughfare in the central city. The goal was to turn Market Street into what planners call a 'complete street' – a road that is more amenable to walking, biking and slower vehicular speeds. By using both cheap and readily available materials, the idea behind the demonstration project was to allow residents to experience a rendering of proposed changes before having to make any 'substantial financial or political commitments' (City of Poughkeepsie, 2017). This planning approach is termed tactical urbanism. In other contexts it has been called 'guerilla urbanism', 'pop-up urbanism', 'DIY urbanism', 'everyday urbanism', 'planning by doing' or 'urban prototyping' (Chase et al, 1999; Bishop and Williams, 2012; Iveson, 2013; Lydon and Garcia, 2015; Douglas, 2018). While materials may differ, at the heart of this approach is a commitment to 'using short-term, low cost, and scalable interventions to catalyze long-term change' (Streets Plan Collaborative, 2016: 11).

Some argue that tactical urbanism and urban prototyping are simply the end result of decades of austerity, state retrenchment and neoliberal restructuring (Mould, 2014; Brenner, 2017). In the face of declines in both federal and state spending on infrastructure, the use of hay bales and chalk paint is less a sign of local ingenuity than a sign of diminished ambitions and the compunction to simply 'do more with less' (Mould, 2014; Brenner, 2017). At the same time, and given its emphasis on incremental change, reversibility and non-expert knowledge, something like 'tactical urbanism' is also the clearest rebuke of the hubris that defined mid-century planning.

Whether the Poughkeepsie City Center Connectivity Project is simply a symptom of austerity or a genuine attempt at promoting 'location-specific solutions', few believe that chalk paint and hay bales will be sufficient to reverse the legacy of the city's arterial highways. Similarly, where planners are limited to traffic cones and planters, the risk of repeating the mistakes of mid-century planning seem even more remote. In short, today's John Lindmarks and Emma Maroneys have little to fear.

Projects like the Poughkeepsie City Center Connectivity Project offer yet another perspective on the 'tragedy of development'. On one hand, such projects not only speak to the incapacity of the city to reverse something like urban renewal, but the incapacity to even make minor adjustments to city's layout. In some ways this fact is common knowledge. In a 2017 interview, Poughkeepsie Mayor Rob Rolison offered what seemed a sober assessment of what was actually possible.

> It's not like cities are creating new roads, those days have kind of come and gone for the most part. We may be re-aligning, going from one way to two way [roads]. But the actual physical of construction of new streets – other than when there is construction and you need to do that – most of it is where it is and it's probably not going away. (Nasso, 2017)

Despite persistent calls to rethink the arterials, or to address the traffic collisions and fatalities associated with the north–south arterial's half-cloverleaf exchange built in the 1960s, the resources have not been forthcoming (Debald, 2020). Rather than the Faustian tragedy of noble intentions gone awry, here the tragedy is that whatever noble intentions exist, there is little likelihood that they may find expression. On the other hand, in Poughkeepsie, the tragedy of development can also be located in what appears to be a paradox. That paradox is evident in the fact that reversing the legacies of the arterial highways will not only require more than chalk paint and hay bales but it may require adopting the hubris, scope and utopian protocols that have long been the target of critique (Davidson, 2020). The paradox is also evident in the reverse, the fact that adopting 'location-specific solutions developed in partnership with the people that inhabit them' (Larson,

2021) may mean abandoning the project of reversing the legacy of post-war planning – a project that is necessarily regional in scope.

Conclusion

In November 2021, the President of the United States signed into law the Infrastructure Investment and Jobs Act. Priced at $1.2 trillion, the bill will mark the largest infusion of federal dollars in the nation's infrastructure since the 1950s. Around half of the bill is dedicated to new spending. This new allotment includes $110 billion for roads, bridges and other major projects as well as significant outlays for public transit and broadband internet (White House, 2021). The bill also includes a $1 billion set aside for the *Reconnecting Communities Act* – a small but symbolically significant pilot programme providing federal support for projects 'aimed at either removing, retrofitting, or mitigating pieces of highway and similar infrastructure' that are shown to have hampered the connectivity of communities (Vakil, 2021). While the full impact of the bill on Poughkeepsie remains to be seen, at least at the moment it offers the potential for significant and otherwise ambitious changes to the city's ageing infrastructure.

City planners and leaders in Poughkeepsie have spent decades seeking to reverse the legacy of the highway era and to 'atone for their sins' – to quote one city planner (Hughes, 2019). In most instances, however, the opportunity for atonement has been limited. While the passage of the new federal infrastructure bill is unlikely to result in the demolitions that defined the mid-century, many, especially lawyers, still expect an uptick in eminent domain cases (Rikon, 2021). If money for significant changes is made available, planners and city officials in Poughkeepsie will look back at the construction of the city's first major highway project as a lesson and as a warning. In that quest, they may stumble upon the Lindmark case, or the comments of Emma Maroney. Others, in turn, may read the speeches of Mayor Dietz or Mayor Graham. In almost every case, they will be forced to confront the 'tragedy of development' anew and to consider how the nature of that tragedy has changed over time.

As this chapter has argued, debates about the arterial highways – as well as their legacy – provide a window to how the 'tragedy of development' has evolved. At moments that tragedy has been, drawing on Berman, about noble intentions gone awry. In other instances, it can be found in the necessity of planning cities through abstractions and the contrast between the people that populate planning manuals and the Emma Maroneys that populate actual cities. In an unequal society, the burdens and costs of development invariably fall on the poorest and the least powerful. And this too is part of the tragedy. The tragedy of development is also the tragedy of noble ambitions that go unexpressed, or that collapse under the burden of avoiding the mistakes of the past. While the details and scope of the new infrastructure bill remain to be seen, in Poughkeepsie, the most optimistic view is that planners and city leaders may have yet another opportunity to use infrastructure to redefine the 'tragedy of development' and to once again answer the question asked by Richard Blouin in 1963: 'what kind of people live in Poughkeepsie, anyway?'

Acknowledgements

In the process of researching and writing this paper I drew on the support of any number of colleagues and friends. Of these, I am especially grateful to Kira Thompson, Emily Dozier, Paul Hesse, Susan Grove, Roy Budnick, Reecia Orzeck, and Angela DeFelice. I am also deeply appreciative for the patience shown to me by the editors of this volume and the initial suggestions provided by Theresa Enright, Alan Wiig and Kevin Ward.

References

Anderson, M. (1964) *The Federal Bulldozer: A Critical Analysis of Urban Renewal, 1942–1962*, Cambridge, MA: MIT Press.

Barnard, P. (2015) 'Reimagine, rethink', Poughkeepsie Journal, 7 June, p G1.

Berger, J. (1998) 'Poughkeepsie, in long tailspin, now copes with clouded image', New York Times, 5 October, p B1.

Berman, M. ([1982] 1988) *All that Is Solid Melts into Air: The Experience of Modernity*, 2nd edn, New York: Penguin.

Berzon, A. (2000) 'Panel discusses direction development should take in Poughkeepsie', *The Miscellany News*, 129(9): 10.

Bishop, P. and Williams, L. (2012) *The Temporary City*, Abingdon: Routledge.

Blouin, R. (1963) Letter to the editor, Poughkeepsie Journal, 5 May, p 12A.

Brenner, N. (2017) 'Is "tactical urbanism" an alternative to neoliberal urbanism? Reflections on an exhibition at the MoMA', in P. Petrescu and K. Trogal (eds) *The Social (Re)Production of Architecture: Politics, Values and Actions in Contemporary Practice*, Abingdon: Routledge, pp 113–28.

Budds, D. (2019) 'How four small cities are fighting the effects of urban renewal', *Curbed*, 16 October. Available from: archive.curbed.com/2019/10/16/20915450/urban-renewal-mass-design-fringe-cities [Accessed January 3 2023].

Candeub & Fleissig Planning Consultants (1960) *Master Plan Report 4: Traffic Plan*, February, Poughkeepsie, NY: City of Poughkeepsie.

Chase J., Kaliski, J. and Crawford, M. (1999) *Everyday Urbanism*, New York: Monacelli Press.

Chicago Tribune (1963) 'Dump books like trash: dealer is ousted in New York road feud', Chicago Tribune, 27 April, p 3.

City of Poughkeepsie (2017) *Poughkeepsie City Center Connectivity Project*, December, p 4. Available from: https://www.cityofpoughkeepsie.com/DocumentCenter/View/345/PCCCP-Final-Report-PDF [Accessed 10 November 2022].

City Chamberlain (1957) 'Approval of plans', *Minutes of the Poughkeepsie Common Council 1957*, 4 March, Poughkeepsie, NY: Common Council, p 128.

City Chamberlain (1958a) 'Reports of committees: Arterial Highway Committee', *Minutes of the Poughkeepsie Common Council 1958*, 15 September, Poughkeepsie, NY: Common Council, pp 435–7.

City Chamberlain (1958b) 'Reports of Committees', *Minutes of the Poughkeepsie Common Council 1958*, 3 September, Poughkeepsie, NY: Common Council, p 410.

City Chamberlain (1960) 'Letters to Common Council', *Minutes of the Poughkeepsie Common Council 1960*, 21 March, Poughkeepsie, NY: Common Council, p 181.

Davidson, J. (2020) 'The Mid-Century Misfire That Was "Slum Clearance" Tore Down Much More Than Tenements', *New York Magazine*. 8 January. Available from: http://nymag.com/intelligencer/2020/01/fringe-cities-center-for-architecture.htm [Accessed January 3 2023].

Debald, M. (2020) 'Poughkeepsie 9.44.55: rethinking the arterials and interchange', *Plan On It: A Dutchess County Planning Federation eNewsletter*, 1–6 October. Available from: https://www.dutchessny.gov/Departments/Planning/Docs/October2020-Poughkeepsie94455-printerfriendly.pdf [Accessed 10 November 2022].

Douglas, G.C.C. (2018) *The Help-Yourself City: Legitimacy and Inequality in DIY Urbanism*, Oxford: Oxford University Press.

Dwarka, K. (2014) Poughkeepsie City Center Revitalization Plan Draft: *Working Paper 1: Existing Conditions*, 31 March, Poughkeepsie, NY. Available from: https://www.cityofpoughkeepsie.com/DocumentCenter/View/113/Poughkeepsie-City-Center-Revitalization-Plan-PDF [Accessed 10 November 2022].

Edison, T. (1966) 'Vietnam: what should we do?' New York Times, 16 October, p 199.

Elmira Star Gazette (1922) 'Proposed new highway bridge across Hudson', Elmira Star Gazette, 14 December, p 12.

Flad, H. (1987) 'A time of readjustment: urban renewal in Poughkeepsie 1955–1975', in C.

Flad, H. and Griffen, C. (2009) *Main Street and Mainframes: Landscape and Social Change in Poughkeepsie*, Albany, NY: SUNY Press.

Griffen (ed) *New Perspectives on Poughkeepsie's Past*, Poughkeepsie, NY: Dutchess County Historical Society, pp 152–80.

Hughes, C.J. (2019) 'A Hudson river city that's worked hard for its revival', Poughkeepsie Journal, 16 June, p 6RE.

Iveson, K. (2013) 'Cities within the city: do-it-yourself urbanism and the right to the city', *International Journal of Urban and Regional Research*, 37(3): 941–56.

Jacobs, J. (1961) *The Death and Life of Great American Cities*, New York: Vintage.

Journal-News (1963) 'City burning books owner left on walk', *Journal-News*, 23 May, p 1.

Larson, J. (2022) 'Poughkeepsie: Real Renewal', *Chronogram*, 1 February. Available from Chonogram.com/hudsonvalley/poughkeepsie-real-renewal/ [Accessed January 3 2023].

Lydon, M. and Garcia, A. (2015) *Tactical Urbanism: Short-Term Action for Long-Term Change*, Washington, DC: Island Press.

Mould, O. (2014) 'Tactical urbanism: the new vernacular of the creative city', *Geography Compass*, 8(8): 529–39.

Mowrer, E.A. (1963) 'So it couldn't happen here?', Lowell Sun, 3 May, p 6.

Mumford, L. (1955) 'The sky line: the roaring traffic's boom – III', The New Yorker, 16 April, p 78.

Myers, H. (1960) 'Signs tell the story along artery route', Poughkeepsie Journal, 4 December, p 1C.

Myers, H. (1961) 'Cloverleaf slated in union square hub', Poughkeepsie Journal, 1 January, p 1C.

Nasso, R. (2017) 'The complex roads of Poughkeepsie', The Groundhog, 10 April. Available from: https://medium.com/thegroundhog/the-complex-roads-of-poughkeepsie-d85fac424b68 [Accessed 10 November 2022].

New York Department of Transportation (nd 1973) *Draft Environmental/Section 4(f) Statement Poughkeepsie East–West Arterial*, Albany, NY: NYDT.

O'Brien, E. (1961) 'Lindmark has only 12 days left to move 800,000 books from artery path', Poughkeepsie Journal, 6 December, p 52.

O'Brien, E. (1963a) 'Moving of Lindmark books marks end of era in city', Poughkeepsie Journal, 2 May, p 34.

O'Brien, E. (1963b) 'All ages paw through Lindmark books, tumbling neat stacks piled by workmen', Poughkeepsie Journal, 26 April, p 1.

Opdycke, S. (1990) 'With prosperity all around: urban issues in Poughkeepsie, N.Y., 1950–1980', *Dutchess County Historical Society Year Book*, 75: 62–80, Poughkeepsie, NY: Dutchess County Historical Society.

Poughkeepsie Eagle (1922) 'Poughkeepsians urge support of highway bridge movement', Poughkeepsie Eagle, 8 March, p 1.

Poughkeepsie Journal (1952) 'Stevens vows full hearing on holy comforter appeals', Poughkeepsie Journal, 3 July, p 1.

Poughkeepsie Journal (1957a) 'Chamber urges artery plan to solve traffic congestion', Poughkeepsie Journal, 21 February, p 26.

Poughkeepsie Journal (1957b) 'Text of Graham's statement', Poughkeepsie Journal, 17 February, p 8A.

Poughkeepsie Journal (1958a) 'Rise in values if forecast if city approves artery plan', Poughkeepsie Journal, 24 June, p 7.

Poughkeepsie Journal (1958b) 'An artery for the queen city', Poughkeepsie Journal, 16 September, p 6.

Poughkeepsie Journal (1960) '57 families ask assistance', Poughkeepsie Journal, 9 October, p 9B.

Poughkeepsie Journal (1961) 'Artery will save lives, state official tells court in Lindmark ouster case', Poughkeepsie Journal, 20 December, p 14.

Poughkeepsie Journal (1962a) 'State acts to release wrecker from Lindmark demolition job', Poughkeepsie Journal, 15 August, p 1.

Poughkeepsie Journal (1962b) 'Bergman reports: Lindmark demolition delay imposes hardship on firm', Poughkeepsie Journal, 15, April, p 4.

Poughkeepsie Journal (1963a) 'City burns Lindmark books in incinerator', Poughkeepsie Journal, 22 May, p 1.

Poughkeepsie Journal (1963b) 'Decision in Lindmark case reported by Judge Haven', Poughkeepsie Journal, 4 April, p 22.

Poughkeepsie Journal (1964) 'Artery work starts Monday', Poughkeepsie Journal, 4 January, p 1.

Poughkeepsie Journal (1966) 'Scenes of artery which opens Friday', Poughkeepsie Journal, 28 August, p 5B.

Poughkeepsie Journal (1969) 'State accepts city plan for Urban Renewal relocation', Poughkeepsie Journal, 25 September p 12.

Poughkeepsie Journal (1971) 'Relocation payments complete', Poughkeepsie Journal, 23 October, p 2.

Poughkeepsie Journal (1979) 'East–west arterial highway is open … almost', Poughkeepsie Journal, 6 November, p 10.

Rikon, M. (2021) 'The infrastructure package means business for eminent domain lawyers', Law.com. Available from: https://www.law.com/newyorklawjournal/2021/12/23/the-infrastructure-package-means-business-for-eminent-domain-lawyers/ [Accessed 10 November 2022].

Ronall, J.O. (1963) 'Bookshop's razing assailed: to the editor of the New York Times', New York Times, 1 May, p 38.

Salisbury, H. (1959) 'Study finds cars choking cities as "urban sprawl" takes over', New York Times, 3 March, p 1.

Sells, C., Bonaparte, C. and Tallamy, B. (1947) *Report on State Arterial Highway in the Poughkeepsie Urban Area*, Albany, NY: Department of Public Works.

Scott, J.C. (1998) *Seeing Like a State: How Certain Schemes to Improve the Human Condition Have Failed*, New Haven, CT: Yale University Press.

Stevens, J. (1963) 'Bookseller's library trampled as shop makes way for road', New York Times, 27 April, p 27.

Streets Plan Collaborative (2016) *Tactical Urbanists Guide to Materials and Design*. Available from: http://tacticalurbanismguide.com/ [Accessed 10 November 2022].

Tobin, T. (1993a) 'Early urban renewal programs leave trail of unfulfilled promises', Poughkeepsie Journal, 9 April, p 8E.

Tobin, T. (1993b) 'History dotted with miscues', Poughkeepsie Journal, 9 April, p8E ★.

Vakil, C. (2021) 'Advocates see pilot program to address inequalities from highways as crucial first step', The Hill, 26 November. Available from: https://thehill.com/policy/transportation/583066-advocates-see-pilot-program-to-address-highway-inequalities-as-crucial [Accessed 10 November 2022].

White House (2021) Fact Sheet: The Bipartisan Infrastructure Deal, 6 November, Washington DC: The White House. Available from: https://www.whitehouse.gov/briefing-room/statements-releases/2021/11/06/fact-sheet-the-bipartisan-infrastructure-deal/ [Accessed 10 November 2022].

Whyte, W.H. (1980) *The Social Life of Small Urban Places*, New York: Project for Public Spaces.

3

Temporalities of the Climate Crisis: Maintenance, Green Finance and Racialized Austerity in New York City and Cape Town

Patrick Bigger and Nate Millington

Introduction

Cities built for the 20th century are increasingly reckoning with 21st century realities that cut across social, economic and environmental registers. A critical confluence lies in the question of how to pay for the infrastructure needed to adapt to changing socio-environmental conditions precipitated by climate change. The infrastructures built to respond to previous climatic regimes no longer appear capable of providing services, protecting from environmental calamities, and ensuring safety and dignity to all residents. At the same time, it must be noted that in many cities, especially but not exclusively in the Global South, infrastructures were never universal. Instead, infrastructures have long been marked by inequality and unevenness, both between cities but also within them, reflecting patterns of uneven development and uneven investment. In the current moment, these specific inequalities are being stretched even further, as pressures from a changing climate intersect with forms of service delivery that prioritize cost recovery through seemingly ever-increasing tariffs and fares. As Furlong makes clear, infrastructure and its financing are intimately linked: 'infrastructure can act both as a foundation for economic development and social inclusion, and as an instrument of wealth extraction, enhanced inequality and potential crisis' (Furlong, 2020: 572). Attention to the specificities of infrastructure is subsequently critical to understanding contemporary cities, as it is one of the key sites through which inequality is experienced and one of the key mechanisms through which urban landscapes are made. This is especially true across binaries of Global North and South, where the capacity of states to drive investment is a key component of how climate change can and will be responded to at the municipal level.

In the current moment, municipalities must come to grips not only with sea-level rise, less predictable weather and growing urban populations, but also the complicated legacies of uneven, often racialized, development in and between cities. The funding requirements to adapt to new environmental realities are astronomical, running into the hundreds of billions of US dollars per year globally (UNEP, 2016). Some cities have begun to anticipate the new infrastructure that climate change will require, while others have been forced to adapt in real time. This chapter focuses on two cities where climate change has materialized in spectacular as well as mundane ways: New York City and Cape Town, South Africa. Both were marked by experiences of what have been commonly referred to as climate crises: Superstorm Sandy drenched New York City in October 2012 and Cape Town was impacted by a drought-induced crisis of water scarcity from 2016 to 2018. In addition to these examples of high-profile environmental crisis, both cities are also increasingly marked by changing environmental pressures in their everyday operations and functions. New York City has been marked by dangerous and devastating climatic events in recent years – most notably the flooding associated with Hurricane Ida in 2021 – but the city is also impacted by a persistent maintenance crisis due to increasingly regularized problems with water. In Cape Town, the drought and resulting water shortages created budgetary shortfalls that needed to be made up in the months and years following the crisis, and a necessary commitment to water demand management continues to come up against intractable governance challenges. These challenges play out on a landscape of extreme infrastructural inequality, where previous forms of infrastructural cross-subsidization are increasingly at risk (Shepherd, 2019; Millington and Scheba, 2021).

While cities of the Global North and South are often analysed separately, a relational approach rooted in questions drawn from Southern urban theory can shed light on how seemingly distinct cities are nevertheless reflective of shared processes (Lawhon et al, 2016; Caldeira, 2017; Hart, 2018; Roy, 2009, 2017). Asking supposedly 'Southern' questions of the North, and 'Northern' questions of the South, can make clear how contemporary urban geographies are best understood comparatively and across binaries of North and South. Infrastructure is the materialization of uneven geographies of investment and disinvestment, and this focus invites consideration of how the urban is unevenly produced and how unevenness can be expressed at both planetary scales as well as local or regional ones. Attention to the expression of urban inequality via infrastructure between cities but also within cities can allow for analyses that take seriously the variegated but nevertheless still shared experiences of a changing climate – and its municipal manifestations.

In this chapter we explore the ways that municipalities have opted in part to finance their response to a changing climate using debt, in particular through the use of green bonds, a type of debt specifically designated for environmental ends. The New York Metropolitan Transit Authority (hereafter MTA) and the City of Cape Town have been pioneers in the municipal green bond market. The bonds issued by MTA and Cape Town are certified to the Climate Bonds Standard, which requires the identification of the use of proceeds and an external verification by an auditor of those green bona fides. It does not, however, guarantee that any greater environmental benefits will accrue than would have otherwise happened, nor does it necessarily impact the cost of capital for borrowers. Green bonds also do not require that these bonds will pay for transformative investments in infrastructure. Instead, in both New York City and Cape Town, green debt has largely been used to refinance existing projects.

We argue that the use of green debt for climate change adaptation in cities that are already feeling its impact threatens to deepen racialized infrastructural geographies of financial and environmental risk. While Cape Town is perhaps the prototypical case of racialized inequality given its enduring apartheid spatialities, the constitution and distribution of environmental and financial risk play out in broadly similar ways in both cities due to the histories and processes through which racial capitalism materializes in specific sites (Fredrickson, 1981). Finance does not alter existing geographies and dynamics despite its framing as a vehicle for building more resilient cities. That finance can keep systems running without fundamentally changing them draws attention to one of the central tensions of climate finance across scales, that those least responsible for emissions are facing the brunt of the climate crisis. Cape Town's hydroscape is defined not simply by an absolute water shortage but reflects enduring inequalities that bifurcate the population into over- and under-consumers of water (see Rodina, 2016; Millington and Scheba, 2021; Yates and Harris, 2018). The inequalities of public transportation provision in New York are similarly indexed against historical and contemporary social difference, as the poor, women and communities of colour disproportionately bear the risks of poor transportation access and reliability.

Undoing inequities of service provision that have built up over decades and centuries is not the aim of green bonds, but the temporal structure of finance needs to be considered when imagining particular development trajectories linked to climate change. Bond markets are predicated on the assumption of certain futures which then get built into the present, with implications for those who make payments – in particular ratepayers and urban residents who receive (and pay for) infrastructural services. The turn to (green) debt as a mechanism for responding to the future and present threat of climate change has implications for how infrastructural temporalities are conceptualized and experienced, with claims made on the future impacting on the present.

We argue in this chapter that the turn to capital markets for adaptation finance threatens to narrow the possibilities for radical changes needed for a just transformation. By piling on additional debts in which investors generally have senior claims on future revenues, municipal borrowing to fund projects that are already in process forecloses more fundamental actions in the present and future. While all forms of debt financing inherently constitute and distribute risk, we are concerned that the 'greening' of municipal debt may occlude retrograde social processes that heap addition risks onto those least able to bear them. By this, we mean that the 'green halo' (Sörqvist et al, 2015) of environmental finance may distract observers not attuned to day-to-day realities of people who are indelibly dependent on public infrastructure – for example, New Yorkers who have few choices for transportation except subways and buses, or Capetonians without the means to afford new water tariffs levied in response to the city's crisis. In both cases, crisis response mediated through green debt can leave these communities in more, rather than less, risky positions.

At the same time, these cities, like most, have few good options when it comes to paying for adaptation. Decades of austerity, rising inequality, the spatialization of explicitly racist policies and the costs associated with disaster recovery all impose financial burdens on top of already spiralling costs for infrastructure maintenance and provision. While marginalized communities in both cities have long suffered infrastructural deprivation in comparison to favoured parts of each city, the contemporary expression of municipalized austerity has distinctly different origins despite outcomes that bear key similarities. In short, many of the effects of austerity and the growing power of financiers in the global economy have left city bureaucrats with little recourse to institutions other than capital markets if they are to make the best of an impossible situation within existing political-economic arrangements. Adaptation in the city cannot be reduced to questions of municipal fiscal management; it requires sustained investment from other fiscal scales coupled with systemic changes to how risks, environmental and economic, are produced and distributed.

Green debts and climate crisis

The consolidation of capital in increasingly smaller hands means that many neighbourhoods, cities and nation states are starved of funds for day-to-day maintenance or the expansion of vital services, never mind transformative infrastructural retrofits that could produce inclusive communities that are less exposed to environmental and economic risks. In cities, this starvation has been produced through municipal austerity and has resulted in racially explicit infrastructural deprivation, further complicated by environmental change. Adaptation needs impose additional costs on cities and drive them to increased borrowing and service charges, fuelling a cycle of indebtedness and intensifying spatialities of risk. While other studies of financialization have linked state austerity across juridical scales to the introduction of financial practices and logics in governance (Peck, 2012), links between austerity and the financialization of nature have been notable in their absence (Calvário et al, 2017; Bigger and Dempsey, 2018).

As urban climate policy becomes increasingly interwoven with finance capital, the forms through which those policies are articulated are globally significant (Long and Rice, 2019). Attention to the specific forms of those changes is critical if we are to contest looming eco-apartheid prefigured by the constitution and distribution of environmental/economic risk (Cohen, 2017). This interest, in turn, leads us back to recent work on racial capitalism, and how the meteoric growth of financial markets and deployments of financial logics (in nature and otherwise) are not simply an economic phenomenon, but are intensely social-spatial processes to which racism and White supremacy, historical and contemporary, are inextricably bound (Kish and Leroy, 2015; Bledsoe and Wright, 2019). If urban austerity is marked by a bio/necro-politics of abandonment articulated through race (McIntyre and Nast, 2011; Ranganathan, 2016) while the extent and intensification of financialization also operates through race (Arestis et al, 2013), it stands to reason that financial responses to urban climate crises will be shot through with racialized dynamics of risk. We build on insights from Christophers's (2018: 146) analysis of bonds that financed Washington, DC's sewerage system refurbishment. In his analysis, environmental and financial risks associated with debt will have potentially harmful impacts on residents who bear environmental risks from a changing climate as well as through their role as the primary funders of debt-servicing obligations through their tariffs and fees. We extend this argument by noting that urban residents do not bear environmental and financial risks equally, and the distribution of those risks breaks down on well-worn raced and classed lines.

We do this largely through attention to labelled green debt, one of the financial tools utilized by municipalities to make up for budgetary shortfalls and broader austerity dynamics. Green debt was the domain of development banks until 2014, when municipalities and corporations began borrowing for less carbon-intensive projects. By the end of 2017, annual green bond issuance exceeded US$160 billion, nearly topping all other types of finance explicitly designated to mitigate or adapt to climate change combined. Green bonds increasingly form a component of mainstream investment portfolios and help define what kinds of climate change–related projects get funded (Bracking, 2015). Proponents of green bonds claim that if even a sliver of all bonds were 'greened', the funding gaps for the provision of urban infrastructure designed for the rigours of climate change could be filled overnight (Climate Bonds Initiative, nd). As a result, there is legitimate interest among some debt buyers for investment-grade bonds that have a credible claim to creating environmental benefits.

Both Cape Town and New York City have issued green bonds in response to ongoing socioecological crisis and officials in both cities reported that labelling increased orders for debt as new investors are attracted to bonds they might not have previously considered (Issuer interviews, October 2018). That increasing interest by new buyers will 'crowd in' green finance is one of the animating hypotheses of green bond advocates; when labelled green debt outperforms unlabelled debt, green bonds will create a pricing premium. In turn, this would lower the cost of environmentally conscious projects and create a 'virtuous cycle' of more and more green projects (Reichelt and Keenan, 2017). While there is preliminary evidence that this 'greenium' may be starting to emerge (Partridge and Medda, 2018), research participants in Cape Town's municipal finance division, in New York directly involved with the MTA's green borrowing, and other market interlocutors in Copenhagen and London expressed scepticism that any such discount existed. Indeed, with added costs of verifying the environmental criteria of a bond, issuance may be more, rather than less, expensive. This echoes Christophers's (2018) observation that the use of exotic green financial mechanisms in Washington, DC actually increased borrowing costs for utilities, and hence for ratepayers.

These added expenses with no guaranteed price premium are two of the shortcomings we might attribute to green bonds (see Bigger and Millington, 2019 for a more detailed analysis). Additionally, while some green bonds are certified to comply with standards that have developed, there are no legal definitions of 'green' in green bonds. The failure to achieve stated environmental goals in any issuance is legally unpunishable. Further, and more directly relevant to the story we want to tell, green labelling does not entail any promise that funding raised will be more environmentally beneficial than what would have happened otherwise; in the language of carbon markets, there is not necessarily any additionality. This means that green debt can be, and frequently is, used to pay for projects that have already been completed by refinancing bank debt, or to pay for projects that are already planned. This is the case in both New York and Cape Town, where green bonds have largely refinanced existing debt.

As such, paying attention to dynamics of 'green' finance has implications not just for work in political ecology but also for understanding contemporary urban and infrastructural governance in an era of deepening austerity, climate crisis and what Long and Rice (2019) call 'climate urbanism'. Climate finance offers unique insight into contemporary governance challenges facing cities and municipalities (Bulkeley, 2010; Taylor and Aalbers, 2022). While Rebecca Lave (in Bigger and Dempsey, 2018) is right that much of the focus on environmental finance has prioritized novelty over effect, the degree to which cities are positioned as the primary actors within climate change adaptation and mitigation is increasingly hard to overstate and suggests the need for critical inquiry into climate-induced budgeting in multiscalar contexts of austerity (Long and Rice, 2019).

New York: managing austerity with debt

In the summer of 2017, then-Governor of New York Andrew Cuomo announced that the New York subway system was in a state of emergency (Fitzsimmons, 2017). Given the magnitude of the damage to the subway system created by Superstorm Sandy in 2012, estimated at around $5 billion, one might suppose the storm was the proximate cause of a lingering crisis (Hinds, 2012). Sandy certainly contributed to reliability problems that saw on-time performance slip to 58 per cent in early 2018 (Hu, 2018), but the roots of the transportation crisis can be traced back to New York's fiscal crisis of the 1970s (Harvey, 2005). Since the early 1970s, the MTA has see-sawed between financial famine and comparative feast. Each successive renaissance, however, has come with the burden of more debt as relative state appropriations fell, fares rose, antiquated signalling degraded and the system was rendered unprepared – both physically and financially – for an external shock like Sandy. While Sandy was dramatic in its intensity, water is a constant struggle for the MTA: 14 million gallons of water are pumped out of the system on dry days alone (Hu and Barnard, 2021).

The unequal provisioning of infrastructure is built into the fabric of New York City. Transportation, as much as redlining or restrictive covenants, was and is a key component to the spatialization of race in the city (see Winner, 1980). Robert Moses, New York's City Planning Commissioner (among his many titles) throughout the mid-20th century, promoted car-led development, which often had racially deleterious consequences. Moses was responsible for vast demolitions and dispossessions targeting neighbourhoods of colour; up to 500,000 people were displaced, directly or indirectly, by Moses's 'slum clearance' (Caro, 1974). These dispossessions facilitated the construction of motorways that eased (White) car-commuting from suburbs while displacing communities of colour to further-flung parts of the boroughs with less access to public transit. The processes of displacement and redlining contributed to the racial unrest of the 1960s (Freilla, 2004). This, in turn, was followed by new rounds of disinvestment in neighbourhoods throughout the city, helping format New York's contemporary spatialities of inequality.

Now, even the parts of the city that are historically well served by transportation suffer from reliability issues. For some New Yorkers, the subway's poor on-time performance is merely an annoyance (if a vexing one). But for communities dependent on public transit, a grouping that includes many low-income workers, often women, people of colour and immigrants, a late train can mean losing a job, missing a doctor's appointment for which they will be charged, or sending a child to disciplinary proceedings for tardiness. This is especially true for service industry workers (again, disproportionately women and people of colour), whose transportation needs are even less well served than New Yorkers who travel during peak hours. The flexibilization of work has not been matched by an increase in trains and buses during non-peak times (Stringer, 2018). In this way, the risks produced by the subway system crises of maintenance and funding, inflected by Sandy's damage to the system, are unevenly borne across axes of social difference. These points are made explicitly by transit advocacy organizations like Straphangers as well as anti-racist movements like Swipe it Forward, who explicitly connect the maintenance crisis with the heightened policing of fare-evaders. For Swipe it Forward, 'Punishing fare-evaders IS a criminalization of poverty, and it adversely affects black and brown people in the city' (Swipe it Forward, 2021). Transportation infrastructure shapes racialized inequality in multiple ways.

New York's mass transit system was 'financialized' from its genesis, as the various subway lines were built by the city and then leased to private operators (Hood, [1993] 2004). The system was subsequently brought under state ownership in the 1940s, but by the early 1980s was taking on ever-increasing debt while government appropriations waned. Following the municipal financial crisis that was part of the wider economic downturn in the early 1970s, New York City's transit system infamously fell into disrepair, especially the subway. Graffitied MTA trains became synonymous with racialized urban blight (Dickinson, 2008), and with the US 'urban crisis' more generally. In 1981, when the MTA began to dig itself out of the hole created by austerity, it did so both through marginally higher state appropriations and through expanded borrowing powers (Rivera, 2008). In 1981, MTA carried no long-term debt; by 1999 outstanding debt stood at US$17.5 billion (Rivera, 2008). Debt levels stabilized briefly, but in 2002 the debt was restructured, dramatically prolonging the repayment period on existing debt (NY Torch, 2010). This meant greater capital availability and increased headroom for further borrowing in the short term, but the trade-off was an ever-increasing debt burden that would be borne by multiple generations of transit users. Debt issued in the early 1990s would not be paid off until 2032 (Rivera, 2008).

Following the 2002 restructuring, MTA's debt load began to grow even more rapidly, reaching nearly US$30 billion in 2009 (PCAC, 2012), an increase of nearly 60 per cent in a decade, and a pace which MTA has maintained. Including its $6.2 billion in green bonds, MTA debt now stands at nearly $50 billion. Debt service is MTA's second largest cost after labour and is growing at twice the rate (Braun, 2018). Because of this deteriorating financial situation, MTA's credit rating was downgraded in August 2018 to A by Standard and Poor's, closer to non-investment grade than prime (Scaggs, 2018). This, perversely, will further raise borrowing costs on future issuances, exacerbating the austerity-fuelled hole in which it finds itself.

To address challenges of funding and to highlight the positive environmental impacts of mass transit, in 2016 the MTA turned to what was at the time a relatively untested tool to finance its operating expenses and capital spending in the form of its initial green bond offering. The issuance came soon after the MTA's 'fix and fortify' programme in the wake of Sandy that identified critical upgrades needed in indispensable parts of the system. Observers reckon that the 'fix' part of the programme, which was paid for primarily through US federal disaster recovery funds, went reasonably well, though it is difficult to parse considering the overarching maintenance crisis (deMause, 2016). However, the 'fortify' part of the equation has been much slower to materialize, remaining an aspiration tied to the MTA's underfunded capital budget. To fund fixes and fortifications, while also simply raising enough capital to keep transit running, the MTA has continued to issue debt, much of which now bears a green label. The MTA offers half of each bond issuance to retail investors, and even conducts marketing campaigns in stations for some issuances (interview with MTA official, October 2018). Part of this marketing effort around the green bond was to entice younger buyers, as millennials are thought to be shifting towards 'impact investing', or investments that promise to deliver desirable social or environmental outcomes (interview with MTA official, October 2018).

As Rosenman (2019) and Kish and Leroy (2015) demonstrate, impact investing (of which green bonds might be considered a part) is a way that the life chances of the poor and people of colour come to be further imbricated with financial logics. Offering bonds to retail investors, and advertising them to commuters is, in effect, a way for New Yorkers with investable income to extract rents from New Yorkers dependent on public transportation. Given that a substantial proportion of the 60 per cent of New Yorkers who live pay-cheque-to-pay-cheque are also reliant on mass transit (Afridi, 2016), and the majority of passengers are women, people of colour and immigrants (Kabak, 2010; Saska, 2015), the use of debt to fund mass transit operations represents an intra-urban reverse subsidy where the poor and communities of colour indirectly transfer rents to people with investable money.

Meanwhile, these communities disproportionately bear the environmental risks of the next storm. People with investable income are more likely to be able to afford other means of transportation in response to crises of mobility, both ordinary and extraordinary, particularly through on-demand ride hailing, the growth of which is driving down subway ridership (Colon, 2018). The combination of unreliable service and taxi deregulation is fuelling what was recently pronounced a 'death spiral' (Durkin, 2018), as the maintenance crisis drives middle-class passengers to ride-hailing apps, in turn reducing fare revenues, leading to further constrained budgets and deteriorating borrowing conditions and, ultimately to fare increases and further borrowing. That is without adding the next storm into the equation, or the ongoing COVID-19 pandemic.

In New York, conservative think tanks and some in the media are pinning the blame for rising costs and the maintenance crisis on workers' salaries and pensions, signalling increased risks for workers through new rounds of austerity and calls for union busting (for example, Gelinas, 2011). This is doubly significant because of the demographic profile of New York transit workers. In 2007, 70 per cent of transportation workers were people of colour; African Americans constituted more than 40 per cent of the workforce despite being a quarter of the city's population at the same time (LMIS, 2009). Meanwhile, the median annual earnings for MTA employees was around $90,000 per year in 2015 (Knocke, 2016), significantly higher than most blue-collar jobs. Therefore, any attack on workers is explicitly an attack on communities of colour, who will be disproportionately impacted by job losses or cuts to pay and benefits. By pursuing adaptation through debt rather than broad-based taxation at the federal and state level to fund radically increased appropriation to the system, the books will be balanced on the backs of the workers and transit users.

This follows a broader pattern of the racialized impacts of austerity. Federal austerity in the US has trans-scalar impacts because of the importance of intergovernmental transfers. Austerity has hastened the shift from government to governance, a well-trod feature of neoliberalization more broadly (Peck, 2012); a less well explored dimension is who lost jobs as parts of the state have contracted. Given that federal and some states desegregated work early compared to much of the private sector, public sector employment was a cornerstone of African American class ascendancy in the US in the 1960s and 1970s (Laird, 2017). However, as these workers retired or were laid off and their positions were contracted out, employment was rendered precarious, less well paid or simply unfulfilled. The loss of government jobs has been a contributor to growth of the racial wage gap. In 1979, Black men's average hourly salary was 22 per cent lower than that of White men. By 2015, the gap had grown to 31 per cent (Redden and Kasperkevic, 2016). The MTA's financial precarity, maintenance crisis and environmental vulnerability disproportionately impacts the everyday lives of people of colour, and increased debt service will increase pressure to make cuts elsewhere, most likely on the salary and benefits of a workforce that disproportionately comprises people of colour.

Meanwhile, capital spending activities are unevenly distributed. Work continues on the massively expensive Hudson Yards extension that will primarily serve new corporate banking headquarters in west Manhattan. While cost estimates to shore up the subway in the next ten years come in around $40 billion, the proposed responses have been insufficient, piecemeal and often regressive. The newest initiative would see the introduction of a congestion charge levied on cars entering the central business district of Manhattan, with proceeds ring-fenced mostly for the subway. The new fee is projected to raise $800 million to $1.5 billion annually over the next decade but, importantly, advocates note that the revenue could be leveraged into further bond issuances worth as much as 17 times the value of the congestion charge (Fitzsimmons, 2018). As Huber (2016) has shown, however, tying environmental funding to dedicated revenue sources, rather than drawing from general state obligations that can be funded through progressive taxation is risky because those mechanisms are easily reversed and can experience wild swings. The MTA does look to benefit considerably from the Infrastructure Investment and Jobs Act passed in 2021 by the Biden Administration, but the projected amounts are broadly insufficient to the system's needs. While the details are still being discussed, the MTA expects to receive around $10 billion to upgrade accessibility and make other long-needed changes (Gold et al, 2021). With ridership still only at 60 per cent of pre-pandemic levels as of May 2022 (Woodhouse, 2022), however, significantly more financing is undoubtedly needed if the system is to continue running.

Cape Town: municipal autonomy and household debt impairment

Cape Town is marked by enduring and dramatic inequality materialized in the city's infrastructures (Jaglin, 2008). While the inability to access drinkable water is statistically insignificant, the everyday dynamics of water access are more complex given the city's highly differentiated urban form. Accessing water in the city is complicated by broader dynamics of informality, insecurity, and uneven tenure (Rodina, 2016). The city has made impressive strides in extending water provisioning, but the intensity of segregation and inequality in the city means that consistent water access is a challenge for many, especially when access overlaps with broader dynamics of insecurity, informality, and indebtedness (Figure 3.1). Finding ways to reduce water demand has been a priority of the municipality since 2007 at least, largely owing to population growth and potential limitations on surface water due to climate change (City of Cape Town, nd, Ziervogel, 2019).

These dynamics were pushed to their limit between 2016 and 2018, when the city of Cape Town reached the precipice of a water crisis that nearly resulted in citywide rationing under the spectre of 'Day Zero'. The city

Figure 3.1: Public art in Cape Town, 2018

Source: Nate Millington

was narrowly able to avoid a full-scale crisis of water delivery through huge reductions in personal water consumption by urban residents, the negotiation of significant water transfers from the agricultural sector and, ultimately, the return of rain (Figure 3.2). Reductions in personal water usage were unprecedented: Capetonians reduced their water footprint by roughly 50 per cent over the course of two years through a combination of punitive tariffs, voluntary reductions and technical approaches including pressure reductions in pipes (for an overview of the crisis and the municipal response, see Ziervogel, 2019).

Declining revenues resulting from reduced water consumption created a complex fiscal situation for the city, as the crisis reduced the city's revenue, inhibiting forms of cross-subsidization that have been critical to post-apartheid governance in South Africa. In early 2018 the city proposed a drought levy to make up for reduced income from tariffs because of the crisis. This levy would have subsidized the budget through a system based not on water usage but on property values. A complex coalition of rich and poor actors aggressively pushed back, arguing that the proposal unfairly affected residents who had lowered their water consumption considerably. The levy was scrapped (Kamaldien, 2018). As a result, the city released a budget that included a significant increase in water cost, with tiered pricing based on water usage. While the new tariffs were politically unpopular, they

Figure 3.2: References to the water crisis at Cape Town International Airport, 2018

Source: Nate Millington

were justified as being necessary due to the combined situation of reduced water income and increased costs due to new water augmentation strategies including groundwater extraction and desalination.

The city's water crisis fits into a longer dynamic of increased pressure on the municipality from continued in-migration, worries about water availability because of climate change, and limited federal investment in the water sector. South African municipalities have a large degree of financial autonomy, especially in the domains of human settlement (including water) and public transportation. This gives municipalities licence to operate semi-independently, but also requires that they find ways of funding their operations. The bulk of municipal revenues comes from their own revenue streams, mainly service charges and property taxes (SACN, 2018: ii). In Cape Town, for the budget year 2016/17, 82 per cent of the city's revenues came from their own sources (SACN, 2018: 7), with toughly 10 per cent of the city's operating budget coming from water tariffs. Gaps in revenue that are available to municipalities to fund infrastructure and critical services are growing, however, and municipalities are being increasingly encouraged by the national government to increase their borrowing. The Development Bank of South Africa's Municipal Infrastructure Investment Framework has outlined the capital requirements for South Africa's municipal services, including water supply (see Palmer et al, 2017: 142). In the case of water supply, the estimated capital needs roughly double the actual capital spent, and municipal funding gaps are expected to grow in the next decade (SACN, 2018: v). As Palmer et al (2017: 156) note, '[T]here remains a gap in the availability of capital that applies across the municipal spectrum. This ... means that poor households are deprived of adequate services, and too many are left to live in underserved informal settlements and depressed rural settlements'.

The use of debt finance is one means of plugging this gap. The City of Cape Town issued a green bond in July 2017. Although issued during the water crisis, the decision to issue a green bond had been made beforehand and formed part of the city's longer-term strategy to issue bonds in recognition of declining financial resources at the federal level (interview with Western Cape provincial government employee, October 2018). In describing the bond itself, representatives of the treasury department noted that its issuance was part of the then-mayor's strategy to articulate a green or sustainability strategy in the years preceding the crisis (interview with Representatives of Cape Town Treasury Department, July 2018). The extra cost of processing the bond was justified as a material demonstration of the city's commitment to green ambitions. As the city possesses high rates of creditworthiness in relation to other municipalities in South Africa, accessing capital presents little difficulty for Cape Town (interview with Western Cape provincial government employee, October 2018). As such, bonds have proved an effective means of raising capital in the context of federal austerity, economic slowdown and increasing levels of political dysfunction in South Africa.

Interviews with treasury department representatives suggest that projects were largely selected post hoc; once a decision to use a green bond had been made, the challenge was then to locate projects that fit the criteria (interview with Representatives of Cape Town Treasury Department, July 2018). As a result, the bond has largely been used to refinance existing projects and infrastructures, which were discovered through an audit of the city's existing projects. Funds were mainly directed towards water supply infrastructure for improvements to reservoirs, alongside the development of technologies to give the city more control over the water system, effectively heightening the city's ability to reduce water pressure and reduce water losses from leaks. Critically, significant funding from the green bond was earmarked for the continued installation of household flow regulators or water management devices (WMDs; see Figure 3.3). WMDs deliver an allotment of water before cutting off, resetting the next day. They are designed to regulate water demand while also minimizing household debt. Starting in 2001, all South

Figure 3.3: A water management device, 2018

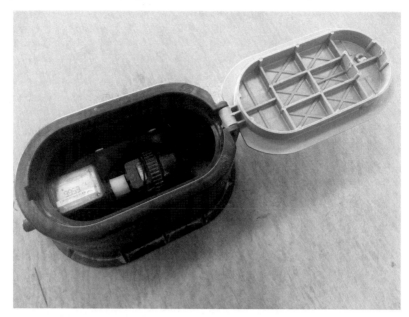

Source: Nate Millington

African citizens have been guaranteed at least 25 litres of water per person per day or 6 kl per household per month as part of the county's Free Basic Water programme (Yates and Harris, 2018; Enqvist and Ziervogel, 2019). WMDs are designed to provide Free Basic Water while ensuring that residents do not use more water than they can afford. The rollout of WMDs began in 2007, and an estimated 250,000 had been installed by 2018 (Roeland, 2018; Yates and Harris, 2018).

The installation of WMDs is increasingly linked to a changing regulatory understanding of Free Basic Water. While the first 6 kl per household per month was previously delivered free of charge, all water is now chargeable on a tiered basis (Yates and Harris, 2018: 79). For residents to receive their free water, they need to register as indigent (and re-register every 12 months). Indigent households cannot refuse the installation of WMDs. Registration, however, can be burdensome, requiring residents to prove their poverty (SERI, 2013: 44). As a result, Yates and Harris (2018) estimate that many indigent households are not formally registered. Activist organizations like the Water Crisis Coalition have argued that WMDs disproportionately impact poor households due to their installation in homes where water bills have gone unpaid. While WMDs are designed to hold people to their allotted Free Basic Water – and in this sense are formally in line with South Africa's constitution – the intersection of WMDs with other inequalities

Figure 3.4: Residents queue to collect water from a natural spring, Cape Town, 2018

Source: Nate Millington

complicates this simple calculation. Residents of townships and informal settlements often subdivide their homes and rent out their backyards as an income-generating strategy in the context of extreme unemployment, and so household sizes may vary considerably. As such, many who are in possession of WMDs are at risk of receiving less water than their guaranteed allotments due to overlapping infrastructures of informality and inequality (SERI, 2013: 64; Figure 3.4). Additionally, WMDs are marked by breakdown and uncertainty, and residents regularly complain about their functionality, flagging the similar if differentiated crises of urban infrastructure hit by climate change in Cape Town and New York.

Reining in household debt has animated a number of interventions into infrastructural governance in Cape Town, in particular the usage of WMDs and other forms of technology-based demand management currently in development (Scheba et al, 2021). Debt, and the incapacity of many to pay their water bills regardless of the cost, has been a central preoccupation of Cape Town's water demand management reduction policies. Water demand management projects have 'been as much about cost recovery as they have been about drought mitigation – until recently the City targeted indebted households rather than high volume consumers in general' (Yates and Harris, 2018: 81). Municipalities need to cover costs through payments made by users of municipal services, who are one of the primary sources of revenue for the city. The need to recover costs has largely come to be framed not through a lack of funding but rather of non-payment, particularly by low-income residents. The ultimate effect of this condition and framing is that new water demand management strategies become punitive through changes to tariff structures and restrictions on water usage. Critically, Cape Town's debt was not used to fund new expansive infrastructures for decarbonizing water provisioning or levelling access, but rather formed a component of a broader strategy to manage demand through technological means. The deployment of municipal green debt as a way of responding to environmental change threatens to further entrench debt and finance in the running of the city, with implications both for how cross-subsidization occurs and how risk is distributed.

Differentiated exposure to risk is entrenched by green debt through the continued deployment of WMDs as means of conjoined demand reduction and debt recovery. But the risks are more expansive. Green debt links efforts to reduce household indebtedness to the issuance of debt at the municipal level, constituting indebted households as necessary subjects of new financialized logics. Like subway passengers in New York City, the tariffs have become a wealth transfer from poor to rich, this time mediated by the profound inequality between Global North and South. Climate debt in this case mirrors ongoing dynamics of austerity but adds a layer of risk given the city's dependency on tariffs to fund its operations. These include other social services for the city's most vulnerable, who are impacted by shifting financial priorities in the context of climate crisis. The linkage between debt recovery, demand management and climate change adaptation threatens to deepen processes of uneven water access in the city by shifting the valuation of water to and heightening the comparative burden on poor households (see Yates and Harris, 2018). This has implications not just for water but for municipal services more broadly, as South African cities continue to face the challenge of finding ways to fund redistribution in the context of the COVID-19 driven economic slowdown and ongoing climatic uncertainty.

Conclusion

The climate crisis is here, and the infrastructures to respond have not yet been created. The transformative changes required to ensure that climate change does not disproportionately impact the most vulnerable are yet to be seen, and the infrastructural response to climate change has so far focused on the maintenance of existing systems rather than their remaking or repurposing. Finding ways of financing infrastructures that are capable of responding to a changing climate is a key contemporary task, and one that will entail a broad rethinking of governance at both local and global scales.

Infrastructure is a bridge between past and future, not merely through forms of path-dependency but also through its capacity to anchor different futures.

We argue in this chapter that municipal water users in Cape Town and New Yorkers dependent on public transportation are doubly at risk from a changing climate. First, they are endangered by increasing climate instability that threatens to disrupt the provision of essential public services, rendering access to water or transport more difficult, if not impossible. At the same time, residents are financially endangered as growing debt burdens, increasing costs of borrowing associated with credit rating downgrades and global interest rate increases, and rising rates or fares to pay for each are applied to service users who have no other options. While the wealthier can opt out, as they do in New York through ride-hailing apps, and in Cape Town as the rich are able to buy virtually unlimited supplies of bottled water, the poor are locked into paying for the service, and in turn contribute to the rents extracted by each utilities' creditors.

Debt is one of the few mechanisms that municipalities have for attempting to manage the financial and ecological crises magnified by climate change, and this debt is increasingly carrying explicitly environmental aspirations. The rush to financial markets to support critical social services should give us pause, however. The phenomenon of green bonds prompts us to flag not only the power accorded to financiers for coping with all sorts of critical and emergent issues, but also the extent to which cities have been cast adrift by austerity and devolution. Quotidian struggles around access reflect elaborations of twinned environmental and financial risk, and marginalized communities who are endangered through the risks manifested through the issuance of debt, green or not. New forms of finance or municipal governance are not producing entirely new socio-environmental outcomes, but are intensifying existing inequities of service provision and associated economic and environmental risks for marginalized communities.

In this chapter we have highlighted the ways that climate finance yields increasingly dangerous geographies for urbanites subject to racialized austerity and environmental change across and through operations and experiences of infrastructure. Municipal green finance is framed as a mechanism for enabling sustainable transitions, but it is structured through existing racialized geographies of inequality. By drawing together Cape Town and New York City, we highlight the need for fine-grained, comparative analysis of racial capitalism in spatially distant cities to understand the relational geographies of climate change and associated patterns of differentiated infrastructural adaptation. Attention to municipal governance can render apparent the deep linkages between finance, austerity and racialized inequality in cities (Jenkins, 2021; Ponder, 2021) – linkages that cut across binaries of North and South and reveal the need for more relational forms of comparison (Hart, 2018). Cape Town and New York City are radically different cities with differing state capacities. But comparative analysis makes clear that existing approaches that crudely split Global North and Global South infrastructures can limit possibilities for understanding contemporary conjunctures of inequality, climate change and infrastructural provisioning, points that Prince Guma expands on in Afterword 2.

Municipal debt, whether green or not, serves to aggravate entrenched inequality and displace environmental and financial risks onto those least able to bear them. While we would challenge municipal finance and planning offices to radically reconsider priorities and the types of programmes that are earmarked for funding, our concern is primarily located with higher order political scales where borrowing and redistribution can create more progressive and broad-based socialities of risk (Christophers et al, 2020). WMDs are no more the socially or environmentally just solution for Cape Town than raising fares for business-as-usual service is for New York. Instead, federal officials and multilateral pools of capital must make large volumes of concessionary money available for creative, huge and democratic interventions in cities that will reduce risks for the many who are least able to manage them.

The expansion of leveraged multilateral flows in the South or municipal borrowing in the North both serve to entrench extant regimes of financial and environmental risk for non-elites, and particularly marginalized communities across infrastructures. This critique is applicable to the field of 'green finance', or even the 'green economy' more broadly, as financiers and states grasp with increasing desperation for business-as-usual solutions to capital's socioecological contradictions. Thus far, climate-financial interventions to slow the pace of environmental degradation or prepare communities for new climate realities have largely failed; our research demonstrates how new risks are produced and distributed through financial interventions, rather than ameliorated. Producing new and more egalitarian regimes of risk is critical if we want to avoid discovering what the realization of racially inflected climate-financial risk looks like, over and over again.

Acknowledgements

Funding for this paper came from the Economic and Social Research Council–Department for International Development joint fund for poverty alleviation research ES/M009408/1, for the project titled 'Turning Livelihoods to Rubbish? Assessing the Impacts of Formalization and Technologization of Waste Management on the Urban Poor' and Swedish Research Council project grant, 'Climate Change and Transformations of Financial Risk' (#2015-01694).

Thanks to Ilias Alami and Brett Christophers for comments on earlier drafts, two anonymous reviewers, and Suraya Scheba for conversation and collaboration throughout the research process. This chapter draws on the authors' previously written paper: P. Bigger and N. Millington (2020) 'Getting soaked? Climate crisis, adaptation finance, and racialized austerity', *Environment and Planning E: Nature and Space*, 3(3): 601–23.

References

Afridi, L. (2016) 'How is economic opportunity threatened in your neighborhood?', New York: Association for Housing and Neighborhood Development. Available from: https://anhd.org/report/how-econo mic-opportunity-threatened-your-neighborhood-2016 [Accessed 11 November 2022].

Arestis, P., Charles, A. and Fontana, G. (2013) 'Financialization, the Great Recession, and the stratification of the US labor market', *Feminist Economics*, 19(3): 152–80.

Bigger, P. and Dempsey, J. (2018) 'Reflecting on neoliberal natures: an exchange', *Environment and Planning E: Nature and Space*, 1(1/2): 25–75.

Bledsoe, A. and Wright, W.J. (2019) 'The anti-Blackness of global capital', *Environment and Planning D: Society and Space*, 37(1): 8–26.

Bracking, S. (2015) 'Performativity in the Green Economy: how far does climate finance create a fictive economy?', *Third World Quarterly*, 36(12): 2337–57.

Braun, M.Z. (2018) 'MTA's rising debt and payroll cost take toll on bond rating', Bloomberg, 12 March. Available from: https://www.bloomberg. com/news/articles/2018-03-12/mta-s-rising-debt-and-payroll-costs-take-toll-on-credit-rating [accessed 22 November 2018].

Bulkeley, H. (2010) 'Cities and the governing of climate change', *Annual Review of Environment and Resources*, 35: 229–53.

Caldeira, T.P.R. (2017) 'Peripheral urbanization: autoconstruction, transversal logics, and politics in cities of the Global South', *Environment and Planning D: Society and Space*, 35(1): 3–20.

Calvário, R., Velegrakis, G. and Kaika, M. (2017) 'The political ecology of austerity: an analysis of socio-environmental conflict under crisis in Greece', *Capitalism Nature Socialism*, 28(3): 69–87.

Caro, R. (1974) *The Power Broker: Robert Moses and the Fall of New York*, New York: Knopf.

Christophers, B. (2018) 'Risk capital: urban political ecology and entanglements of financial and environmental risk in Washington, D.C.', *Environment and Planning E: Nature and Space*, 1(1/2): 144–64.

Christophers, B., Johnson, L. and Bigger P. (2020) 'Stretching scales: risk and sociality in climate finance', *Environment and Planning A: Economy and Space*, 52(8): 88–110.

City of Cape Town (nd) *Our Shared Water Future: Cape Town's Water Strategy*, Cape Town: Water and Sanitation Department of the City of Cape Town. Available from: https://resource.capetown.gov.za/documen tcentre/Documents/City%20strategies,%20plans%20and%20frameworks/Cape%20Town%20Water%20Strategy.pdf [Accessed 11 November 2022].

Climate Bonds Initiative (n.d.) 'The 10 point case'. Available from: https://www.climatebonds.net/projects/promotion/10-point-case [Accessed 4 July 2019].

Cohen, D.A. (2017) 'The other low-carbon protagonists: poor people's movements and climate politics in Sao Paulo', in M. Greenberg and P. Lewis (eds) *The City is the Factory: New Solidarities and Spatial Strategies in an Urban Age*, Ithaca, NY: Cornell University Press, pp 140–57.

Colon, D. (2018) 'Who's to blame for MTA's declining ridership?' *Curbed New York*. 25 July. Available from: https://ny.curbed.com/2018/7/25/17613 544/nyc-subway-mta-ridership-decline [Accessed 16 September 2019].

deMause, N. (2016) 'The MTA's climate change dilemma: how do you plug a million holes?', Village Voice, 13 December. Available from: https://www.villagevoice.com/2016/09/13/the-mtas-climate-change-dilemma-how-do-you-plug-a-million-holes/ [Accessed 21 December 2018].

Dickinson, M. (2008) 'The making of space, race and place: New York City's war on graffiti, 1970–the present', *Critique of Anthropology*, 28(1): 27–45.

Durkin, E. (2018) 'New York City subway and bus services have entered 'death spiral', experts say', The Guardian, 20 November. Available from: https://www.theguardian.com/us-news/2018/nov/20/new-york-city-subway-bus-death-spiral-mta-fares [Accessed 16 September 2019].

Enqvist, J.P. and Ziervogel, G. (2019) 'Water governance and justice in Cape Town: an overview', *Wiley Interdisciplinary Reviews: Water*, 6(4): art e1354. Available from: https://doi.org/10.1002/wat2.1354 [Accessed 11 November 2022].

Fitzsimmons, E.G. (2017) 'Cuomo declares a state of emergency for New York City subways', New York Times, 29 June. Available from: https://www.nytimes.com/2017/06/29/nyregion/cuomo-declares-a-state-of-emerge ncy-for-the-subway.html [Accessed 21 December 2018].

Fitzsimmons, E.G. (2018) 'Can charging drivers really solve the subway crisis?', New York Times, 12 October. Available from: https://www.nytimes.com/2018/10/12/nyregion/congestion-pricing-subway-mta.html?rref=collection%2Fbyline%2Femma-g.-fitzsimmons [Accessed 5 July 2019].

Fredrickson, G. (1981) *White Supremacy: A Comparative Study of American and South African History*, Oxford: Oxford University Press.

Freilla, O. (2004) 'Burying Robert Moses's legacy in New York City', in B. Bullard, G.S. Johnson and A. Torres (eds) *Highway Robbery: Transportation Racism and Routes to Equity*, Cambridge, MA: South End Press, pp 75–96.

Furlong, K. (2020) 'Geographies of infrastructure 1: economies', *Progress in Human Geography*, 44(3): 572–82.

Gelinas, N. (2011) 'The MTA's too-nice pay', New York Post, 13 July. Available from: https://nypost.com/2011/07/13/mtas-too-nice-pay/ [Accessed 29 December 2018].

Gold, M., Zaveri, M. and Wong, A. (2021) 'What the Infrastructure Bill means for the New York region', New York Times, updated 16 November. Available from: https://www.nytimes.com/2021/11/15/nyregion/infrastructure-bill-new-york.html [Accessed 11 November 2022].

Hart, G. (2018) 'Relational comparison revisited: Marxist postcolonial geographies in practice', *Progress in Human Geography*, 42(3): 371–94.

Harvey, D. (2005) *A Brief History of Neoliberalism*, Oxford: Oxford University Press.

Hinds, K. (2012) 'Totaling Sandy's losses: how New York's MTA got to $5 billion', WNYC, 27 November. Available from: https://www.wnyc.org/story/286877-totalling-sandy-losses-how-new-yorks-mta-got-to-5-billion/ [Accessed 4 July 2019].

Hood, C. ([1993] 2004) *722 Miles: The Building of the Subways and How They Transformed New York*, centennial edn, Baltimore, MD: Johns Hopkins University Press.

Hu, W. (2018) 'New York subway's on-time performance hits new low', New York Times, 19 March. Available from: https://www.nytimes.com/2018/03/19/nyregion/new-york-subways-on-time-performance-hits-new-low.html [Accessed 18 January 2019].

Hu, W. and Barnard, A. (2021) 'Why the New York subway has a water problem', New York Times, 9 July. Available from: https://www.nytimes.com/2021/07/09/nyregion/nyc-subway-flooding-climate-change.html [Accessed 11 November 2022].

Huber, M. (2016) 'The carbon tax is doomed', *Jacobin*. Available from: https://www.jacobinmag.com/2016/ 10/oil-fossil-fuel-climate-cap-trade-tax-renewables/ [Accessed 10 May 2018].

Jaglin, S. (2008) 'Differentiating networked services in Cape Town: echoes of splintering urbanism?', *Geoforum*, 39(6): 1897–1906.

Jenkins, D. (2021) *The Bonds of Inequality: Debt and the Making of the American City*, Chicago: University of Chicago Press.

Kabak, B. (2010) 'MTA demographics: a glimpse at who rides and how we pay', Second Avenue Sagas, 20 October. Available from: http://secondavenuesagas.com/2010/10/20/mta-demographics-a-glimpse-at-who-rides-and-how-we-pay/ [Accessed 5 July 2019].

Kamaldien, Y. (2018) '#WaterCrisis: funds drought as levy scrapped', Weekend Argus, 20 January. Formerly available from: https://www.iol.co.za/weekend-argus.

Kish, Z. and Leroy, J. (2015) 'Bonded life: technologies of racial finance from slave insurance to philanthrocapital', *Cultural Studies*, 29(5/6): 630–51.

Knocke, J. (2016) 'The MTA loses six billion dollars a year and no one cares', Medium, 6 July. Available from: https://medium.com/@johnnyknocke/the-mta-loses-six-billion-dollars-a-year-and-nobody-cares-d0d23093b2d8 [Accessed 5 July 2019].

Laird, J. (2017) 'Public sector employment inequality in the United States and the Great Recession', *Demography*, 54(1): 391–411.

Lawhon, M., Silver, J., Ernstson, H. and Pierce, J. (2016) 'Unlearning (un) located ideas in the provincialization of urban theory', *Regional Studies*, 50(9): 1611–22.

LMIS (Labor Market Information Service) (2009) *Employment in New York City Urban Transport*, May, New York: LMIS. Available from: http://www.nyc.gov/html/sbs/wib/downloads/pdf/urban_transit.pdf [Accessed 5 July 2019].

Long, J. and Rice, J.L. (2019) 'From sustainable urbanism to climate urbanism', *Urban Studies*, 56(5): 992–1008.

McIntyre, M. and Nast, H.J. (2011) 'Bio(necro)polis: Marx, surplus populations, and the spatial dialectics of reproduction and "race"', *Antipode*, 43(5): 1465–88.

Millington, N. and Scheba, S. (2021) 'Day zero and the infrastructures of climate change: water governance, inequality, and infrastructural politics in Cape Town's water crisis', *International Journal of Urban and Regional Research*, 45(1): 116–32.

NY Torch (2010) 'Back at the scene of the crime', Empire Center, 26 March. Available from: https://www.empirecenter.org/publications/back-at-the-scene-of-the-crime/ [Accessed 20 December 2018].

Palmer, I., Moodley, N. and Parnell, S. (2017) *Building a Capable State: Service Delivery in Post Apartheid South Africa*, London: Zed Books.

Partridge, C. and Medda, F. (2018) 'Premium in the primary and secondary U.S. municipal bond markets', SSRN, 22 August. Available from: http://dx.doi.org/10.2139/ssrn.3237032 [Accessed 4 July 2019].

PCAC (Permanent Citizens Advisory Committee to the MTA) (2012) *The Road Back: A Historic Review of the MTA's Capital Program*, New York: PCAC. Available from: https://pcac.org/report/road-back-2012/ [Accessed 11 November 2022].

Peck, J. (2012) 'Austerity urbanism: American cities under extreme economy', *City*, 16(6): 626–55.

Ponder, C.S. (2021) 'Spatializing the municipal bond market: urban resilience under racial capitalism', *Annals of the American Association of Geographers*, 111(7): 2112–29.

Ranganathan, M. (2016) 'Thinking with Flint: racial liberalism and the roots of an American water tragedy', *Capitalism Nature Socialism*, 27(3): 17–33.

Redden, M. and Kasperkevic, J. (2016) 'Wage gap between White and Black Americans is worse today than in 1979', The Guardian, 20 September. Available from: https://www.theguardian.com/us-news/2016/sep/20/wage-gap-black-white-americans [Accessed 18 December 2018].

Reichelt, H. and Keenan, C. (2017) The Green Bond Market: 10 Years Later and Looking Ahead, Washington, DC: World Bank.

Rivera, R. (2008) 'M.T.A. and its debt, and how they got that way', New York Times, 26 July. Available from: https://www.nytimes.com/2008/07/26/nyregion/26mta.html [Accessed 17 January 2019].

Rodina, L. (2016) 'Human right to water in Khayelitsha, South Africa: lessons from a "lived experiences" perspective', Geoforum, 72: 58–66.

Roeland, M. (2018) 'Water curbs: a tale of rich and poor', GroundUp, 7 March. Available from: https://www.groundup.org.za/article/water-curbs-tale-rich-and-poor/ [Accessed 4 July 2019].

Rosenman, E. (2019) 'The geographies of social finance: poverty regulation through the "invisible heart" of markets', Progress in Human Geography, 43(1): 141–62.

Roy, A. (2009) 'The 21st-century metropolis: new geographies of theory', Regional Studies, 43(6): 819–30.

Roy, A. (2017) 'Dis/possessive collectivism: property and personhood at city's end', Geoforum, 80: A1–A11.

SACN (South African Cities Network) (2018) State of City Finances Report 2018, Johannesburg: SACN.

Saska, J. (2015) 'SEPTA has largest percentage of female riders – 64% – among large transit agencies', PlanPhilly, WHYY, 26 January. Available from: http://planphilly.com/articles/2015/01/26/septa-has-largest-percentage-of-female-riders-64-among-large-transit-agencies/ [Accessed 14 December 2018].

Scaggs, A. (2018) 'New York's MTA downgraded by S&P', Financial Times, 9 August. Available from: https://www.ft.com/content/5eca988c-9c03-11e8-9702-5946bae86e6d [Accessed 14 December 2018].

Scheba, S., Meyer, F., Benson, K., Karunananthan, M., Farr, V. and Green, L. (2021) 'Cape Town's drip system plan will entrench water apartheid', University of Cape Town News, 28 May. Available from: https://www.news.uct.ac.za/article/-2021-05-28-cape-towns-drip-system-plan-will-entrench-water-apartheid [Accessed 11 November 2022].

SERI (Socio-economic Rights Institute) (2013) Targeting the Poor: An analysis of Free Basic Services (FBS) and Municipal Indigent Policies in South Africa, Johannesburg: SERI. Available from: https://www.seri-sa.org/images/Targeting_the_Poor_Nov13.pdf [Accessed 4 July 2019].

Shepherd, N. (2019) 'Making sense of "day zero": slow catastrophes, Anthropocene futures, and the story of Cape Town's water crisis', *Water*, 11(9): art 1744. Available from: https://doi.org/10.3390/w11091744 [Accessed 11 November 2022].

Sörqvist, P., Haga, A., Langeborg, L., Holmgren, M., Wallinder, M. and Nöstl, A., et al (2015) 'The green halo: mechanisms and limits of the eco-label effect', *Food Quality and Preference*, 43: 1–9.

Stringer, S.M. (2018) Left in the Dark: How the MTA Is Failing to Keep Up with New York City's Changing Economy, New York: New York City Office of the Comptroller. Available from: https://comptroller.nyc.gov/reports/left-in-the-dark-how-the-mta-is-failing-to-keep-up-with-new-york-citys-changing-economy/ [Accessed 11 November 2022].

Swipe it Forward (2021) 'About us'. Available from: https://swipeitforward.nyc/about-us [Accessed 11 November 2022].

Taylor, Z.J. and Aalbers, M.B. (2022) 'Climate gentrification: risk, rent, and restructuring in Greater Miami', *Annals of the American Association of Geographers*, 112(6): 1685–701.

UNEP (UN Environmental Programme) (2016) *The Adaptation Finance Gap Report 2016*, Nairobi: UNEP. Available from: https://unepccc.org/publications/the-adaptation-finance-gap-report/ [Accessed 11 November 2022].

Winner, L. (1980) 'Do artifacts have politics?', *Daedalus*, 109(1): 121–36.

Woodhouse, S. (2022) 'NYC subway riders return to outer boroughs while business areas lag', Bloomberg, 25 May. Available from: https://www.bloomberg.com/news/articles/2022-05-25/nyc-subway-riders-return-to-outer-boroughs-business-areas-lag [Accessed 21 July 2022].

Yates, J.S. and Harris, L.M. (2018) 'Hybrid regulatory landscapes: the human right to water, variegated neoliberal water governance, and policy transfer in Cape Town, South Africa, and Accra, Ghana', *World Development*, 110: 75–87.

Ziervogel, G. (2019) Unpacking the Cape Town Drought: Lessons Learned: Report for Cities Support Programme Undertaken by African Centre for Cities, February, Pretoria: National Treasury. Available from: https://www.africancentreforcities.net/wp-content/uploads/2019/02/Ziervogel-2019-Lessons-from-Cape-Town-Drought_A.pdf [Accessed 4 July 2019].

4

Emerging Techno-ecologies of Energy: Examining Digital Interventions and Engagements with Urban Infrastructure

Andrés Luque-Ayala and Jonathan Rutherford

Introduction

The modes and implications of the digital transformation of urban infrastructures are an increasingly crucial issue for understanding urban futures. They matter, we argue, for how we conceptualize the role of infrastructures and the associated ecological flows (such as water and energy) in the making of contemporary urbanity. Critically, as we discuss in this chapter, they matter for how we understand the already complex relationship between city and nature. Regardless of whether we think of this as the arrival of the smart city or as the intensification of an already pervasive computational urbanism, the well-recognized mediation that networked infrastructures offer between nature and the city (see, for example, Kaika and Swyngedouw, 2000) has been problematized by the increasingly ubiquitous and ever deeper presence of computational systems in their management and use. From smart electricity meters to waste collections scheduled through sensors, among many others, algorithmic processes and the 'data revolution' are becoming essential features of the city's infrastructural flows (Kitchin, 2014; Shahrokni et al, 2015; Moss et al, 2021). Water and energy, for example, are no longer simply material flows in the city. Rather, they have become datafied ecologies, simultaneously constituted through physical components and relations, immaterial datafication processes, and algorithmic calculations – a recombinant materiality of pipes/wires, circulating fluids and digital information exchanges that, notably, reopens questions of how people come to know and engage with infrastructurally mediated urban natures.

In this chapter, we look at the digitization of urban infrastructures and their attendant ecological flows. We examine how this leads, first, to new ways of knowing urban natures and, second, to a broader set of agencies and subjective engagements in the active ongoing infrastructural making of cities. We examine this question through an analysis of recent interventions in energy infrastructures in Bristol, a UK city where since the early 2010s a variety of stakeholders have sought to advance greater sustainability by both increasing the city's capacity for renewable electricity generation and improving the energy efficiency of the city's housing stock. They have done so notably, we argue, by mobilizing and managing digital and ecological flows and processes in tandem – in this way, infrastructuring an urban future through digital engagements. We focus on a combined set of digital-physical material processes through which actors' capacity to intervene in, and understanding of, the techno-ecological flows of energy systems appear to be shifting. The digital intervention enables non-human entities to be crucially entangled in these processes, forging infrastructural futures that emerge across an evolving plane of intelligibility between ecological and digital flows and human activities.

We use this framing to take an in-depth look at the city of Bristol's aim of becoming a 'smart-energy city' by redeploying digital energy as a substantive means through which a low carbon and sustainable future can be achieved. We focus on three small-scale interventions where computational processes are becoming intertwined in the working of urban infrastructures for the realization of renewable electricity (via photovoltaic installations) and energy efficiency optimization (via thermal insulation). Our proposed framing develops an understanding of urban infrastructure as hybrid techno-nature – a combinatory form, mode and device constituted by increasingly indissociable physical-digital materiality. Increasingly, such hybrid techno-nature is mobilized towards the realization of urban sustainability and low carbon ambitions.

Exploring city–nature relations through physical-digital materialities: infrastructures as hybrid techno-natures

Within urban studies, infrastructures have been recognized as the critical mediator of the city–nature relationship. Urban political ecology scholars, for example, drawing on their analysis of urban infrastructures, have shown us that the city–nature relationship is a 'messy socio-spatial continuum'; a 'continuous flow of natural elements (water, electricity, gas, etc.) from the countryside into the city and finally into the modern home' (Kaika, 2005: 4). Infrastructure networks, rather than making cities independent from nature, weave nature and city together, in a continuous process referred to as 'the urbanization of nature': a dialectical analysis of how humankind, through its actions, produces both city and nature as part of the same process. Here, both nature and city are hybrids; never 'purely human nor purely natural' (Kaika, 2005: 7; see also Gandy, 2003; Swyngedouw, 2006). The result is an urban world that is necessarily a cyborg world, 'part natural part social, part technical part cultural, but with no clear boundaries, centres, or margins' (Swyngedouw, 2006: 118). Nature and the city are conjoined hybrids, through connective infrastructures and the ecological flows they enable.

Increasingly, this infrastructural mediation between city and nature occurs through digital registers: by and through data collection, algorithmic calculations, sensing technologies and a growing ecology of digital tools and practices (see, for example, Gabrys, 2014). Arguably aimed at optimizing infrastructure networks and their flows, these tools and practices also seek to increase their efficiency, expand their functionality and, at times, repurpose them. Urban computation has emerged as an infrastructural form, whereby 'smart' city processes not only depend upon but also transform traditional networked infrastructures and urban ecological flows (Luque-Ayala and Marvin, 2020). Luque-Ayala and Marvin argue that the computational city puts in place a new generation of urban infrastructures that are both digital and corporeal, and that operate thanks to the mutability afforded by processes of datafication, digital sensing and algorithmic recombination. In the computational city, digital systems and material infrastructures are co-constituted through the affordances of each other: 'an intelligence incarnate of the urban' (Luque-Ayala and Marvin, 2020: 6). While digital sensors fragment the ecological flow into tightly timed micro-measurements, data emerges as a common language across multiple urban processes and infrastructural flows. The digital intervention in infrastructural domains renders calculative intelligibility across urban processes, making it clear that data in the city gains agency through its materialization in the form of urban infrastructures.

The digital thus produces a potentially transformational change in the roles and capacities of different actors that operate in and through infrastructures, while at the same time the agency of the computational city is the effect of its organic materialization by way of infrastructures. The hybridity of the 'cyborg city' (compare Gandy, 2005) is, then, reaffirmed through digital processes and practices (compare Kinsley, 2014). White and Wilbert (2009: 5) conceptualized this evolving machine-organism compact through a notion of 'technonatures' that captures 'the anthropogenic reach of modern humanity' as our knowledge of and practices in worlds are increasingly mediated by technology. Technology and digital processes are enveloped or folded into systemic urban flows to such an extent that it is no longer possible to meaningfully separate ecological flows and data information systems through which urban infrastructure is managed. This framing develops an understanding of urban infrastructure as hybrid techno-nature, a form/mode/device constituted by increasingly indissociable physical-digital materiality through which 'sustainability' and 'low carbon' goals can, it is claimed, be advanced. The urbanization of nature now takes place through entwined smart/digital and physical processes and techniques that recombine resources/wastes and data/code as a new hybrid urban materiality, albeit unevenly deployed and unequally experienced.

Rethinking agency in (infra)structures: enabling im/possibilities of intervention

The centrality of these infrastructures and metabolic flows to urban life render them crucial sites and arenas of social struggle and political conflict. But, regardless of the digital intervention, the natural and technical components and processes are not necessarily inert parts of these struggles. Urban studies scholars increasingly draw on new materialist perspectives, wherein infrastructures emerge as 'vibrant matters' and 'lively things', acting 'as quasi agents or forces with trajectories, propensities, and tendencies of their own' (Bennett, 2010: viii). This forges a politics of active urban materiality that refuses to see the matters and materials of the city as neutral or inactive (Latham, 2016). This perspective acknowledges the role of infrastructure in producing or enabling im/possibilities of intervention that, transcending (infra)structural constraints, play out alongside and become entangled with the habitually studied political effects of human agency (see Rutherford, 2020). Thus, the production and reproduction of cities as a 'hybrid' affair is neither subjected to structural determination nor just operated by people, but equally by other more 'fluid' to 'more-than-human' presences (see Whatmore, 2002; Latour, 2005). In examining the resulting interplay between agencies that matter, we are called *in fine* 'to explore the way these materials combine in particular instances with particular forces, and to scrutinize how this play of effects and affects produces particular urban formations' (Hubbard, 2006: 248). Bennett's case study of the North American electricity blackout of 2003 is a prime example of sociotechnical analysis which decentres (but does not disregard) both structure and human agency, foregrounding the effects of materials, flows and forces – usually in the infrastructural background – to consider the complex interplay of always associated humans and non-humans. For her, avoiding 'presupposing the priority of human intentions, projections or even behaviours' (Bennett, 2005: 456), allows natural-technological materialities a more active role. As she argues, 'There was never a time when human agency was anything other than an interfolding network of humanity and non-humanity. What is perhaps different today is that the higher degree of infrastructural and technological complexity has rendered this harder to deny' (Bennett, 2005: 463).

So what happens when these 'non-humans' are either digital devices or ecological flows that enter a plane of intelligibility (and thus find a 'voice') through digital materialities and practices? As we become 'ever more entangled with things, with technological, cultural, urban, and ecological networks and diverse hybrid materialities and non-human agencies', a complex social-ecological-technological and political field is opened up away from narrow, disenfranchising views of nature/ecology/sustainability as outside of, or separate from, technologized societies and social relations that actually fully involve and rely on a host of 'active and lively partners' (White and Wilbert, 2009: 6; see also Hinchliffe, 2007).

Datafied ecologies: making digital energy in Bristol

We now turn to an examination of how the processes of digitization of infrastructures and ecological flows play out in practice, becoming folded into a conjoined physical-digital materiality that shifts how actors come to know and engage with urban natures. We focus on three recent, ostensibly small-scale, energy interventions in the city of Bristol that seek to test conditions for expanding renewable energy and increasing energy efficiency through eco-digital energy configurations. These initiatives contribute more widely to urban sustainability efforts and aim at reducing CO_2 emissions. Our analysis targets the emerging points of connection between, or hybridization of, digital systems and datafication and functioning and circulation of ecological – principally energy – flows.

Our specific focus on electricity derived from renewable energy (as opposed to that derived from fossil fuels) and energy efficiency as management of stored heat matters here. We approach energy flows as inherently lively matter, constituted in the case of electricity of 'a stream of electrons moving in a current ... because its essence is this mobility, it always is going somewhere' (Bennett, 2005: 450, 451). Both electrons and heat molecules are constantly in motion in our living environments, as opposed to an energy matter which is buried in latent and inactive state in the form of fossil fuels in the subsurface. As well as this particular form of urban nature, there is then an immediate, material dimension to renewable energy and energy efficiency in urban environments in the way in which they manifest through immersive or experiential engagement of users. As we explore later, this needs to be constantly produced/reproduced and maintained (through particular tasks and efforts), reflecting the ongoing infrastructuring of urban futures. This infrastructuring in turn opens up urban configurations to (further) digital-physical intervention.

We focus on Bristol because it is a pertinent example of a city where, in a context of urban sustainability policies, a host of actors and initiatives are seeking to leverage the multifaceted possibilities of intervening in and reshaping the city's smart energy systems. Bristol's recent history is forged by progressive urban sustainability thinking and practice, as demonstrated by the city being the Green Capital of Europe in 2015. Urban environmental and energy policies in recent years have endeavoured to increase the capacity of the city government and other associated local actors to actively rework infrastructure systems such as energy for social, economic and ecological benefits (see, for example, Bristol City Council, 2015). In the UK's electricity system, for example, the constrained position of the city in south-west England at the 'end' of long distance electricity supply lines (and therefore dependent on wider grid reliability) has been a driver for proposals from both the city and the local/regional electricity distribution company, Western Power, that aim to improve resilience through acting both on supply and demand sides and by using digital technology to monitor, manage and increase local availability and use of power. Empirically, we draw on interviews with local policy actors and energy system specialists supplemented by analysis of strategic documents and project reports concerning the initiatives we focus on.

The city has long held an ambition of becoming a hub for low-carbon industries, and as part of the work leading to the European Green Capital award, a range of stakeholders including the city council embraced the idea of becoming a Smart Energy City by 2020 (Centre for Sustainable Energy, 2015). In this urban policy context, a number of initiatives have sought, through engaging with digital technologies, to orchestrate 'smart use, smart distribution and smart supply of heat and power across the city' (Centre for Sustainable Energy, 2015: 6). Three of them are examined here. First, *SoLa Bristol*, a research and development initiative by Western Power, the regional electricity distribution network operator, in collaboration with Bristol City Council. SoLa Bristol examined the impacts of high-density photovoltaic solar power generation on the district network operator's low-voltage network, the possibilities of domestic battery storage, and customer responses to variable tariffs for electricity use. Second, the *C.H.E.E.S.E. Project*, a social enterprise specializing in non-profit, domestic energy efficiency survey drawing on the use of relatively popular digital technologies such as smart mobile phones. Third, the *Bristol Energy Cooperative*, a community-owned business set up in 2011 to develop renewable electricity has sought power purchase agreements with virtual i.e. digital aggregators for optimizing the sale of electricity to the grid.

Table 4.1 captures some of the main points from the three initiatives that we develop in the rest of this chapter. We have divided our analysis according to the specific questions we asked at the start of the chapter about the modalities and implications of digitization/datafication processes for actors' engagement with urban natures. First, we look at the emerging intelligibility

Table 4.1: Summary of the Bristol initiatives in relation to our focus. Key question: How have digital technologies transformed the ways people engage with urban natures?

	Aims, rationale	Actors involved	Material (physical–digital) components	Knowing	Agency, subjectivities	Emerging techno-natural engagements
SoLa Bristol	Testing impacts of photovoltaic (PV) solar power generation on low-voltage distribution network, possibilities of domestic battery storage, customer responses to variable tariffs	Bristol City Council, Western Power (distribution utility), local residents	PV panels installed on home roofs, battery storage in lofts, use of tablets for consumption tracking, grid connection	Awareness of material flows through data flows, kWh translated into £. Temporal and device specific data on home energy use (utility)	Active residents: enrolled as labour for grid functioning, rewarded through managing their energy use and sale to grid. Active energy–data flows	Through activating consumers in physical–digital infrastructure
C.H.E.E.S.E.	Home energy efficiency surveys to make energy losses visible	Non-profit entity, volunteers working as 'energy tracers', residents	Heating systems, blower doors/fans, iPhone and thermal camera, tablet	'Tracing' and visualization, embodied sensing and feeling of flows	Engagement with energy flows through digital interface, creates capacity for intervention. Digital makes energy flows into an active subject; evidences a 'dialogue' between interior and exterior atmospheres	Through atmospheric exposure and configuration of resident, airflow and digital interface
BEC	Community-owned cooperative developing local renewable electricity generation	Cooperative members, technicians and engineers, virtual aggregator companies	Solar and wind infrastructure, digital metering/monitoring, aggregation platforms, algorithms for optimizing grid input	Digital metering enables check on functioning and spatio-temporal aggregation possibilities	Passive cooperative seeking monetary return, aggregation actively manages flows. Active materiality of electrons and data representation	Through spatio-temporal optimization of energy flows (electrons and data)

of interventions, where we examine how and where digital processes and practices transform how urban ecological flows – and through that urban nature – come to be known and capable of being acted upon. Second, we home in on the agencies and subjectivities that both emerge and are at stake in the digital reconfiguration of ecological flows. Here we analyse how household residents change their positions and capacities in energy systems by engaging/enrolling (or becoming engaged/enrolled) in particular projects or interventions. Through these we explore shifting forms of transactionality in initiatives, outlining how human and non-human actors and components of digital energy systems interact in testing and seeking out new collective arrangements that merge, blur or hybridize nature–society relations.

SoLa Bristol

SoLa Bristol was active between 2011 and 2016 and involved Bristol City Council alongside Western Power, the regional electricity distribution network operator. Funded through the UK government's Low Carbon Network Fund, it was one of a handful of projects around renewable energy that the city council, through a local community media centre, took part in as an outreach and engagement exercise with the aim of investigating ways of reducing energy bills in low-income neighbourhoods. For the distribution network operator it was more about testing: (1) the impacts of low-carbon technologies (specifically, high-density photovoltaic solar generation) on their low-voltage network, particularly in terms of network peaks and thermal overloads; (2) the possibility of domestic battery storage, demand response and home direct current (DC) networks (low voltage, as opposed to the more traditional high voltage alternating current (AC) networks) as a solution for network peaks and thermal overloads; and (3) the possible mutual benefits (and financial feasibility) of network operators and customers sharing battery storage on DC networks, a process to be modulated through the use of variable tariffs (where customers purposefully shape their energy consumption patterns in response to different pricing at different times of the day) (Western Power interview, March 2017; Western Power Distribution, 2016).

The SoLa Bristol project provided 30 homes with rooftop solar panels, 2 kW of battery storage and a DC microgrid that ran from the battery. The project relied therefore on access to, uptake and reuse of some spaces of the home, as batteries had to be physically located in lofts, and cables and connections hooked up between lofts and the ground floors of homes to enable the microgrid to run and control various energy devices. These homes had the ability to operate lighting and USB charging points via either solar panels or battery storage. Any excess energy stored in the batteries could be exported to the grid at peak times in exchange for monthly payments to households, a feed-in to the grid provision that aimed to push households to shift some of their consumption away from the peak. Similar arrangements were provided for five commercial buildings and schools. In this case, battery storage had a greater capacity (8 kW), and the DC microgrid lighting and information technology equipment.

Data collection and digital systems were integral to the combined physical-digital material intervention. The project placed a particular emphasis on collecting data associated to its performance, aimed at enabling the network operator to conduct extensive analyses on potential benefits to customers and the electricity network. In the view of the operator, 'obtaining good quality data was a key factor of success for SoLa Bristol' (Western Power Distribution, 2016: 11). The data that flowed between homes and Western Power provided the grounds for both long-term analysis and learning as well as near real-time interventions in the resulting energy system. Digital communication modules allowed grid managers to charge/discharge batteries according to particular constraints caused by excess of load or of generation. These data were also fed to homeowners through the provision of a tablet computer with a purposefully developed energy management app – in this way, advancing a key project aim: to actively involve homeowners in the energy management process. The tablet operated as a user-friendly smart-energy monitor, using a simple graphic interface showing customers in real time the amount of energy generated by the photovoltaic panels installed in their roof as well as their levels of energy consumption. The app translated energy units (kilowatt-hours, kWh) into 'pounds and pennies', in this way using the calculative practices involved in the monetization of the energy flow as the means through which a common language between energy users, energy providers and the system itself could emerge.

In terms of modes of knowing urban natures in SoLa Bristol, energy users gained a new awareness of the material flow of energy – from the sun and rooftop photovoltaic cells, through batteries located in their lofts and domestic energy-consuming devices, and out to the grid. This awareness was produced via a flow of data between the emerging electricity assemblage and the tablet computer. The tablet's display of electricity quantities translates energy units into monetary units. In the words of a homeowner involved in the project, digital visualization through a tablet played a role in 'simplifying' the knowledge so that 'we all can understand it' (Knowle West Media Centre, 2016) – in effect, providing novel channels for energy knowledge while also altering the required forms and levels of expertize to engage with the ecological flows of the city. Residents also gained new sensibility to the temporal variation of electricity production and availability. They could see in real time the performance of their photovoltaic panels and battery storage and thus know, for example, when to run energy-consuming devices for lower cost. Viewed from the perspective of the energy company (primarily interested in more temporally efficient energy use for grid optimization), the enrolment of residents into the project through provision of a tablet and digital translation of otherwise complex processes can be seen as a way of obtaining demand-side labour that helps with overall grid functioning without much additional effort.

In terms of changing subjective engagements, the household here is no longer simply a passive energy consumer at the end of a complex material flow system over/within which it has no control. Households have also become producers with an active involvement in managing the energy flow. They gained an awareness of energy that allowed them to, in the first instance, reduce their consumption by seeing in the tablet the difference that practices such as switching lights off or unplugging devices makes for energy levels in batteries. The translation of energy units from kilowatt-hours to pounds and pence coupled with differential energy tariffs linked to periods of peak demand across the city sparked changes in energy practices, leading them to, for example, do laundry at night. On the one hand, this is an energy flow that is more malleable for the user. On the other, the optimal operation of the emerging configuration of the flow relies on the incorporation of the user as a manager of energy processes through a change in consumption practices. This is an important change in subjectivities, enrolling the user as a new labour force rewarded through its ability to enable the sale of renewable energy to the grid at the right time.

C.H.E.E.S.E. project

The second intervention we examine in Bristol is the Cold Homes Energy Efficiency Survey Experts (C.H.E.E.S.E.) project, a non-profit community energy initiative supporting Bristol's homes in increasing energy efficiency through accessible, low-cost and digitally mediated survey techniques. The project, active since 2015 and winner of a Community Energy national award in 2018, provides internal home thermal imaging surveys achieved via an Apple iPhone enabled with miniature FLIR infrared thermal cameras (Figure 4.1). As at 2018, the project had carried out a total of 172 surveys, 56 of them free surveys to low-income households.

The surveying techniques that C.H.E.E.S.E. applies are intimately connected with atmospheric conditions and seasonal patterns in nature. The project uses a precise protocol to show residents the energy losses in their homes. This protocol is followed in situ by so-called energy tracers. Surveys can only be carried out in winter, when the difference in temperature between inside and outside is greater The survey starts with a particular atmospheric intervention in the home. This involves preheating the house to 10° Celsius above the ambient outside temperature, then lowering the air pressure using a 'blower door' to pull the air out the house – a large fan installed in an external door,

Figure 4.1: Thermal imaging via mini infrared camera attached to an iPhone, 2017

Source: Andrés Luque-Ayala and Jonathan Rutherford

extracting air and thus reducing the air pressure of the sealed envelope. The fan's reduction in air pressure draws cold air from the outside via draughts resulting from poor thermal insulation and gaps in the fabric of the building. This in effect establishes a particular material interaction between the internal and external atmospheres of the home. The temperature differential, as materialized through the exchange of cold and warm air, is made visible via an ecosystem of relatively low-cost and popular digital technologies. Through an iPhone with a thermal imaging camera attached and a custom app, the energy tracer and the householder can 'see first-hand how heat moves around [the] home and where it is lost' through draughts or poor insulation for example (project managers interview, March 2017). Digital technologies also play an important role in providing a recording of the 'tracing', and, through that, enabling possibilities for learning and transformation. In this way, the survey is done with residents following the process 'immersively' on a tablet computer. The video, photos and audio recording of the conversation between the 'energy tracer' and the resident, discussing potential energy saving measures, is left with the householder via a USB memory stick. Thus, tracing airflows and heat circulation and losses in the internal home space produces new knowledge about building energy efficiency through an atmospheric immersion enabled or mediated by digital techniques.

As with SoLa Bristol, a similar process of residential engagement with energy through a digital interface is observed within the C.H.E.E.S.E. project, where an iPhone visualizes heat flows through 'an immersive experience', and where the user gains the ability to physically experience the energy flow (project managers interview, March 2017). In this case, knowing this urban ecological flow is not a matter of counting and enumerating (as would be the case with smart-energy meters), but a more embodied process of directly sensing and feeling the flow. In contrast to SoLa Bristol, where knowing the flow results from a numeric quantification (via digital energy meters) that is mathematically visualized (via charts) and mentally accessed via rational thinking, the C.H.E.E.S.E. Project mobilizes digital imaging for the creation of a temporary device that 'measures' flows without placing an emphasis on exactitude via numeric quantification. Rather, the mode of knowing energy here relies first on digitally mediated 'tracing' process and then on user confirmation via the senses: what the homeowner can (digitally) see, but also feel and touch (the draughts), and the sensorial and intuitive experience of atmospherically being in the flow. The combination of the digital and physical enables, in this case, the identification of flows (heat loss) to be eliminated to make a home more energy efficient.

Critically, the digitalization of energy allows for the consideration of non-human subjectivities – and through this, a novel conceptualization of nature in the process of infrastructuring urban futures in Bristol. The case of the C.H.E.E.S.E. project reveals the emergence of energy as a lively agent. Here, beyond the significant capacities that households gain over energy flows (by way of visualizing how energy circulates), what is at stake is the interaction between two active agents: the household and heat. Energy, in the form of heat that is differentially flowing through the house and between the house and the outside, emerges as a subject, surrounding and entangled with the user while also sharing with them a perpetually changing atmosphere. The digital mediation of tracing airflow and temperature reveals energy as experienced through visual and tactile sensation. This digitized energy is not about rational calculation but atmospheric immersion, with digital tools creating the conditions for users to be able to experientially immerse themselves in the flow; an 'exposure to the elemental' (McCormack, 2015). It is a digital-physical, material intervention that explicitly brings active nature into the home, via an awareness of otherwise invisible ecological flows in the city; an awareness generated by and through a digitally enabled dialogue between external and internal atmospheric conditions.

Bristol Energy Cooperative

The third intervention in Bristol is the Bristol Energy Cooperative (BEC), a community-owned energy cooperative that was set up in 2011 to focus on local, green and affordable energy provision. In their words, 'we're a people-owned power station for Greater Bristol!' (BEC, 2020). A mix of loans, public funding from share offers, and the use of a crowdfunding platform had raised more than £10 million at the time of fieldwork in 2017. This enabled BEC to develop two 4 MW solar farms outside Bristol and install rooftop solar on a number of buildings in the city. Their annual electricity output from these solar installations is almost 10,000 MWh, 'enough to power over 3000 average homes' (BEC, 2020). They use digital metering technology to monitor their solar installations and to measure the difference between generation and onsite use for billing purposes. In their search for financial sustainability and a sound business model, they have had a Power Purchase Agreement with a company that specializes in doing virtual energy aggregation, or the digital gathering together of electricity generated from different sites and companies for sale on the market at economies of scale. Here, digital technology behind the scenes is allowing increasingly agile, near real-time adjustment of generation profiles and flexible tracking of price variations to 'target the peak as a sales strategy' (BEC interview, March 2017).

Energy aggregators are new intermediaries in energy systems, operating so-called virtual power plants as a temporary grouping of dispersed sites of energy production to enable this intermittent, often small-scale production to service the centralized grid. Their activities depend on real-time information about production, storage, demand and fluctuating grid provision (from other sources) that enables them to match available distributed production and potential shortfalls in meeting demand at peak times (see, for example, IRENA, 2019). Aggregators develop their own algorithms and digital control management system aimed at facilitating and optimizing schedules and the sending of commands to units of production like BEC's solar panels, as well as the integration of forecasts over time of kilowatt-hours available and needed in relation to shifting grid prices. Here then we have an emerging energy system in which flows of electrons and kilowatt-hours through production, storage and transmission grids are increasingly controlled and hybridized with digital capacities and parallel flows of information.

Knowing the energy flow via the spatio-temporal aggregation enabled by digital metering is particularly relevant in the case of the BEC. However, it is worth noting that, in the context of electricity, the novelty of the datafication of energy as an urban ecological flow is relatively limited: for over 100 years, electricity flows have been known 'at a distance' via metering – specifically, through the use of numbers and processes of enumeration and quantification (Kragh-Furbo and Walker, 2018; see also Espeland and Stevens, 1998). Metering, whether digital or nondigital, produces a trace of energy use via forms of spatial and temporal aggregation. However, in the nondigital arrangement, detail is kept hidden; 'the work done by what devices, to which ends and as part of which practices' remains obscured. With digitization, in contrast, the 'electricity flow materialises then as an apparently far more countable and accountable phenomenon' (Kragh-Furbo and Walker, 2018: 9).

It is important to point out that what is aggregated via metering is not the materiality of the flow, but a numeric representation. Data is thus acting as a proxy for the flow. This dematerialization allows for the flow to be recalculated via mathematical operations encoded in algorithms (from simple addition or subtraction to more complex numerical operations). It also allows the energy flow to be known across past and future temporalities, via an algorithmic combination of historical statistical records on energy production and current and predicted weather flows (for example, cloud cover and rain forecasts) – leading to future estimates of energy generation that can be mobilized in financial energy markets. Here the energy flow gains a new physical-digital materiality, co-constituted via electrons and data operating in tandem.

Critically, it was digitally metering the flow that allowed BEC to sign an energy purchase agreement with the virtual energy aggregator. The latter's digital platform groups together dispersed renewable loads from small producers, such as BEC's solar installations, for aggregated sale to the grid. Aggregation creates economies of scale while their 'nimble' real-time management and control of generation and battery storage means they can optimize the sale of energy during periods of high demand, thus giving a small energy generator like BEC a generally better price than if they had done their own feed-in to the grid (BEC interview, March 2017). Knowing the energy flow across future temporalities, a function of the digitally metered flow recombined with other ecological flows by way of algorithmic calculation, is of particular relevance in the relationship between BEC and the energy aggregator. Here, past and present energy flows (statistical data and real-time information on energy generation) are recombined via specialized software and artificial intelligence with data from other ecological flows (such as current and predicted weather patterns) in order to predict with some level of accuracy the future energy flow and performance of the photovoltaic installations owned by BEC – resulting in a speculative form of dematerialized (yet nonetheless highly agentic) energy flow.

Compared to SoLa Bristol and the C.H.E.E.S.E. project, the BEC initiative reveals a third and different mode of subjectivity with regard to the urban ecological flows. Here it becomes clear that the flow that matters is no longer the sole material flow of energy, but a new flow that is made of both energy and data, co-constituted through the materiality of electrons and their numeric quantification in the form of data. This reconfigured flow reveals a hybridized nature – an ecological flow that is almost remade anew via a dematerialized flow of data. However, BEC has less of an active role in this digital-physical circulation process (when compared to, for example, the energy users in the other two projects examined in this chapter): once the solar panels are in place and functioning, and their production fed into a digitally enabled virtual aggregation contract, then the digital monitoring and algorithmic optimization of flows carried out by the energy aggregation company become the primary management and control instruments behind the mobilization of renewable energy, leaving BEC staff funding mainly focused on the financial side of operations, such as balancing and loan engagements across their portfolio of installations.

In summary, looking across these three initiatives (Table 4.1) we have a sense that they may be pointing to new ways through which urban ecological flows are configured and conceptualized through a range of material-digital interactions, relations and practices. Perhaps the clearest change in the coupling of urban infrastructures and digital systems, primarily by way of datafication processes, is a transformation in the way in which ecological flows come to be known. In all three cases discussed in this chapter, the datafication of energy provides the stakeholders involved with new capabilities to come to know the flow and engage with it.

Furthermore, the digitization of energy and the emergence of a combined physical-digital material configuration results in shifts in the agencies and subjective engagements involved in creating and maintaining the three project interventions. To a large extent, an increase in the capacity of human agents to operate with and through energy flows is the primary aim of the digital intervention. In all three cases the primary users of the flow have gained, deepened or reinforced their capacities of engagement with dynamic energy flows. Engaging with the energy flow as a data flow, for example, has given agents greater flexibility over their use of energy and malleability of the energy flow itself. How these new techno-natural engagements have emerged though differs across the three projects, from the activation of previously passive users through physical-digital infrastructure (SoLa Bristol), to the atmospheric visibility of the home and resulting entanglement of residents, airflow/heat and digital interfaces (C.H.E.E.S.E.), and the search for spatio-temporal optimization of energy production and aggregation that hybridizes electrons and data as an indissociable techno-nature (BEC).

Conclusion

The chapter has explored some of the forms and implications of urban digital natures currently emerging as energy and other infrastructure systems become increasingly layered and combined with digital, datafied processes and logics that fundamentally transform their functioning and capacity. This hybridization problematizes views of infrastructure as mediators *between* nature and the particular city if that distinction is collapsed from the outset by a techno-ecological fusion in which and ecological data flows cannot be meaningfully disarticulated as the former are continuously known, made visible, monitored, managed and calculated/recalculated by the latter. In short, energy flows no longer materialize in the built environment without the digital processes through which they are always already constituted and directed. Energy becomes an increasingly datafied ecology made and calculated through fused digital–physical flows and materialities.

Using vignettes of three ongoing initiatives around digital energy in the city of Bristol, we analysed what these emerging techno-ecological urban natures allow or produce that may be distinctive from previous urban energy initiatives and interventions. Across the projects, on one level, the digital is primarily about utilizing and improving the possibilities of renewable energy and energy efficiency in the built environment. Tracing, monitoring and managing the capture of energy from the sun or reduction of energy consumption and heat loss in the home becomes a way of activating energy components and flows (solar, heat particles, airflow) that both atmospherically coexist with and co-create urban environments, and in parallel act as a disruptive force to traditional and well-embedded metabolic flows that are based on fossil fuel extraction. Yet, as the projects seek to mobilize and manage digital and ecological flows and processes together, we argue furthermore that this appears to shift how actors come to know, understand and engage with the techno-ecological flows of energy systems. As well as making energy flows visible and actionable in new ways, critically, the encounter between and merger of physical infrastructures and digital practices generates possibilities for a wider perspective of agency within infrastructural processes. Digital engagements provide novel capacities that transform subjective positions within the energy system, foregrounding the human agencies of infrastructural arrangements. But, in meaningfully engaging with the energy flow itself and a variety of associated material entities, they also point to a pre-existing, but often unaccounted for, non-human agency. Infrastructuring in this instance captures the opening of a shared plane of intelligibility across which humans and non-humans dialogue, interact and struggle to shape urban techno-ecological systems that are the evolving outcomes of these transactions.

The contribution of the chapter has therefore been to identify how digital technologies, processes and practices are constituting new ways of knowing urban natures and novel subjective engagements with the active infrastructural making and remaking of cities. We suggest that there is an emerging politics of digital energy in the city that stems from these processes of intelligibility (how energy flows are known and made actionable) and engagement (how subjects change positions and capacities to act in energy systems). More understanding of these processes may help to get beyond the 'limited purchase of smart grids' (Powells et al, 2016: 141) in activating more inclusive and sustainable infrastructure configurations. The outcomes for urban infrastructural futures may be more flexibility for the variety of stakeholders in understanding and dealing with what appear to be increasingly complex techno-natural entanglements, and being aware of the possibilities (and limits) of human agency in shaping and reclaiming digital urban natures as part of progressive political strategies.

References

Bennett, J. (2005) 'The agency of assemblages and the North American blackout', *Public Culture*, 17(3): 445–65.

Bennett, J. (2010) *Vibrant Matter: A Political Ecology of Things*, Durham, NC: Duke University Press.

BEC (Bristol Energy Cooperative) (2020) 'About', Bristol Energy Cooperative. Available from: http://bristolenergy.coop/about/ [Accessed 10 November 2021].

Bristol City Council (2015) Our Resilient Future: A Framework for Climate and Energy Security, Bristol: BCC.

Centre for Sustainable Energy (2015) Towards a Smart Energy City: Mapping a Path for Bristol, Bristol: CSE.

Espeland, W.N. and Stevens, M.L. (1998) 'Commensuration as a social process', *Annual Review of Sociology*, 24: 313–43.

Gabrys, J. (2014) 'Programming environments: environmentality and citizen sensing in the smart city', *Environment and Planning D: Society and Space*, 32(1): 30–48.

Gandy, M. (2003) *Concrete and Clay: Reworking Nature in New York City*, Cambridge, MA: MIT Press.

Gandy, M. (2005) 'Cyborg urbanization: complexity and monstrosity in the contemporary city', *International Journal of Urban and Regional Research*, 29(1): 26–49.

Hinchliffe, S. (2007) *Geographies of Nature: Societies, Environments, Ecologies*, London: Sage.

Hubbard, P. (2006) *City*, Abingdon: Routledge.

IRENA (International Renewable Energy Agency) (2019) Innovation Landscape Brief: Aggregators, Abu Dhabi: IRENA.

Kaika, M. (2005) *City of Flows: Modernity, Nature, and the City*, Abingdon: Routledge.

Kaika, M. and Swyngedouw, E. (2000) 'Fetishizing the modern city: the phantasmagoria of urban technological networks', *International Journal of Urban and Regional Research*, 24(1): 120–38.

Kinsley, S. (2014) 'The matter of "virtual" geographies', *Progress in Human Geography*, 38(3): 364–84.

Kitchin, R. (2014) *The Data Revolution: Big Data, Open Data, Data Infrastructures and Their Consequences*, London: Sage.

Knowle West Media Centre (2016) SoLa Bristol Final (short project film), YouTube. Available from: https://www.youtube.com/watch?v=7ukU nKDowvY [Accessed 29 October 2021].

Kragh-Furbo, M. and Walker, G. (2018) 'Electricity as (big) data: metering, spatiotemporal granularity and value', *Big Data & Society*, 5(1). Available from: https://doi.org/10.1177/2053951718757254 [Accessed 14 November 2022].

Latham, A. (2016) 'Materialities', in M. Jayne and K. Ward (eds) *Urban Theory: New Critical Perspectives*, Abingdon: Routledge, pp 183–92.

Latour, B. (2005) *Reassembling the Social: An Introduction to Actor-Network-Theory*, Oxford: Oxford University Press.

Luque-Ayala, A. and Marvin, S. (2020) *Urban Operating Systems: Producing the Computational City*, Cambridge, MA: MIT Press.

McCormack, D.P. (2015) 'Envelopment, exposure, and the allure of becoming elemental', *Dialogues in Human Geography*, 5(1): 85–9.

Moss, T., Voigt, F. and Becker, S. (2021) 'Digital urban nature: probing a void in the smart city discourse', *City*, 25(3/4): 255–76.

Powells, G., Bulkeley, H. and McLean, A. (2016) 'Geographies of smart urban power', in A. Luque-Ayala, S. Marvin and C. McFarlane (eds) *Smart Urbanism: Utopian Vision or False Dawn?*, Abingdon: Routledge, pp 125–44.

Rutherford, J. (2020) *Redeploying Urban Infrastructure: The Politics of Urban Socio-Technical Futures*, Cham: Palgrave Macmillan.

Shahrokni, H., Lazarevic, D. and Brandt, N. (2015) 'Smart urban metabolism: towards a real-time understanding of the energy and material flows of a city and its citizens', *Journal of Urban Technology*, 22(1): 65–86.

Swyngedouw, E. (2006) 'Circulations and metabolisms:(hybrid) natures and (cyborg) cities', *Science as Culture*, 15(2): 105–21.

Western Power Distribution (2016) *Project SoLa Bristol Closedown Report*, Bristol: WPD.

Whatmore, S. (2002) *Hybrid Geographies: Natures Cultures Spaces*, London: Sage.

White, D.F. and Wilbert, C. (eds) (2009) *Technonatures: Environments, Technologies, Spaces, and Places in the Twenty-First Century*, Waterloo, ONT: Wilfrid Laurier University Press.

5

Infrastructural Reparations: Reimagining Reparative Justice in Haiti and Puerto Rico

Mimi Sheller

Introduction

Infrastructural citizenship – the idea that there is a political relationship between people and those infrastructures that shape their lives, and that they, in turn, shape – is a key area of inquiry in contemporary infrastructure studies (Lemanski, 2019, 2020). For some groups the promise of infrastructural citizenship as an everyday claim upon the state is far more precarious than others: not only is access to infrastructure uncertain, but also the underlying promise of a functioning state and access to citizenship remains in question. Especially for those living in the wake of slavery, the violence and negation of the afterlives of slavery demands more than infrastructural repair to empower 'living blackness' within the 'unfinished project of emancipation' (Sharpe, 2016: 2, 5). This chapter will instead foreground *infrastructural reparations*, as a form of what Sharpe calls 'wake work' as a kind of 'imagining otherwise' and '*hard insisting*' (Sharpe, 2016: 17–19, original emphasis). Reimagining infrastructural reparations calls into question the violence of anti-Blackness that underlies the 'North Atlantic universals' (Trouillot, 2021: 142) of the citizen, the state, the human, determining who has the right to live and who will be left to die. That is to say, insofar as White supremacy and coloniality exploit and dispose of Black bodies *as infrastructure for White self-reproduction*, the evident ideals of state, citizenship and infrastructural citizenship must themselves be pried open as analytical fictions through insistent projects of reparative infrastructural justice.

Infrastructure has an inherently uneven capacity to connect and to provide for some people certain goods and particular flows of information, while at the same time disenfranchising and dehumanizing other people through the very processes of (dis)connecting elements of the urban condition (including urbanization that extends beyond cities and encompasses offshore islands such as those in the Caribbean). Such (dis)connections are the subject of various tactics not simply of repair, but of infrastructural reparations that exceed the universal framework of states and citizenship. Reparative infrastructural justice insists on overturning the violence of the infrastructural dispositions that have long upheld White supremacy by dehumanizing Black, Brown and Indigenous people, and other people of colour. Existing studies of infrastructural citizenship have focused on physical infrastructure such as oil pipelines (Appel, 2019), water systems (De Coss-Corzo, 2021) and energy grids (Tormos-Aponte et al, 2021), as well as the labour-intensive reproductive work of care, social reproduction and 'people as infrastructure' (Simone, 2004). The design, the governance, the promise and the failings of infrastructure are all determined by, and determinative of, social relations of power and political agency (Anand et al, 2018). Yet beyond these political struggles to repair failing infrastructure, I seek to recognize a radical politics of infrastructural reparations that imagines infrastructure otherwise by disrupting or appropriating infrastructural (dis)connections.

As Anand (2015, 2017), Gandy (2008, 2014) and others have argued, the cities of the Global South are sites of fractured modernity, where infrastructure, risk and disease are distributed unequally, and where class and racial inequality follow lines of uneven water and sanitation access, and uneven access to energy grids and communications networks. There is an evident coloniality of uneven infrastructure that reproduces the global 'color line', as W.E.B. Dubois called it, i.e. 'the relation of the darker to the lighter races of men in Asia and Africa, in America and the islands of the sea' (Dubois, 1903: 10). The colour line is also an infrastructural chasm that divides the descendants of the White settler slaveholding regimes from those 'wretched of the earth' (Fanon, 1990) who were subjected to the system of slavery and now inhabit the 'underdeveloped' 'shanty towns' and 'slums' of the Global South as well as the ghettoes, exurbs, prisons and migrant detention centres of the Global North (Wynter, 2003). The major global provision of infrastructure brings oil, water, gas and energy flowing into the privileged spaces and elite neighbourhoods of the Global North, the seats of colonial power, the imperial metropoles, the core of the world economy, and the preferred 'liveable cities' and suburbs of White gentrification. The same systems of infrastructural provision simultaneously extract from, pollute and foreshorten life in the global peripheries and racialized spaces of the disprivileged: the colonized, 'dependent', 'underdeveloped' (Rodney, [1972] 2018) peripheries and the brownfield, fenceline, sacrifice zones foisted on Black, Brown and Indigenous neighbourhoods. These two systems are entangled and mutually constitutive, thus we cannot speak of infrastructure in cities of North America without considering their 'global shadows' (Ferguson, 2006) – shadows that may also fall closer to home in the racialized dispossession that punctures spaces of accumulation with zones of extraction and disposability. In the 'otherwise modern' AlterNative Americas where 'North Atlantic universals' do not hold (Trouillot, 2021: 142), the study of infrastructural citizenship remains incomplete if it does not grapple with the coloniality of citizenship, and the racialized populations relegated to second-class citizenship or non-citizenship and who hold a different relationship to infrastructural citizenship. Those with no claims upon the state to provide the basics of life – 'with no state or nation to protect us, with no citizenship bound to be respected' (Sharpe, 2016: 22) – must go beyond repair or maintenance, seeking instead infrastructural reparations and reparative justice as material conditions for living.

In addition to the contributions of radical Black thinkers such as DuBois, Rodney and Trouillot, and theorists of infrastructural repair in the Global South like Anand, Gandy, Simone and de Coss-Corzo, my approach builds on theories of 'infrastructuring' as an active practice, along with materialist approaches to media that emphasize the material geographies and dispositions of power embedded within communication infrastructures (Star, 1999; Parks and Schwoch, 2012; Parks, 2014). I understand infrastructure, following Heather Horst, as 'a dynamic process that is simultaneously made and unmade' (Horst, 2013: 151) and, we could add, that simultaneously connects and disconnects various users. Infrastructuring thus involves the daily struggle for patching together missed connections or creatively appropriating that which is available (de Souza e Silva et al, 2011). Such infrastructuring takes place both as strategies of the powerful to build infrastructural futures, and as tactical interventions 'from below' especially within the structures of coloniality and racial capitalism. More generally, though, these active processes also involve crossing over and through *multiple kinds* of infrastructure. Rather than a study of one or another system, for example water or electricity alone, I seek to show their entanglements with each other, and of the physical infrastructure with the digital, the communicational, the financial and the social infrastructures of reproduction, politics and migration.

Beyond repair: conceptualizing infrastructural reparations

In this chapter I will reflect on some of the tactics of flexible, provisional, infrastructural reparations that have emerged in the Caribbean, drawing on my work on Haiti and Puerto Rico in the wake of slavery, colonialism and climate disaster. My studies of historical popular democratic movements and public claim-making in Jamaica and Haiti in the 19th century (Sheller, 2000, 2012) sensitize me to the subaltern politics of contesting exclusionary citizenship regimes in the post-slavery Caribbean. Likewise, wider work on the histories of US relations of extraction with the Caribbean region (Sheller, 2003, 2014) demonstrate the exploitation of Caribbean land and people for the benefit of the Global North. While Jamaica, Haiti, Puerto Rico, the Dominican Republic and Cuba have experienced very different forms of (dis)connectivity and incorporation into the international system, differing patterns of urbanization, and varied ways of building and governing infrastructure systems, in each case there have been struggles for radical reconstruction and reparations to address the deep-seated coloniality and denial of citizenship, including infrastructural citizenship.

Infrastructure space is an active form of organizing capacities for life (and death). Physical systems for water, sewage and energy, along with communication systems such as the undersea cable network, mobile phone masts, satellite transmission and the mobile internet form what Keller Easterling calls infrastructure space. Easterling describes the 'political character of infrastructure space' based on 'accidental, covert, or stubborn forms of power' that hide in its folds (Easterling, 2016: 73; and see Parks and Starosielski, 2015; Starosielski, 2015). Uneven (dis)connectivity is a key form that such power takes, that generates creative efforts at appropriation. Infrastructure space is not mere background but takes active forms, argues Easterling, through the organization of components into dynamic mechanisms. (Dis)connection is always an ongoing active process, an activity of simultaneous connection and disconnection, that occurs within the activation of dispositions within any infrastructure space. Racialization, I suggest, is a disposition of infrastructural (dis)connectivity that is one of the fundamental bases of White supremacy, grounded in indigenous genocide, transatlantic slavery and (neo)colonial extraction.

Incomplete and failing infrastructure is a constant reminder of the uneven temporalities of infrastructural building, maintenance and repair, which are always embedded in colonial relations and racialized global economies that etch ever more deeply the lines of life and death in the Anthropocene. Nikhil Anand's chapter on Mumbai's water supply and hydraulic publics in *The Promise of Infrastructure* (Anand et al, 2018), for example, depicts how citizenship is achieved transactionally and infrastructurally, as those on the margins demand access to water. Tormos-Aponte et al (2021) show how post-disaster restoration of power grids in Puerto Rico after Hurricane Maria was driven by clientelism and political affiliations, rather than need. Patrick Bigger and Nate Millington (this volume) show how the anticipations of new infrastructures is a relation of power in regard to who designs futures: who waits and for whom? Infrastructural injustices shape times, time horizons and life cycles. There is a lack of synchronicity in the time horizons of durability, materiality, engineering and financialization of infrastructure versus the immediate needs of living people and communities – but there is also need for a longer time horizon that acknowledges the demand for historical reparations in addition to immediate needs.

Recent studies of infrastructure have highlighted practices of maintenance and repair, and one way to think about this is in terms of a patchwork construction. In a study of workers in the water system of Mexico City, Alejandro de Coss-Corzo develops the concept of patchwork: 'I define patchwork as a repair practice, enabled by workers' embodied expertize ... and practical knowledge ... as a repair logic, adaptive and improvisational; and as a socio-material form, related both to the materiality of infrastructure and to the relations that are enabled through it' (de Coss-Corzo, 2021: 238).

Highlighting 'improvisation, adaptation and incrementalism' (de Coss-Corzo, 2021: 239) within repair practices, he argues that patchwork is a logic of infrastructural adaptation that allows for the endurance of urban modernity within contexts of austerity and socio-material change. De Coss-Corzo shows that repair practices 'are always already political, entangled with the maintenance of relations of power and inequality across different scales and among different actors, including the state, informal neighborhoods, private providers, and international experts' (de Coss-Corzo, 2021: 243). But what if 'modern' urban infrastructure is not yet there? And what if there is no state agency to engage in repair, public–private partnerships are failing and international experts are not helpful?

What I will call patching, in contrast, is not a question of repair of existing infrastructure, but rather an action of attracting, stealing or 'patching into' a partial infrastructure to which a community is not already connected, while simultaneously patching together a state that is not functioning and forms of citizenship that do not exist. Patching is a form of appropriation that may also intersect with forms of urban violence and extortion; infrastructure, in that sense, may be beyond repair, leading instead to efforts to patch together, steal or improvise autonomous ways of sustaining life. In those places and among those people who have been most subject to infrastructural (and state) neglect and disconnection, there arises of necessity alternative means of infrastructuring from below: seizing the means of connection, patching together systems of provision, appropriating the levers of infrastructural power, whether calling on the state or escaping its grip.

Building and maintaining infrastructure requires constant physical repair, especially following the cascades of natural disaster that have become so commonplace in the human-made climate disruption that some call the Anthropocene, but also in the slower disasters of developmental abandonment and toxic 'territories of urban relegation' (Wacquant, 2016: 1077; see also Auyero, 2012; Auyero and Swistun, 2009). As AbdouMaliq Simone puts it in his now classic essay on Johannesburg, South Africa, this involves not only physical infrastructure but also human infrastructure as a platform of practices:

> African cities are characterized by incessantly flexible, mobile, and provisional intersections of residents that operate without clearly delineated notions of how the city is to be inhabited and used. These intersections, particularly in the last two decades, have depended on the ability of residents to engage complex combinations of objects, spaces, persons, and practices. These conjunctions become an infrastructure – a platform providing for and reproducing life in the city. (Simone, 2004: 407–8)

Building on this notion of complex combinations of objects, spaces, persons and practices, I deploy the term 'reparations' in a multivalent way, including the histories of racialized exclusion and infrastructural neglect – indeed denial of access to life – that demand more explicit reparative justice. This ranges from reparations for slavery to the demand for climate reparations by small island states that contributed the least to greenhouse gas emissions but suffer the worst consequences of climate change. So infrastructural reparations are concerned with not only the immediacy of day-to-day needs for survival, but also organizing life differently in the wake of historical relegation. Infrastructural reparations might involve physical objects and systems, but also reorganize (or mobilize) diverse spaces, relations and practices in reparative ways.

In the following sections I will focus on two moments and *tactics* of infrastructural reparations – in de Certeau's sense (1984) as also picked up by Simone (2004) – in Caribbean cities experiencing periods of natural disaster, political conflict and states of emergency: Port-au-Prince, Haiti, after the 2010 earthquake and ongoing political turbulence since; and San Juan, Puerto Rico, caught in both the sudden disaster of Hurricane Maria in 2017 and the ongoing slow disaster of coloniality, debt and austerity. Caribbean cities have deep ties to the Global North – indeed were central in the making of Northern urbanization (Sheller, 2003, 2014) – and I would argue cannot be thought of or theorized outside of the global infrastructures of (dis)connectivity. These include the background physical infrastructure of sea lanes, air space, fossil fuel and communication infrastructures such as undersea cables and satellites (all of which are ultimately subject to US military power in the Caribbean), as well as crucial financial infrastructures and software for internet connectivity used for 'offshoring' various kinds of data-based service work such as the offshore banking sector, call centres or internet-based services (Freeman, 2000; Lewis, 2020).

First, using the example of physical infrastructural repair in post-earthquake Haiti, I will show how the improvised *patching* of infrastructure (for water, energy and communication) was always present there, yet became ever more of a necessity in the face of infrastructural collapse and state disappearance after the shock of the 2010 earthquake. Patching infrastructure became a means of dealing with this unliveable situation of an absent state, impunity for violence, endless insecurity, and rising costs of living that in 2021 culminated in the assassination of President Jovenel Moïse and a constitutional crisis (Katz, 2013; Beckett, 2019; Johnston, 2022), which has resulted in an ongoing infrastructural collapse today. Then, building on my earlier work on the 'infrastructuring of imagined islands' (Sheller, 2009a, 2009b), I will consider how the emergence of 'encrypted geographies' in the Caribbean (Simpson, 2021; Simpson and Sheller, 2022) leverages Puerto Rico for libertarian crypto-experimentation in new financial and political infrastructures based on blockchain technology. I seek to show how the connections between physical and digital infrastructure, real and imagined states and territories, sovereignty and non-sovereignty all suggest the ways in which our theoretical imaginaries of infrastructure must extend beyond liberal discourses of universal citizenship and progressive (but failing) narratives of inclusion and humanitarian repair, and move instead towards critical practices of radical reparations and reparative justice.

Patching together life in post-earthquake Port-au-Prince, Haiti

Infrastructure is at one and the same time a necessity for daily life's social reproduction and an essential institution enmeshed in the exploitation and expropriation that are constitutive of global, racial capitalism. In Port-au-Prince, Haiti – a city named after its colonial port and those who controlled it – with a population of at least 2.8 million people, there is only partial provision of public infrastructure for water, energy, transport and communication. Self-provisioning and community-based tactics to access these basic life systems were intensified by the devastating impact of the 2010 earthquake and subsequent cholera epidemic, and the evident failure of the international 'Build Back Better' promise of post-earthquake reconstruction, which was never realized (Katz, 2013; Beckett, 2019; Sheller, 2020). Today, a political crisis has led to a complete collapse of the urban infrastructure, which has been blockaded by armed gangs.

The structural violence of Haitian urbanization was already deeply shaped by the US Occupation of 1915–34, the Duvalier Dictatorship that followed, the suppression of democratic movements and the imposition of neoliberal structural adjustment policies, all of which displaced rural communities and drove rapid urbanization and uncontrolled growth of Port-au-Prince since the 1980s (Arthur and Dash, 1999). This left the population dwelling in hastily built shanties with no public services especially vulnerable to the

Figure 5.1: Children collecting water from a humanitarian distribution centre, Port-au-Prince, Haiti, 2010

Source: Mimi Sheller

earthquake, as well as to frequent flooding, hurricanes and droughts. When the 2010 earthquake wiped out many communal water standpipes that were the sole source of water, and people were displaced to temporary tent camps, water had to be trucked in and distributed by humanitarian organizations. Often they relied on women and children to do the work of provisioning water (see Figure 5.1).

Before the earthquake many communities in Haiti had (and continue to have) no piped water provision (nor sewage treatment). The majority purchased treated potable water by the sachet or bucket, or resorted to point-of-use purification with bleach. Middle-class neighbourhoods in Port-au-Prince were served by the public agency CAMEP [Centrale Autonome Métropolitaine d'Eau Potable] and later formed public–private partnerships that provide metered water in association with the national water agency DINEPA [Direction Nationale de l'Eau Potable et de l'Assainissement]. Poorer neighbourhoods organized *Komite Dlo* (water committees) that worked with DINEPA and with nongovernmental organizations (NGOs) to build and maintain communal standpipes or water kiosks. The water committees collected fees from users, paying some back to the public water authority while keeping some for maintaining the system, for the committee itself, or for community projects in some cases (Sheller et al, 2013). In the absence of an effective state, however, such community-controlled arrangements can come to resemble something more like strong-arm extortion by gangs who in some neighbourhoods have taken over policing functions. Patching together the promise of infrastructure thus draws on what Chelsey Kivland (2020) calls the 'street sovereignty' of the 'makeshift state in urban Haiti'.

The latest crisis of reproduction of civil society and infrastructural citizenship in Haiti is marked by reverberating political crises, urban *ensekirite* [insecurity], and rampant kidnapping, leading finally to the assassination of President Jovenel Moïse in July 2021, followed by ongoing murky debates over the legitimacy of the current government led by Prime Minister Ariel Henry (Johnston, 2022). Today, some areas have access to the electric grid, but service is irregular and even in middle-class or better-off neighbourhoods many households must resort to diesel-power generators for electricity. Poorer 'informal' neighbourhoods seek to gain access to transformers connected to local substations and then wire in multiple illegal electrical hook-ups, often resulting in power overloads and fires (Kivland, 2020). It is a patchwork energy system, constantly breaking down, and it also requires an extensive infrastructure for the use of kerosene lamps and the production and delivery of charcoal for cooking. Diesel for generators and vehicles has also been a constant source of political conflict and high prices, especially following the demise of the Petrocaribe deal with Venezuela, which led to fuel shortages, soaring prices, investigations of government corruption and massive street protests in 2019. The blockade of fuel deliveries by armed gangs in 2022 led to calls for foreign intervention.

What does infrastructural repair look like in this context? In the years after the 2010 earthquake, the local and international response unfortunately consolidated the governmental and international NGO use of partial-access premium infrastructure for post-disaster logistics and communication, rather than supporting the building of broad public infrastructure (Sheller, 2013, 2019). The UN bases of so-called 'peace-keeping' forces, for example, built their own highly secured satellite communications towers that were not locally connected (see Figure 5.2). While military and humanitarian responders travelled from many countries and brought as much portable temporary infrastructure as they could, the reconstruction effort dismally failed to make any difference in building back infrastructure for those in the informal neighbourhoods of Port-au-Prince, who suffered an absence of housing and saw few improvements in public infrastructure for water, energy or communications (Katz, 2013; Sheller, 2020). Post-earthquake infrastructures of attempted connection and repair thus simultaneously entailed disconnectivity, political frustration and widespread despair (Beckett, 2019).

Figure 5.2: UN MINUSTAH (United Nations Stabilization Mission in Haiti) base in Leogane, Haiti, 2010

Source: Mimi Sheller

When existing infrastructures for transport and communication are disrupted by a disaster, people usually make efforts to reconnect, that is, by rebuilding roads, repairing pipes or installing powerlines or phone masts; but the installation of new infrastructure after a disruption may also lead to what Graham and Marvin (2001) refer to as 'bypassing' and 'splintering', in which some groups or regions are connected over, above, and at the expense of, others. Infrastructures of connection function as implicit geographies of disconnection in ways that usually reinforce existing structural exclusions and racialized inequities. This was very much the case in post-earthquake Haiti, where infrastructural reconstruction could never be separated from fierce competition for *any* connections to the local state, NGOs, to foreign aid contractors and to 'street sovereigns', all of whom could offer different possibilities for infrastructural connection, but always in fragmented and incomplete ways.

Furthermore, communication infrastructures and locational technologies are also enrolled into – indeed are the basis for – uneven global assemblages of power that have more, or less, democratizing effects depending on how they are performed. Digital connection also requires *physical infrastructure* such as mobile phones, phone masts, satellites, Wi-Fi, underground cables, phones and electricity; *institutional infrastructure* such as a network of services providers, government regulations, legal codes and engineering protocols; and *social infrastructure* such as literacy, numeracy and technical know-how. Emergency interventions following the earthquake brought new kinds of physical connectivity (such as satellite-based mobile communications systems) that bypassed national public infrastructure (such as Haiti's national public telecom company, which was privatized and sold off to a Vietnamese company) and only extended connectivity to those empowered with privileged institutional and social infrastructure. Using temporary communication infrastructures to respond to disasters only works if there are communities organized to appropriate technology and adapt it to their needs in ways that can be extended into longer-term provision. Infrastructural access requires physically, institutionally *and* socially joining up connected locations where people and communities can maintain *ongoing access* to energy, water and communication systems. This requires not only repair or maintenance of community-based connectivity, but reparative justice to overcome historical exclusions.

Kivland (2020) describes how young men in the informal neighbourhood of Bel-Air in Port-au-Prince form organizations of 'street sovereignty', which attempt to stand in for the state and bring needed infrastructure to their neighbourhoods. Without public provision of infrastructure by the state, such groups refer to themselves not as gangs, but as *baz* [base], employing an infrastructural term for their own formation. The *baz* sought to call forth the state and seize the powers of the state, by bargaining with political candidates for their votes, or with NGOs to provide a workforce and grassroots legitimacy for their community-based projects. Yet the collapse of the state and its reliance on armed groups (known as *chimè*, or spooks) also brought waves of conflict, including gun violence, rape and kidnapping in poor neighbourhoods (which eventually spilled over into the middle-class neighbourhoods and the kidnapping of foreigners too). NGOs delivering free water, or installing electrical transformers in neighbourhoods without power, are also creating systems that are destined to fail unless they build human and social infrastructure too.

Some gang leaders emerged as politicians themselves, leveraging infrastructural citizenship to claim political leadership. The 'G9 and Family' gang controlled by former police officer Jimmy Chérizier, alias 'Barbecue', was closely allied with the ruling PHTK [Parti Haïtien Tèt Kale], against the *baz* in Bel-Air, who were aligned with the Lavalas party. G9 and Family engaged in various forms of extortion, demanding payments from street vendors and public transportation drivers, as well as through kidnappings. They took control over local police forces and public services such as electricity and water provision for payment. The control of such infrastructure became a key form of political manoeuvring for legitimacy and mobilization of a political 'base'. Although implicated in numerous extrajudicial killings (including the infamous La Saline Massacre in which at least 71 people were killed), Chérizier began to style himself as a revolutionary leader of a popular political movement fighting for the poor and marginalized, issuing public proclamations and leading marches after the July 2021 assassination of his ally President Jovenel Moïse (Insight Caribbean, 2021). The state has effectively disappeared in Haiti (Beckett, 2019), yet the demand for infrastructural reparations remains.

These dynamic constellations of infrastructural politics can be imagined as patches of connectivity amid fields of disconnectivity. But infrastructural patching has its dangers, especially when it rests on threats and acts of violence from the *baz*. In the absence of state provision and the failures of transnational aid, democratizing infrastructure requires paying close attention to the demonstrated capabilities that communities already have for potential connection, but also awareness of the wider infrastructures of state violence in which poor communities are enmeshed, including state complicity in the illicit weapons and transnational drugs trade which run their own underground (and at sea) infrastructural channels through Central America and the Caribbean, with Haiti serving as a key node in the network. Protecting and expanding patchy forms of insurgent 'connectivity from below' demands that we ask how local appropriations of infrastructure might be built on in ways that strengthen local actors' autonomy and agency, allowing for reparations of everyday *mizè* (misery) without entrenching the use and abuse of armed coercion. Either way, it is clear that the makeshift anti-infrastructures of street sovereignty are not a glitch: they are a feature of violently won infrastructural futures.

While the strategy of patching is suggestive of scrappy underdogs configuring infrastructural resources from below within violent situations, another related tactic appropriates infrastructural reparations through the practice of the scam. Jovan Scott Lewis (2020) has shown how 'scammers' in Montego Bay, Jamaica, seized on the physical and human infrastructure of call centres as an opportunity to turn the tables on global capital accumulation. They leveraged enhanced connectivity to funnel money from North Americans back into their own pockets. If patching is about finding *work-arounds* to access infrastructures from which one is otherwise disconnected (by stitching together alternative makeshift infrastructures and leveraging elite alliances through force), scamming is about exploiting good infrastructural connectivity to *reverse the flow* of goods/services/money back towards one's own location. Building on Lewis's insights about this kind of reparative justice, I turn in the next section to the arrival of cryptocurrency entrepreneurs in Puerto Rico as another possible site for infrastructural reparations. For those who are not the protected infrastructural citizens of the imagined state, what expanded capacities might the new dispositions of digital infrastructure space afford?

Encrypting libertarian utopias in San Juan, Puerto Rico

After the destructive impacts of Hurricanes Irma and Maria in 2017, a group of cryptocurrency entrepreneurs landed in San Juan, Puerto Rico, with claims to restarting the economy and repairing the damaged island. In contrast to infrastructuring from below, these initiatives came from outside the region and are not associated with reparative justice. Yet they do suggest a continuation of tactics of piracy and exit from the nation-state system, which have long attracted Caribbean participants. Crypto-utopias play with Caribbean histories of 'marronage' and piracy that leverage interstitial island spaces to seize new possibilities. Here I focus on another tactic of infrastructural reparations related to the rise of 'encrypted geographies' (Simpson, 2021) in the Caribbean, built on the blockchain and leveraging the symbolism of 'offshore' tropical islands as sites of freedom, experimentation and escape from the state.

While digital divides have attracted much critical attention, more recently the increasing 'datafication' of society and algorithmic culture differentiates between 'traditional digital inequalities', or digital divide – access, usage, outcome – and 'new digital inequalities' (knowledge, database, treatment) that are forming an 'algorithmic divide' (Ragnedda 2020: 93–4). Data systems are implicated in the production of 'code/space' (Kitchen and Dodge, 2011; Kitchen et al, 2018) in ways that reinforce and reproduce mobility injustices (Sheller, 2018). Data justice approaches emphasize that infrastructure design and decision making are intrinsically bound up with data, algorithms and, increasingly, AI, with many inequitable results. Software-enabled tourism destinations and luxury architecture on private islands in the Caribbean, for example, have leveraged virtual cyber-technologies to support tourist mobility and accessibility, while marginalizing non-citizens such as Haitian migrants working in tourism-dependent economies across the Caribbean (Sheller, 2009a).

In reshaping forms of mobility, property, sovereignty and citizenship this software-supported tourist infrastructuring also leverages US military power to control the Caribbean (Sheller, 2021). Infrastructural studies therefore needs to join together earlier studies of splintered urbanism (Graham and Marvin, 2001) and code/space (Kitchen and Dodge, 2011) with the new transnational geographies of tourism, militarism, finance capital, offshore territoriality and fantasies of extraterritorial escape that have become so prominent within emerging new configurations of Web3 cyber-infrastructure, blockchain and 'crypto-islands'.

Few studies of code/space foresaw the arrival of blockchain-based cryptocurrencies, non-fungible tokens (NFTs), and their potential for massive disruption of existing models not only of finance and banking, but also of states, cities, citizenship and belonging. The arrival of blockchain technologies takes the questions of agency, autonomy and democracy raised in infrastructure studies, software studies and mobility studies to an entirely new level. If traditional infrastructural connectivity was about centralized public networks of connectivity, such systems were always in tension with decentralization and local provision. Graham and Marvin (2001) noted the splintering of once national aspirations for public infrastructures into premium infrastructure space for the elite; yet the experience in the cities of the Global South was more often that decentralization was the norm, in the absence of centralized public infrastructures for water treatment or electricity or communications. This made these locations especially susceptible to the infiltration of 'decentralized finance' (defi) entrepreneurs.

Implicit in infrastructural reparations is not so much the demise and repair of once centralized systems of infrastructural provision and control, but rather as already described, the opportunities presented to improvise new infrastructural connections by breaking into that which exists. It is less a case of splintering what was once there, and more a case of *fractalizing and redistributing emerging infrastructural possibilities*. This kind of inventiveness is related to the 'inventive political technologies' of infrastructuring that Simone describes for Jakarta, wherein '[i]nfrastructure exerts a force – not simply in the materials and energies it avails, but also the way it attracts people, draws them in, coalesces and expands their capacities' (Simone, 2013: 243). What forces and energies are coalescing around the capacities of crypto-imaginaries generated by blockchain technologies and its imagined inventive political technologies?

Libertarians, many on the right wing of the political spectrum, have also embraced the demise of centralized power and political belonging through their embrace of 'start-up societies' that exit from existing forms of state and financial regulation and invent their own forms of horizontal infrastructuring, in the form of 'distributed autonomous organizations' as a kind of parallel universe built on the emerging blockchain technology. This implicit fracturing of the state monopoly on territoriality and contract law may come at a high cost to the public realm and citizenries – but might also open new infrastructural affordances for the excluded denizens of the offshore zones of coloniality and racialized exclusion. Some theorists of infrastructure such as Dominic Boyer (in Anand et al, 2018) argue for a revolutionary infrastructure that constructs a future of local development and decentralized forms of power and political belonging. Many green energy advocates, for example, call for distributed community-owned microgrids that can handle multiple inputs of renewable energy. Such ideas of decentralization inspired some of the claims being made by crypto-entrepreneurs in Puerto Rico; however, it is not clear that such rhizomatic infrastructures will necessarily bring forth a more sustainable and just future.

Isabelle Simpson has explored how the start-up societies imaginary is shaped both by blockchain technologies themselves, and by the discourses of decentralization, peer-to-peer network and 'trustless' governance used by developers and cryptocurrencies enthusiasts to describe and promote these technologies (Simpson, 2021). Together we have explored how islands, both natural and human-made, have become prime locations for experimentation with such ventures, which 'often rely on technologies like blockchain and cryptocurrencies to raise capital, experiment with new governance models, attract investors and entrepreneurs, and entice governments with promises of breakthrough regulatory innovation and lucrative business opportunities' (Simpson and Sheller, 2022). The promise of blockchain-based start-up societies is that they can free participants from states, banks and overbearing bureaucratic systems, including national citizenship and border control. They offer an alleged blank slate, within which people can build digitally mediated mechanisms of trust through encrypted and secure transactions kept in the permanent ledger of the blockchain. Yet the preferred location for such start-up societies has heavily leveraged the idea of the tropical paradise island-getaway, and in fact also involves 'escape' to actual islands in the Caribbean.

Several such start-up societies have been attracted to offshore island jurisdictions where there is low or no taxation, including Puerto Rico, and little government regulation, allowing them to experiment with 'defi' while defying state regulation. We argue that 'islands are particularly attractive to proponents of start-up societies precisely because their imagined interstitiality ... allows these would be city-builders and political entrepreneurs to exploit island space and island imaginaries to "exit" and strategically position themselves as "outside" the reach of the state, but still advantageously within the global economy' (Simpson and Sheller, 2022). Simpson (in Hagen and Diener, 2022; Simpson, 2021) develops the concept of 'encrypted geographies' to describe such hybrid spaces designed to provide an exit from the state and a path (supposedly) 'beyond politics' (Thiel, 2009). Moreover, the crypto-utopian vision claims that blockchain microtransactions will enable new forms of infrastructuring, by which services like water, electricity or data can be bought in small amounts, serving small consumers and informal neighbourhoods as much as the rich elite.

Following the decimation of several Caribbean islands by Hurricanes Irma and Maria in autumn 2017, technology, business and innovation leaders from outside the region stepped forward with ideas for reinventing Puerto Rico as a crypto-utopia. One such initiative, initially named Puertopia, but rebranded as Sol, consisted of a group of crypto-investors led by Brock Pierce, a former child actor, now a crypto-entrepreneur who also ran as independent for US president in 2020. They proposed using 'blockchain infrastructure' to renew urban development in Puerto Rico after Hurricane Maria (Bowles, 2018;

Watlington, 2019). Dozens of crypto-entrepreneurs, attracted by Puerto Rico's absence of federal personal income tax or capital gains tax, relocated themselves and their businesses to the island (Bowles, 2018; Klein, 2018). The group rented a four-star hotel called the Monastery and in March 2018 held a blockchain summit conference called Puerto Crypto.

Post-disaster Puerto Rico, where the energy grid had collapsed and would take years to repair, offered potentially fruitful opportunities for the creation of interstitial encrypted geographies. In May 2018, the Startup Societies Foundation also held its annual summit at George Mason University in Virginia, under the theme 'Rebuild Puerto Rico' and held a hackathon calling for 'investors, blockchain entrepreneurs, policymakers, green infrastructure companies, real estate developers, NGOs, academics, Special Economic Zone experts, and exponential technology startups to form a consortium to rebuild Puerto Rico with sustainable startup cities' (McKinney 2022). This was at the very moment that Puerto Ricans were not only recovering from Hurricane Maria but were fighting austerity measures associated with the PROMESA legislation (Puerto Rico Oversight, Management, and Economic Stability Act), which had forced cuts in education, pensions and healthcare, and the restructuring of the public electricity utility, known as PREPA. By leveraging the emergency situation, this kind of 'disaster capitalism' (Klein, 2018) reflects the highly unequal 'accumulation by adaptation' (Dawson, 2017: 65) that takes root after natural disasters. Here it could feed seamlessly into speculative crypto-capitalist investments and lucrative land dispossession, displacing Puerto Ricans through a kind of disaster gentrification (Murphy et al, 2022).

As Puerto Rican anthropologist Yarimar Bonilla (2018) explains, Act 20/ 22, originally passed in 2012 and subsequently modified, allowed wealthy investors who spent half the year in Puerto Rico to benefit from 'exemptions from federal and local taxes, capital gains tax, and taxes on passive income until the year 2035'. This proved to be highly attractive:

> Originally designed to attract wealthy financiers, the law has ended up luring tech entrepreneurs, cryptocurrency devotees, digital nomads, and tax dodgers who choose their countries of residence based on economic incentives, regulatory freedom, and 'value opportunities' – rather than on cultural or political ties. Puerto Rico's status as an unincorporated US territory suits these untethered entrepreneurs. As neither a nation nor a US state, it allows arrivals to retain their US citizenship while benefiting from the legal ambiguities of territorial status. (Bonilla, 2018)

Post-Maria Puerto Rico offered an ideal context in which to experiment with technological and cyberlibertarian exit fantasies – as a new stateless infrastructure – in part because of its heavy indebtedness and infrastructural collapse (not unlike Haiti, though positioned differently as a US territory that could attract capital investment). Purposely structured as an interstitial financial and political space where both crypto-secession and crypto-statecraft were possible, the island was especially vulnerable to infiltration, another kind of patching in this moment of emergency recovery.

Puertopians could virtually 'exit' the US and its fiscal regulations while keeping their American citizenship, and present themselves not as foreign colonizers, but as benevolent crypto-capitalists and technology evangelists coming to the rescue of their compatriots. As Bonilla and Klein explain, the crypto-entrepreneurs could tell themselves:

> This is where we need to be, because we can operate within an ambiguous framework. Given Puerto Rico's colonial relationship to the U.S., not all federal legislation applies. And not only that, but we can actually set the terms and create precedents, legislative precedents, of how blockchain and Bitcoin and all these kinds of new technologies are going to be applied. (Bonilla and Klein, 2018)

Thus, the financial infrastructure of the offshore tax-haven, along with the collapsing infrastructure of public provision of energy, water and communications, created the ideal conditions for libertarian experimentation with new forms of decentralized non-state infrastructuring. It was not so ideal, however, for Puerto Ricans.

As Keller Easterling argues, this reveals the kinds of dispositions that are 'hiding in the folds of infrastructure space' (2016: 73), shaping its political character through multiplier effects. The indeterminacy of the extra-state island-space as tax haven, Special Economic Zone and compromised sovereignty played into the hands of the Puertopians to accumulate capital and purchase prime real estate in San Juan, at the very moment that the Puerto Rican public sector was being slashed, and the people of Puerto Rico were being forced by a Congressionally appointed oversight committee to repay the illegitimate debt taken on by the state (Klein, 2018). As one critic argues: 'Although there are no physical walls gating the crypto-utopia in San Juan, there are digital walls and gates that keep anyone out unless they are high net-worth 'accredited investors' ... and on the inside in the "blockchain space"' (Crandall, 2019: 286). Rather than providing infrastructure then, in the sense of public provision, the encrypted geography creates an *anti-infrastructure* that claims to lift infrastructure out of political space, yet potentially leaves the majority population outside the new emerging blockchain space.

In the midst of ruination, and in the absence of any kind of infrastructural reparations to actually provide public financing for water or electricity to the

Puerto Rican population, Puertopia quickly became a blueprint for other such start-up societies and crypto-secessionists, like Honduras Próspera Inc., a controversial charter city project launched in 2017 by a group of American venture capitalists and technology entrepreneurs on the touristic island of Roatán, in Honduras. 'Honduras Próspera is described as a "platform"; both a space and a political and economic interface designed to facilitate economic development, attract investments, and encourage entrepreneurship' (Simpson and Sheller, 2022). These new 'platforms' serve as infrastructures for experimentation in non-state organization and interstitial urbanization, within and beyond the grip of state power. For example, the youthful president of El Salvador, Nayib Bukele, made his country the first to declare Bitcoin the national legal tender, then announced plans to build the world's first tax-free 'Bitcoin City', backed by Bitcoin bonds and powered by volcanic geothermal energy (Renteria, 2021).

The question remains whether such crypto-infrastructures will empower horizontal infrastructural reparations or reproduce the power hidden in its folds. Will Caribbean infrastructural crypto-entrepreneurs be able to leverage the blockchain to patch together encrypted geographies of reparative infrastructure, or will the absence of the state drive further insecurity and violence from what Haitians call the *baz*? Whether these crypto-geographies can ever support Black infrastructural resistance and creativity on a hostile terrain, forming a new kind of 'demonic ground' (McKittrick, 2006) of reparative justice, remains an open question.

Conclusion

Post-disaster reconstruction processes across the Greater Antilles have demonstrated the obduracy of the coloniality of power, its kinopolitical bases and the struggle for alternative futures of infrastructuring (Sheller, 2018, 2020). Tactics of patching, scamming and encrypting are each exemplary of wider ways in which infrastructural futures are being actively remade in experimental innovations of island urbanization that nevertheless build on the ruins of racial capitalism and colonialism. Although imagined as urban peripheries on offshore islands, Caribbean cities are closely connected to the uneven infrastructuring processes of the Global North, which are enmeshed in White supremacy and anti-Blackness. Arising as interstitial spaces of negotiation, appropriation and contestation – especially in the aftermath of disasters and emergencies – makeshift infrastructural futures are already taking shape within the folds and beneath the purview of the sovereign state and outside the realms of citizenship. Inhabiting these hybrid cities on the edges of the fraying international system of modern nation-states, existing without the idealized citizenries of infrastructural access, subaltern people across the Caribbean must seize their own infrastructural reparations for everyday survivance and revival of life in ruins.

Just as the runaway Maroons and pirates of the Caribbean disrupted the smooth operations of plantation space and the transatlantic system of slavery, every infrastructural system has its weak points. Maroons escaped into the interior of mountainous islands or swampy coastal lowlands, while pirates kept on the move, sailing from hidden coves, and hiding on remote islands such as Île de la Tortue off the north-west coast of Haiti. Both Maroons and pirates raided the more structured spaces of circulation that supported the slave plantation economy and spirited away the goods and people whose labour it required. This was a kind of reparative justice, too, but one that the dominant system would not tolerate. Either forced to sign treaties, deported to remote places or hunted out of existence, there was no room for such libertarian/liberationist experiments in the core of the colonial-racial capitalist infrastructure of slavery-based plantations, heavily armed sailing fleets and extractive global trade. Is there space for such experiments today?

I have argued that Caribbean practices of infrastructural reparations today go beyond simple concepts of repair insofar as they too turn the tables on the Global North and global capital by appropriating, infiltrating and profiting from infrastructural gaps in ways motivated by political claims for reparative justice. These same urban island spaces and actors now stand on the cusp of seizing encrypted geographies for disruptive infrastructuring that is horizontally distributed in the blockchain; but the dynamics of violence and insecurity do not bode well. In opening our imagination to wider meanings of reparative infrastructure, I hope to have suggested some ways in which reparations can be extracted in and through infrastructuring from below, which draws on creative agency, social infrastructure and digital as much as physical infrastructure to advance its claims. But this also comes with dangers.

Looming over all of this is the ongoing denial of infrastructural access – and life itself – to African Caribbean and other Caribbean populations in times of planetary climate crisis and global health emergency: stopped at the border, intercepted at sea, denationalized and deported despite the ravages of hurricanes, earthquakes or pandemics. Yet those who have claimed a hard insistence on life will not be snuffed out so easily. Caribbean tactics for infrastructural creativity persist in the wake of global racial capitalism with its unpayable debts, embargoes and extractive economies. Patching and scamming continue unabated and will probably soon be joined by encrypting-from-below, because these infrastructural practices of reparative justice enable people to *chèch lavi* (look for life) amid the ruins of the state, which never wanted them anyway, never cared for them and never provided them with infrastructure. Reparative infrastructural justice, ironically, may demand the demise of North Atlantic universal imaginaries of infrastructural citizenship through the dissolution of existing structures of exclusive connectivity rather than their repair and maintenance. As the centre frays, the edges may prevail.

References

Anand, N. (2015) 'Leaky states: water audits, ignorance, and the politics of infrastructure', *Public Culture*, 27(2): 305–30.

Anand, N. (2017) *Hydraulic City: Water and the Infrastructures of Citizenship in Mumbai*, Durham, NC: Duke University Press.

Anand, N., Gupta, A. and Appel, H. (eds) (2018) *The Promise of Infrastructure*, Durham, NC: Duke University Press.

Appel, H. (2019) *The Licit Life of Capitalism: US Oil in Equatorial Guinea*, Durham, NC: Duke University Press.

Arthur, C. and Dash, J. (eds) (1999) *Libète: A Haiti Anthology*, London: Latin America Bureau.

Auyero, J. (2012) *Patients of the State: The Politics of Waiting in Argentina*, London and New York: Duke University Press.

Auyero, J. and Swistun, D.A. (2009) *Flammable: Environmental Suffering in an Argentine Shantytown*, Oxford: Oxford University Press.

Beckett, G. (2019) *There Is No More Haiti: Between Life and Death in Port-au-Prince*, Oakland: University of California Press.

Bonilla, Y. (2018) 'For investors, Puerto Rico is a fantasy blank slate', The Nation, 28 February. Available from: https://www.thenation.com/article/archive/for-investors-puerto-rico-is-a-fantasy-blank-slate/ [Accessed 15 November 2022].

Bonilla, Y. and Klein, N. (2018) 'Six months after Maria, residents resist efforts to turn island into privatized Bitcoin playground', Democracy Now, 21 March. Available from: https://www.democracynow.org/2018/3/21/six_months_after_maria_residents_resist [Accessed 15 November 2022].

Bowles, N. (2018) 'Making a crypto utopia in Puerto Rico', New York Times, 2 February. Available from: https://www.nytimes.com/2018/02/02/technology/cryptocurrency-puerto-rico.html [Accessed 15 November 2022].

Crandall, J. (2019) 'Blockchains and the "Chains of Empire": contextualizing blockchain, cryptocurrency, and neoliberalism in Puerto Rico', *Design and Culture*, 11(3): 279–300.

Dawson, A. (2017) *Extreme Cities: The Peril and Promise of Urban Life in the Age of Climate Change*, London: Verso.

de Certeau, M. (1984) *The Practice of Everyday Life*, Berkeley: University of California Press.

De Coss-Corzo, A. (2021) 'Patchwork: repair labor and the logic of infrastructure adaptation in Mexico City', *Environment and Planning D: Society and Space*, 39(2): 237–53.

de Souza e Silva, A., Sutko, D.M., Salis, F.A. and de Souza e Silva, C. (2011). 'Mobile phone appropriation in the *favelas* of Rio de Janeiro, Brazil', *New Media & Society*, 13(3): 411–26.

Du Bois, W.E.B. (1903) *The Souls of Black Folk*, New York: New American Library.

Easterling, K. (2016) *Extrastatecraft: The Power of Infrastructure Space*, London: Verso.

Fanon, F. (1990) *The Wretched of the Earth*, trans C. Farrington, London: Penguin.

Ferguson, J. (2006) *Global Shadows: Africa in the Neoliberal World Order*, Durham, NC: Duke University Press.

Freeman, C. (2000) *High Tech and High Heels in the Global Economy*, Durham, NC: Duke University Press.

Gandy, M. (2008) 'Landscapes of disaster: water, modernity, and urban fragmentation in Mumbai', *Environment and Planning A: Economy and Space*, 40(1): 108–30.

Gandy, M. (2014) *The Fabric of Space: Water, Modernity, and the Urban Imagination*, Cambridge, MA: MIT Press.

Graham, S. and Marvin, S. (2001) *Splintering Urbanism: Networked Infrastructures, Technological Mobilities and the Urban Condition*, London: Routledge.

Hagen, J. and Diener, A.C. (eds.) (2022) *Invisible borders in a Bordered World: Power, Mobility, and Belonging*, London and New York: Routledge.

Horst, H.A. (2013) 'The infrastructures of mobile media: towards a future research agenda', *Mobile Media and Communication*, 1(1): 147–52.

Insight Caribbean (2021) 'Jimmy Chérizier, alias "Barbecue"'. Available from: https://web.archive.org/web/20220714223639/https://insightcrime.org/caribbean-organized-crime-news/jimmy-cherizier-alias-barbecue/ [Accessed 21 June 2022].

Johnston, J. (2022) 'They fooled us', Center for Economic and Policy Research, 7 February. Available from: https://cepr.shorthandstories.com/they-fooled-us/index.html [Accessed 15 November 2022].

Katz, J.M. (2013) *The Big Truck that Went By: How the World Came to Save Haiti and Left Behind a Disaster*, New York: Palgrave Macmillan.

Kitchin, R. and Dodge, M. (2011) *Code/Space Software and Everyday Life*, Cambridge, MA: MIT Press.

Kitchin, R., Lauriault, T. and McArdle, G. (eds) (2018) *Data and the City*, Abingdon: Routledge.

Kivland, C.L. (2020) *Street Sovereigns: Young Men and the Makeshift State in Urban Haiti*, Ithaca, NY: Cornell University Press.

Klein, N. (2018) *The Battle for Paradise: Puerto Rico Takes On the Disaster Capitalists*, Chicago: Haymarket Books.

Lemanski, C. (ed) (2019) *Infrastructures of Citizenship: Practices and Identities of Urban Citizens and the State*, Abingdon: Routledge.

Lemanski, C. (2020) 'Infrastructural citizenship: the everyday citizenships of adapting and/or destroying public infrastructure in Cape Town, South Africa', *Transactions of the Institute of British Geographers*, 45(3): 589–605.

Lewis, J.S. (2020) *Scammer's Yard: The Crime of Black Repair in Jamaica*, Minneapolis: University of Minnesota Press.

McKinney, J. (2022) 'Consortium to Rebuild Puerto Rico', updated 4 November 2022. Available from: https://www.trvst.world/charity-civil-society/consortium-to-rebuild-puerto-rico/ [Accessed 6 January 2023].

McKittrick, K. (2006) *Demonic Grounds: Black Women and the Cartographies of Struggle*, Minneapolis: University of Minnesota Press.

Murphy Marcos, C. and Mazzei, P. (2022) 'The rush for a slice of paradise in Puerto Rico', New York Times, 31 January. Available from: https://www.nytimes.com/2022/01/31/us/puerto-rico-gentrification.html [Accessed 15 November 2022].

Parks, L. (2014) 'Walking Phone Workers' in *The Routledge Handbook of Mobilities* (eds) P. Adey, D. Bissell, K. Hannam, P. Merriman and M. Sheller, New York: Routledge, pp 243–55.

Parks, L. and Schwoch, J. (eds) (2012) *Down to Earth: Satellite Technologies, Industries, and Cultures*, New Brunswick, NJ: Rutgers University Press.

Parks, L. and Starosielski, N. (eds) (2015) *Signal Traffic: Critical Studies of Media Infrastructures*, Urbana: University of Illinois Press.

Ragnedda, M. (2020) *Enhancing Digital Equity: Connecting the Digital Underclass*, Cham: Palgrave Macmillan.

Renteria, N. (2021) 'El Salvador plans first "Bitcoin City", backed by bitcoin bonds', Reuters, 21 November. Available from: https://www.reuters.com/markets/rates-bonds/el-salvador-plans-first-bitcoin-city-backed-by-bitcoin-bonds-2021-11-21/ [Accessed 21 June 2022].

Rodney, W. ([1972] 2018) *How Europe Underdeveloped Africa*, London: Verso.

Sharpe, C. (2016) *In the Wake: On Blackness and Being*, Durham, NC: Duke University Press.

Sheller, M. (2000) *Democracy After Slavery: Black Publics and Peasant Radicalism in Haiti and Jamaica*, Warwick: Macmillan Caribbean; Gainesville: University Press of Florida.

Sheller, M. (2003) *Consuming the Caribbean: From Arawaks to Zombies*, London: Routledge.

Sheller, M. (2009a) 'Infrastructures of the imagined island: software, mobilities, and the architecture of Caribbean paradise', *Environment and Planning A: Economy and Space*, 41(6): 1386–403.

Sheller, M. (2009b) 'The new Caribbean complexity: mobility systems, tourism and the spatial rescaling', *Singapore Journal of Tropical Geography*, 30(2): 189–203.

Sheller, M. (2012) *Citizenship from Below: Erotic Agency and Caribbean Freedom*, Durham, NC: Duke University Press.

Sheller, M. (2013) 'The islanding effect: post-disaster mobility systems and humanitarian logistics in Haiti', *Cultural Geographies*, 20(2): 185–204.

Sheller, M. (2014) *Aluminum Dreams: The Making of Light Modernity*, Cambridge, MA: MIT Press.

Sheller, M. (2018) 'Caribbean futures in the offshore Anthropocene: debt, disaster, and duration', *Environment and Planning D: Society and Space*, 36(6): 971–86.

Sheller, M. (2019) 'Locating technologies on the ground in post-earthquake Haiti', in R. Wilken, G. Goggin and H.A. Horst (eds) *Location Technologies in International Context*, Abingdon: Routledge, pp 129–42.

Sheller, M. (2020) *Island Futures: Caribbean Survival in the Anthropocene*, Durham, NC: Duke University Press.

Sheller, M. (2021) 'The geopolitics of offshore infrastructure-space: remediating military bases, tourist resorts, and alternative island futures', in M. Mostafanezhad, M. Cordoba-Azcárate and R. Norum (eds) *Tourism Geopolitics: Assemblages of Infrastructure, Affect, and Imagination*, Tucson: University of Arizona Press, pp 283–305.

Sheller, M., Galada, H.C., Montalto, F.A., Gurian, P.L., Piasecki, M., Ayalew, T. and O'Connor, S. (2013) 'Gender, disaster and resilience: assessing women's water and sanitation needs in Leogane, Haiti, before and after the 2010 earthquake', *wH2O: The Journal of Gender & Water*, 2(1): 18–27.

Simone, A. (2004) 'People as infrastructure: intersecting fragments in Johannesburg', *Public Culture*, 16(3): 407–29.

Simone, A. (2013) 'Cities of uncertainty: Jakarta, the urban majority, and inventive political technologies', *Theory, Culture & Society*, 30(7/8): 243–63.

Simpson, I. (2021) 'Cultural political economy of the start-up societies imaginary', PhD dissertation, McGill University, Montreal.

Simpson, I. and Sheller, M. (2022) 'Islands as interstitial encrypted geographies: making (and failing) cryptosecessionist exits', *Political Geography*, 99: art 102744. Available from: https://doi.org/10.1016/j.pol geo.2022.102744 [Accessed 14 November 2022].

Star, S.L. (1999) 'The ethnography of infrastructure', *American Behavioral Scientist*, 43(3): 377–91.

Starosielski, N. (2015) *The Undersea Network: Sign, Storage Transmission*, Durham, NC: Duke University Press.

Thiel, P. (2009) 'From scratch: libertarian institutions and communities – the education of a libertarian', Cato Unbound, 13 April. Available from: https://www.cato-unbound.org/2009/04/13/peter-thiel/education-libertarian [Accessed 15 November 2022].

Tormos-Aponte, F., García-López, G. and Painter, M.A. (2021) 'Energy inequality and clientelism in the wake of disasters: from colorblind to affirmative power restoration', *Energy Policy*, 158: art 112550. Available from: https://doi.org/10.1016/j.enpol.2021.112550 [Accessed 15 November 2022].

Trouillot, M.-R. (2021) *Trouillot Remixed: The Michel-Rolph Trouillot Reader*, (ed) Y. Bonilla, G. Beckett and M.L. Fernando, Durham, NC: Duke University Press.

Wacquant, L. (2016) 'Revisiting territories of relegation: Class, ethnicity and state in the making of advanced marginality', *Urban Studies*, 53(6): 1077–1088.

Watlington, C. (2019) 'Tales from the cryptos: blockchain visionaries and old colonial scams in Puerto Rico', *The Baffler*, January. Available from: https://thebaffler.com/outbursts/tales-from-the-cryptos-watlington [Accessed 15 November 2022].

Wynter, S. (2003) 'Unsettling the coloniality of being/power/truth/freedom: towards the human, after man, its overrepresentation – an argument', *CR: The New Centennial Review*, 3(3): 257–337.

6

Making Shit Social: Combined Sewer Overflows, Water Citizenship and the Infrastructural Commons

Mark Usher

Introduction

In October 2021, under growing pressure from an incensed public, the UK government orchestrated a policy U-turn by reinstating an amendment to the environment bill for a legal duty on water companies in England to reduce sewage discharges into rivers and seas. In light of growing evidence that water companies were increasingly discharging untreated sewage – illegally, intentionally and repeatedly – into public waterways and protected coastal areas, the Duke of Wellington, a cross-bench peer in the House of Lords, brought a bill to Parliament. As 'sewerage undertakers', water companies would be legally obliged to 'take all reasonable steps to ensure untreated sewage is not discharged from storm overflows' (Hansard, 2021: col 720). Underestimating the level of public anger, the government had initially blocked the amendment due to the estimated costs to water companies, necessitating widespread upgrading of a vast, dilapidating infrastructural system breaking down after decades of underinvestment. In a communication that was widely disparaged for sparing water companies the responsibility for sewage discharges and infrastructural improvement, the government insisted the issue was more historical and systemic than widely reported, where global heating was resulting in increased precipitation that was overwhelming a Victorian infrastructural network no longer appropriate for current population, urban density and rainfall levels. In a statement written on behalf of Conservative MPs rejecting the vote, it was ventured that to 'eliminate storm overflows means transforming the entire Victorian sewage system to a whole new sewage system. It would be irresponsible for any government to spend an estimated preliminary cost of anywhere between £150bn to £650bn to transform the entire sewage system' (Davies, 2021).

Growing numbers of Conservative MPs threatened to rebel against the government in a second Commons vote having been inundated by their constituents angry that water companies – exploiting a regulatory gap created by budget cuts under austerity – were effectively being protected by the state against the public interest. This was after all the same political party that had introduced austerity measures in 2010 in coalition with the Liberal Democrats, which according to UN rapporteur Philip Alston was a 'disgrace ... a social calamity and an economic disaster', rolling back the protections of its own citizens. Alston contended that citizens had been compelled to mobilize independently of the state, as witnessed with food banks, to 'fill holes in government services' (Alston, 2018: 1, 2). Local authorities have seen grants from central government cut by more than half since 2010, significantly impacting on public services and basic infrastructural provision. Austerity has been driven by ideological principles more than fiscal constraints, with then Prime Minister David Cameron conceding that his ambition was for 'building a leaner, more efficient state ... not just now, but permanently' (The Guardian, 2013). In 2011, Cameron wrote a letter to all government ministers to launch the 'Red Tape Challenge', insisting they reduce regulation wherever possible, 'to sweep away unnecessary bureaucracy and complexity, [and] end gold-plating of EU Directives' (PMO, 2011). And indeed, while it was pressure from wealthy constituents that forced Conservative MPs to rebel against the government, much of the impetus came from the wider public via social media platforms, angry against what they perceived as the state's dereliction of duty to regulate effectively and protect its citizens.

While the final version of the environment bill approved by Parliament in November fell short of what campaigners, and the Duke of Wellington, had advocated, the social movement that has coalesced around the issue, encompassing community and recreational lobby groups and conservation organizations, will continue to agitate. The alternative approved amendment commits water companies to a duty of 'progressive reduction in the adverse impacts of discharges from the undertaker's storm overflows' (Environment Act 2021, sec 83(1)), but lacks a strong legal clause and concrete targets. It is noticeable that impacts resulting from discharges, rather than the discharges per se, are to be reduced, indicating that EU law has been watered down, which requires spill avoidance except in exceptional circumstances. The bill received Royal Assent on 9 November 2021 as the Environment Act, having become entangled in the sewage scandal in its final stages, putting combined sewer overflows (CSOs), which have facilitated these surreptitious, frequently illegal discharges by water companies, firmly on the regulatory agenda. When the bill first entered Parliament three years previously, sewer overflows were not even mentioned. Sewer overflows, considered arcane and uninteresting by most MPs, entered into mainstream debate due to pressure from community activists and pressure groups. The state regulators, the Environment Agency (EA) and Ofwat (the Office of Water Services), have launched a major inquiry into water companies after admission of illegal sewage discharges, with 2,000 sewage treatment plants set to be investigated.

It is contended in this chapter that the sewerage network, which typically functions discreetly, the purview of water engineers, has become an unexpected locus of deliberation and contestation of the public realm. Although CSOs have been the focus of campaigns before, particularly during the 1990s in England, they have often gone under the radar of general public concern given their relative obscurity (Finewood, 2016). And indeed, what characterizes this most recent mobilization is its widespread popularity, encompassing a broad range of individuals and groups angered by their state's unwillingness to monitor and regulate CSO usage. In Global North cities, the politics of sanitation is frequently overlooked as sewerage has become taken for granted, with most of the system located underground, remaining largely invisible (Melosi, 2000). As Star (1999) observed, one of the defining characteristics of infrastructure is its pervasive, embedded invisibility, shaping everyday practices, norms and routines imperceptibly, functioning on a largely unconscious level. It is only when the system is disrupted or 'unblackboxed' during floods, droughts or pollution events that users become abruptly conscious of its workings (Graham and Thrift, 2007), when the background is inadvertently foregrounded, temporarily revealing the hidden 'underbelly of the city' (Kaika and Swyngedouw, 2000: 134). What Benidickson (2007) terms a 'culture of flushing' has accompanied the modern sanitation network, where public awareness of excrement effectively terminates at the domestic bathroom, leaving disposal a matter for the authorities. In England, this diminished sense of agency has been heightened with privatization of the water sector, where consumers have become reconstituted as customers rather than citizens, lacking the usual channels of accountability.

After a decade of austerity, the regulatory and monitoring regime installed with the privatization of the sector has been dismantled, emboldening water companies to discharge sewage directly into waterways to reduce operational costs and maximize profits. This has drawn attention to previously concealed material logics inherent in the infrastructural system, where rivers are directly connected to sewerage networks, exposing them to potential maltreatment. The deteriorating condition of rivers since the early 2010s has provided a tangible, concrete expression of state retrenchment and decline of the public realm as a consequence of unbridled market forces. The social movement that has emerged in response has sought to reclaim its stake in the water environment, taking physically to rivers through community monitoring, pollution surveillance and open swimming, re-envisaging them as public commons rather than conveyance channels. This chapter therefore suggests the anti-sewage movement, which has mobilized in and through the physical landscape, driven by grassroots community activism in the space between the state and market, is reflective of 'urban commoning' (Eidelman and Safransky, 2021). What makes commons movements politically distinctive, rural or urban, is not a predefined social agenda but rootedness in local environment, where assertion of rights occurs through engagement with the resource under threat, coordinated by ordinary people seeking to reclaim common goods from private encroachment. In the urban context, this weaving together of community and environment manifests differently from rural commons, in more complex sociotechnical landscapes, offering novel challenges and affordances for mobilization.

The chapter considers the CSO, its material culture and function, which under austerity has been linked to a decline in river conditions. It complicates the prevailing narrative that sewage discharges are the result of a toxic industry culture, situating their overuse in the longer-term demise of the 'modern infrastructural ideal', as centralized, subsidized service delivery has gradually collapsed (Graham and Marvin, 2001). Private water companies inherited a vast dilapidating infrastructural system, which has continued to break down under their management due to continued underinvestment, where shareholder profits have been prioritized over maintenance and improvement. Furthermore, policy reforms and funding cuts as part of the wider austerity programme have significantly reduced the monitoring capacity and mandate of regulators, allowing, indeed encouraging, water companies to discharge sewage more frequently. The oppositional tactics adopted by the anti-sewage movement are then examined, including immersion in water, linking across communities, and citizen monitoring of rivers. Consumers have sought to establish a connection to the water network beyond the household, as active citizens rather than passive customers, making shit a social rather than private individual matter. The chapter concludes by emphasizing the potential role for municipal authorities in the post-Brexit era.

Shit happens: the implicit logic of CSOs

Sewage discharge through CSOs is an entirely legal if provisional measure that allows water companies to temporarily pollute rivers, lakes and seas in a managed way to avoid sewers becoming overwhelmed during periods of heavy rainfall, through allocated permits from the EA. As sewers and drains are part of the same integrated system in England – a legacy of Victorian hydraulic engineering – rainfall and sewage enter into the same underground system before being conveyed for treatment. However, during storm events, heavy rainfall enters the system in large quantities, combines with sewage, and can flow back as mixed wastewater into homes, workplaces and public areas. This has become increasingly likely with more intense rainfall under climate change, growth in impermeable surfaces and increasing water throughput. The Victorian combined system still provides the basis of the network today and during the 20th century sewerage was incorporated into an increasingly centralized configuration administered at the national level. Similar to other major utilities such as electricity, gas and telecommunications, water and sewerage were cross-subsidized based on redistributive economics, administered through supply-side logics, and investment was driven by the provision of basic public goods at affordable prices by the Keynesian welfare state.

As Bakker (2010: 34) contends, water provision and sewage disposal became framed as a civic duty of the municipal then subsequently national state, 'a material emblem of citizenship', underpinning what Graham and Marvin (2001) term the modern infrastructural ideal. Under this sociotechnical ideal all members of society are integrated within a unified network of equal service provision, enabling participation in public life as citizens regardless of ability to pay. In many countries, especially in the Global South, the lack of access to modern sewerage has indeed been conceived as lack of citizenship rights, a status rendered visible by public defecating (Anand, 2017; McFarlane, 2018). As Morales et al (2014: 2824) argue, 'ordinary citizens in fact have the right to be ignorant of the management process beyond the flush of the toilet ... the domain of the state'. A 'culture of flushing' now prevails in the Global North, encouraging widespread ignorance of the disposal process (Benidickson, 2007). Users have effectively become estranged from the functioning and effects of a system that serves them so intimately. In England, this situation has been complicated with privatization of the water sector as consumers became reconstituted as customers rather than citizens (Bakker, 2003), administered not through public right but market payment.

The current scandal surrounding sewage discharge by water companies has foregrounded the hidden world of sewerage, and specifically CSOs, forcing consumers to confront the afterlife and impacts of their waste. CSOs are an infrastructural safety valve that temporarily short-circuits the sewage system, diverting the build-up of mixed wastewater, sewage and stormwater from its intended journey to treatment plants into rivers and coasts. Once the water reaches a specific level it flows over a weir wall located inside the sewerage network and into a dedicated outfall pipe. This mechanism should only legally occur during exceptional periods of heavy rainfall, and with sufficient permits from the EA, as high flows and throughput of water dilute contaminants and distribute them downstream. As the hidden infrastructural switches of this emergency mechanism, CSOs have baked into the urban fabric this implicit logic, which until recently had remained

Figure 6.1: Walwyn Close combined sewer overflow, flowing into the River Mersey, Stretford, Trafford, Greater Manchester

Note: Concealed within a box and hidden behind vegetation is the CSO.
Source: Mark Usher

largely unquestioned by the public, taking place surreptitiously underground in concealed drainage networks. The CSO is not a glitch in an otherwise functioning system but a surface expression of entrenched material logics residing in the wider network. In fact, discharges from CSOs are an indication that the network is functioning appropriately, which are installed to relieve pressure on a hard, static and centralized system.

CSOs – and there are around 15,000 in England – are visually unremarkable, usually located indiscreetly in embankment cleavages, as are the further 3,000 wastewater treatment outfalls (see Figures 6.1 and 6.2). As the water being released by CSOs comprise both wastewater and stormwater, they contain a broad range of harmful contaminants: microbial pathogens, micropollutants, hormones, legal and illicit drugs, pesticides, suspended solids, heavy metals, nutrients and microplastics (Woodward et al, 2021). Fish death, vegetation decline and public health risks are the more immediate indicators of CSO operation, while the longer-term consequences are reduced oxygen levels, increased turbidity, and eutrophication. The sewage scandal has brought to light how rivers function as extensions of the infrastructural system, as sluices for stormwater and raw sewage, often culverted and buried underground (Karvonen, 2011; Usher et al, 2021). In many cases, rivers have been channelled into sewerage networks, stretching their status as waterways to breaking point.

Figure 6.2: Bradley Lane combined sewer overflow, flowing into the River Mersey, Stretford, Trafford, Greater Manchester

Note: This CSO has large covers that temporarily open when in operation.

Source: Mark Usher

A commons in crisis

Previously arcane and overlooked, CSOs now regularly feature in the English national and local mainstream media, prompted by the deterioration of rivers due in large part to sewage discharges by water companies. In 2020 alone, water companies discharged raw sewage in England 400,000 times, amounting to 3.1 million hours overall (The Guardian, 2021a). This indicates that CSOs are being used much more indiscriminately, and illegally, outside of exceptional storm events. One in five CSOs are releasing raw sewage three times as frequently as would otherwise be expected, which would normally be grounds for investigation by the EA. There have been episodes where CSO discharges have had devastating impacts on local ecology and wildlife: Thames Water, the UK's largest water company, was fined £2.3 million in 2016 after pleading guilty to a sewage discharge that killed more than 1,000 fish, doubling the permitted levels of ammonia. The broader consequence of increased CSO use has been a general decline in river water quality. Only 14 per cent of England's rivers, one in seven nationally, are deemed of 'good ecological status' under the EU's Water Framework Directive (see Figure 6.3). In 2020, the EA reported that no single river achieved good chemical status. The EA's latest report reveals that water companies' performance in 2021 was actually the 'worst we have seen in years … shocking' (EA, 2022: Chair's foreword), with serious pollution

Figure 6.3: Liverpool Road/Newhall Avenue combined sewer overflow, flowing into Salteye Brook, Eccles, Salford, Greater Manchester

Note: The brook, largely concealed from public view, is lined with wet wipes, ejected from the CSO.

Source: Jamie Woodward

incidents at their highest level in a decade, and no improvement in sewage discharge compliance. Emma Boyd, Chair of the EA, has consistently impressed that only heavier fines will deter water companies. Southern Water, one of the worst performing water companies, was fined £90 million in August 2021 – the largest ever brought against a water company – for discharging approximately 20 billion litres of raw sewage deliberately into protected coastal seas of Kent and Hampshire.

The EA's investigation, the largest in its 25-year history, revealed very serious widespread criminality, demonstrated by Southern Water's 168 previous offences and ongoing illegal operations, affording the company considerable financial advantage. The problem is a culture of profiteering that has taken root as regulation was rolled back, where sewage discharges have become routine rather than exceptional practice. In 2010, under the Conservative–Liberal Democrat coalition government, it became the duty of water companies themselves to report their own pollution spills and discharges, providing the policy context for a culture of widespread under-reporting. Water companies are discharging sewage at a rate at least ten times greater than EA monitoring suggests, indicating this crisis is significantly worse than it appears (The Guardian, 2021b). This failure to hold water companies to account is largely a result of austerity, as the EA's budget was cut by two thirds from £120 million in 2010 to £40 million, leading to a 45 per cent reduction in river sampling. Between 2019 and 2020, the EA received just £15 million from the government for water quality work, to monitor and enforce on 240,600 kilometres of rivers. The EA only demands summary data from water companies so their analysis is limited, with the appearance of dead fish usually serving as an indicator of a pollution event. According to a leaked internal briefing document, the agency has instructed its staff to systematically ignore pollution reports deemed of lowest risk, to reduce operational costs: of the 116,000 incidents reported in 2021 only 8,000 were attended (The Guardian, 2022). EA call handlers have also been asked to pass on water company pollution reports straight to team leaders, preventing duty officers from triaging these cases.

Since the water sector was privatized in 1989 under the UK's Conservative prime minister, Margaret Thatcher, and ten public water authorities were floated on the London stock exchange, there has been growing criticism of their practices. Over £57 billion in dividends has been paid out to shareholders, half the amount spent on maintenance and improvement. As part of the post-Fordist restructuring of the economy in the 1980s, the private sector was invited to take over key public services in the interests of enhanced efficiency, investment and competitiveness. Water privatization was the most controversial of Thatcher's programmes, opposed by around 75 per cent of the public (Marvin and Guy, 1997). The rationale for privatization – increased efficiency and investment – has not materialized, while bills have gradually increased to over 40 per cent more in real terms than in 1990 (Yearwood, 2018), to cover interest payments on debt raised for dividend payouts rather than infrastructural upgrading.

Ofwat and the EA were established to coordinate nationally across the water companies, manage competition, guide investment, cap customer bills and protect the environment. The intention is to balance the different, often conflicting interests of the customer, shareholder and environment. As Bakker (2000: 17) surmises, the regulators mediate the 'inevitable contradictions between the "logic of capital" and the "logic of citizenship"'. On gaining office in 1997, Labour introduced a windfall tax on profits of privatized utilities to rebalance these logics in response to growing public discontent. Water companies have been the focus of public frustration since privatization, with consumer surveys for Ofwat showing immediate negative opinions around accountability and transparency (Kinnersley, 1994). With regulatory rollback under austerity, corporate malpractice has increased, intensifying public anger. Profits have spiralled above regular commercial returns – Thames Water's operating profit was £638 million in 2017, paying out £100 million in dividends – while investment in infrastructure has declined by 10 per cent per year from 2008 to 2018. In 2018, more than 70 per cent of water companies were owned by organizations from overseas, including hedge funds, sovereign wealth funds and corporations based in tax havens, far removed from the local water environment. Debt has rocketed to around £50 billion, much going to finance shareholder dividends rather than capital expenditure on infrastructure. Excessive CEO salaries have also attracted criticism, which amount to £65 million across the sector between 2016 and 2021. This has been compounded by a culture of tax avoidance: Thames Water paid no corporate tax for a decade.

The demise of an ideal

In the rush to rebuke private water companies, it has largely been overlooked that the infrastructural system they inherited, which allows and indeed requires sewage discharge, has been declining for half a century. The recent sewage scandal is only the most recent development in the gradual breakdown of the modern infrastructural ideal, a slow-motion collapse which began before privatization. Water companies inherited not only assets but the long-standing challenge of maintaining an expensive, resource-intensive, antiquated infrastructural system, buckling under growing fiscal, technical and ecological pressures. This process began in the 1970s when states around the world faced a fiscal crisis triggered by escalating oil prices and the global recession, curtailing their ability to invest in infrastructure (Swyngedouw, 2004). This lent credence, albeit roundly exaggerated, to neoliberal doctrine and privatization, pushed by Margaret Thatcher and Ronald Reagan. In England, ageing water supply, drainage and sewerage networks began to deteriorate, leading to failing culverts, growing leakage rates and a declining water environment (Kaika, 2005; Karvonen, 2011). The breakdown was evinced by worsening water quality, which had become, worryingly for cash-strapped governments, a focal point for new civil society groups.

Rivers and seas had been suffering from pollution for a decade before privatization due to underinvestment, but with the introduction of stringent environmental standards through EU Directives, these downward trends were not only monitored but publicly ranked. In the 1970s, the UK was known as the 'Dirty Man of Europe' due to its poor track record on pollution, especially acid rain and sewage (Rose, 1990). Regulation was essentially in-house, undertaken by the same authorities that administered sewerage, while capital investment halved between 1974 and 1980 (Hassan, 1998). EU Directives created openings for oppositional tactics used by pressure groups in respect to sewage discharges, providing a clear benchmark to evaluate government performance. Pollution became a social and moral as well as a technical issue, salient to those outside the water policy and professional communities (Jordan and Greenway, 1998). Recreational pressure groups became active in the 1990s, most notably Surfers Against Sewage (SAS), who posed in wetsuits with inflatable faeces. The focus of their actions was government incompetence rather than profiteering companies, with clear lines of accountability as representatives of citizens. The government was faced with a twinned crisis of finance and water quality.

These circumstances provided grounds for privatization, transferring the responsibility for upgrading the system to private companies, which inherited a vast degrading infrastructural network and impending crisis. The rationale was that private capital was necessary to meet the stricter demands of EU law, which had not been available through public funds. With EU law and raised public concern, river water quality began to improve after privatization in the early 2000s, reaching levels not seen since the Industrial Revolution (EA, 2001). However, the necessary capital expenditure was not forthcoming, despite this providing justification for privatization, with water companies even attempting to transfer ownership of this declining asset base back to public hands, to concentrate profit-making activity around management. Having been unsuccessful in this endeavour, water companies, as commercial entities, sought other means to maximize shareholder profits, including running it down and reducing water treatment costs through sewage discharges, illegal or otherwise. With the election of the Conservative–Liberal Democrat government in 2010 and its austerity agenda, regulatory safeguards were dismantled, releasing powerful market forces introduced 20 years earlier. The infrastructural system has further declined and problematic logics inherent within it, such as CSOs, are no longer being regulated, enabling water companies to offset treatment and maintenance costs. Consequently, water quality gains have been reversed and the sector is facing a crisis marked by a deteriorating infrastructural system; a retrenched, weakened local state under austerity; and the decline of EU policy influence following Brexit.

Shit is social: commoning through infrastructure

In some respects, the sewage scandal resembles Garrett Hardin's tragedy of the commons, whereby inadequate regulatory oversight over shared resources has allowed water companies to privatize benefits and socialize costs. Yet, while in most countries elected representatives are accountable to citizens in terms of water and sewerage, '[t]here is by contrast a total democratic deficit in the UK' (Hall and Lobina, 2007: 22), with no obvious channel for asserting the public interest. Consumers are also unable to boycott water companies in the conventional way due to their monopoly ownership. This has left citizens feeling powerless, leading to a growing sense that action is required at a broader community scale. Defecation is a highly intimate act, undertaken in the private realm of the domestic toilet, but when sewage enters the public domain, it becomes, quite literally, a social matter. This complicates the relationship between public and private, but from the perspective of a social movement it necessitates an alternative connection with the infrastructural network, established not at the household scale but at the wider system-level. The sewerage network that is typically hidden from view has become the focus of public attention. To borrow the terminology of Amin (2014: 149), sewerage, like other types of infrastructure, becomes 'lively' when it ceases to function invisibly; its latent normativity, 'the very aesthetic and functionality of working commons', is opened up to scrutiny. In the city, commons may look and function very differently from the traditional pasture or woodland, but they nevertheless provide the material basis of shared collective life.

As an alternative schema to neoliberal economics, there has been renewed interest in the idea and practice of the common (Stavrides, 2016; Federici, 2019), and a novel research field focused specifically on urban commons (Borch and Kornberger, 2015; Amin and Howell, 2016). Urban commons, like rural ones, require upkeep and protection in the interest of its users while providing a tangible basis for collective action in defence of the communal good, often occurring in and around infrastructure. As Foster and Iaione (2016: 284) assert, '[t]hese claims consist not simply of the assertion of a "right" to a particular resource; rather, they assert the existence of a common stake or common interest in resources shared with other urban inhabitants as a way of resisting the privatization and/or commodification of those resources'. Urban commoning as a bulwark against austerity has increased in the urban environment, through, for instance, cooperative housing, land trusts, community gardens, libraries, eco-communities and building reuse (Eizenberg, 2012; Bresnihan and Byrne, 2015; Bunce, 2016; Gillespie et al, 2018; Ginn and Ascensão, 2018; Williams, 2018; Apostolopoulou and Kotsila, 2022). Solidarity and mutuality is fostered within a community *in the process* of managing a shared resource, whether this is a brownfield site, public park, allotment or waterway, uniting diverse members around a physical environment held in common.

Seeing commons like a city presents unique challenges for collectivizing in defence of shared means of associational life, including the increased population and infrastructural density; complexity of land use, property relations and existing regulations; and embeddedness in the capitalist economy (Huron, 2015; Eidelman and Safransky, 2021). However, there are also affordances in terms of the networking potential through vast interconnected systems, where infrastructural service provision engenders membership that is at once political, tangible and grounded in everyday life. This offers a very concrete basis for claims-making in respect to everyday matters of concern that affect citizens personally but also collectively, when the ordinarily invisible and technical becomes socially manifest. The infrastructural register matters strategically in terms of mobilizing in and around urban commons, how relationships are established among otherwise unconnected people linked to the same provisioning system. According to Berlant (2016: 408), austerity-driven infrastructural breakdown offers openings for communities to reimagine and reorganize their relationships between one another and their city: 'People are reclaiming bits of nature and of culture, and saying "this is going to be public space" … through the commons concept the very concept of the public is being reinvented now'.

Mobilization through immersion

A significant recent development has been the growth in community campaign groups applying for local rivers to meet legal bathing-water status, in accordance with EU legislation. This places increased pressure on the EA to improve water quality, thereby forcing water companies through alternative means to curtail sewage discharges. If a river is granted bathing-water status, it becomes the legal duty of the EA to monitor sewage and other pollution levels to maintain a water quality deemed safe for immersion. The legal impetus for improved regulation has consequently been enforced from below, from a civil society and community level, in the absence of government pressure. It was the recreational group SAS that initially politicized bathing-water pollution in the 1990s, pursuing what Ward (1996: 331) described as a 'new form of oppositional tactics' to pressure the government to regulate public waters more effectively. Surfers, who unlike the majority of the population immerse themselves in open water regularly, were aggrieved that due to government inaction, poor investment in infrastructure and enforcement of law, they faced unacceptable risks to their health as a result of sewage discharge. In 1994, the group presented their case to the House of Lords Select Committee on the European Communities, which was investigating reform of the Bathing Waters Directive. Their criticism of the poor aspirations of government, which sought only the bare legal minimum in water quality status, were broadly accepted and informed the conclusions of the report, which insisted water companies invest more in sewage infrastructure and treatment (Hansard, 1995). The directive, which legally requires the regular publishing of water quality indicators, henceforth enabled individuals and groups to exert pressure on water companies and government, by embedding this information in their campaigns.

However, the more recent anti-sewage movement, characterized by greater public engagement and community-based activism, has popularized these oppositional tactics, applying them more concertedly at a wider scale, moving the focus from coastal to inland waters. Communities across the country are organizing themselves into campaign groups to apply to Defra (the Department for Environment, Food and Rural Affairs) for their local rivers to be legally identified as a bathing-water destination, to encourage a stricter regime of monitoring, comparable to that for coastal waters, bringing CSOs into question. Bathing-water status is designated by the Secretary of State if a significant number of people immerse themselves in a lake or river, placing the location under Bathing Water Regulations, requiring water quality tests from the EA to enable classification, and local council reports during bathing season, from May until September, on pollutant levels. If water quality does not meet the required standards, the EA will investigate the sources of pollution to identify remedial action (Defra, 2020a). In 2021, Ilkley in West Yorkshire became the first community group to successfully apply for the River Wharfe to be designated, now the only such river in the country, forcing Yorkshire Water and the EA to seek ways to reduce CSO usage.

The intention of the Ilkley Clean River Group (ICRG), comprising local residents, who initiated proceedings, was to trigger a clean-up programme and investment in sewerage, and to reduce CSO usage from 114 to just 3 days a year. The group gathered evidence on numbers of people bathing and paddling in the river, who may ingest water, oversaw a local consultation and sought replies to a later national consultation, finding 998 in favour, 75 opposed. Yorkshire Water has now formed a multi-agency partnership to oversee a clean-up and aims to reduce CSO usage by 20 per cent initially, with the help of smart monitoring technology. The quality of the water has been classified as 'poor', with very high E. coli and intestinal enterococci counts far exceeding all other bathing sites in the country, being described as a 'public toilet', dotted with CSOs (ENDS report, 2021a). There are also reports the EA is failing to properly monitor the CSOs, largely due to funding issues. However, these developments drew increased attention to the prevalence of sewage in the Wharfe and nationally. Community groups across the UK have sought to emulate this success by applying for bathing-water status, on the Thames in Oxford and London, Warleigh Weir in Bath, and the River Almond in West Lothian, Scotland, forming a broader movement. The Rivers Trust has acted as the figurehead organization for the movement, helping with monitoring for applications and providing a platform for mobilization. According to the Chair of the EA, this movement could be a 'game changer' in terms of increasing pressure on government to increase funding to improve water quality, due to greater public expectation and embracing of the water environment (The Guardian, 2020a). The guidance from the EA remains that bathing in rivers presents health risks, due to CSOs in particular, and all are currently unsuitable for swimming.

The most visible expression of this public embracing of waterways is wild or open-water swimming, the popularity of which has rapidly and dramatically increased, further expanding under COVID-19 lockdowns. Wild swimming has become renowned for the visceral, sensuous experience it offers those immersing themselves in the natural world, but just as important, the sense of community that develops in local group networks. Given this profound link between environment and community, wild swimmers have become a key pressure group in the anti-sewage movement and environment bill campaign, who as a society have focused efforts on asserting the right to swim in rivers, lakes and seas, claiming access to a previously concealed, overlooked water commons. The wild swimming movement is seeking to overturn many decades of managing waterways as infrastructural conduits for the conveyance of stormwater and sewage, with the CSO, a private asset of water companies, providing the focal point. Manningtree Mermaids, for instance, a group established in Essex during lockdown, staged a sunrise protest in the River Stour to draw attention to declining water quality due to CSOs. Members of the Whitstable Bluetits, another wild swimming group, created SOS Whitstable to provide a platform for their activism, staging beach protests against what they perceive as overuse of CSOs by Southern Water. Through social media, SOS Whitstable organized a campaign against CSOs, and started a petition supporting the environment bill amendment that received nearly 100,000 signatures. Certainly, wild swimmers are leaving groups due to health risks associated with sewage, including members of the Cambridgeshire and Peterborough Bluetits, who swim in the Great Ouse in St Ives, in response to Anglian Water discharging sewage over 100 times in 2020. While avoiding swimming is an eminently sensible decision for personal reasons, many continue to open swim precisely as this puts increased pressure on the regulator to clamp down on CSO usage, putting their bodies and health at risk to reclaim a social public good, an action of last resort by disempowered citizens frustrated by lack of regulation.

From customer to citizen

This is a form of mobilization reflective of commoning as it is orchestrated in and through physical engagement with the environmental resource the community is seeking to protect. Where common-good groups such as the Levellers flattened hedges and the Diggers cultivated food produce on what they deemed to be common space, wild swimmers in a similarly ordinary, non-violent and performative manner are laying direct physical claim to the water commons. And indeed, water immersion in rivers has taken on a distinctly political dimension, even when orchestrated in the mundane, idiosyncratic form of wild swimming, instigated predominantly by older women. As the Outdoor Swimming Society (2021) recognize, '[t]he focus on swimmers is partly political – a number of environmental groups are turning to swimmers now to try to get their message across ... swimmers may unlock funding for them to achieve their aims'. Bathing-water status designation *requires* that people immerse themselves in water, even if this leads to sickness and diarrhoea, with 380 respondents to the Ilkley consultation reporting regularly swimming in the river to advance the application (Defra, 2020b). The lead applicant for Warleigh Weir in Bath has asserted 'I am trying to make national change ... this is not about me and my kids swimming. This is about rivers being arteries and a metric of the wider environment' (The Guardian, 2020b).

Where the anti-sewage movement in the 1990s was dominated by recreational pressure groups such as surfers, canoeists and anglers, with growing popular interest in urban waterways ordinary citizens have become mobilized, through a recent wave of community activism. This activism is a new phenomenon, driven initially by the strong community togetherness that characterizes wild swimming groups. What connects its members is a perceived material stake in the water commons and a desire to establish a more invested relationship with the network of rivers, lakes and seas, constituted not at an individual household level, as a passive consumer, but on a broader system-level, as an active citizen.

Feeling abandoned by both state and market, aggrieved individuals, unable to effectively assert citizen rights through the marketized regulatory framework, have sought to exert pressure in the capacity of a consumer, using their existing infrastructural connection as bargaining tool. To encourage Southern Water to invest in the sewerage network and reduce CSO usage, water users have mobilized en masse as consumers to collectively withhold payment on wastewater services in a 'ratepayers' revolt', with little other option available to hold the company accountable. Similar tactics were used during a 1995 Yorkshire drought where customers *increased* water consumption against the company directive to reduce usage, to encourage greater investment in infrastructure (Haughton, 1998).

Indeed, water users register as customers rather than citizens in the post-privatization system, where resistance to water company activity appears to be limited to market transactions, primarily fines and bill-paying. During an organized rally, celebrity musician Bob Geldof urged Kent residents not to pay their bills to Southern Water, criticizing the Prime Minister Boris Johnson for its abdication of responsibility (KentOnline, 2021). Conservative councillor Ashley Clark publicly announced he would refuse to pay for an undelivered service, not least as this would contribute to their fine payment for criminal activity. Southern Water have threatened to take action against non-payment including collections activity, citing the Water Industry Act 1991, which residents have countered with recourse to the Consumer Rights Act 2015. At a public meeting on the sewage problem, one third of attendees supported non-payment of bills, with another councillor stating '[water companies] are so unaccountable at the moment. The only thing we can do is withdraw our payments' (ENDS Report, 2021b).

SOS Whitstable has not supported non-payment publicly, adopting a different strategy that effectively scales up their activism from the household tap and toilet to the water network, linking up with a broader community of interest. This is due to legal and credit implications of non-payment, but more importantly, resistance through consumer rights is limited in scope, being individualized, reactive and market-based. SOS Whitstable have linked up with other community groups across the country and coordinated with national recreational and environmental organizations under the #EndSewagePollution coalition, which has become a rallying call on social media. This national mobilization is unprecedented in scale, diversity and community involvement, with all groups sharing a distinct but common interest in improving the condition of waterways. Unlike a traditional common pasture, water and sewerage infrastructure connects vast numbers of people and groups that are geographically distributed, unknown to one another, yet intimately connected. This makes infrastructure extraordinarily sticky, linking household consumers, recreational sportspeople and conservationists, otherwise socially unrelated. The campaign and social movement has mobilized through these networks, conventionally hidden, overlooked and managed by technicians, which have become the focus of political strategic attention, rendered 'lively', reframing shit as a social rather than individual matter. Infrastructure is politically ambiguous; it can individualize and disempower but also collectivize and enable, providing a tangible if often implicit basis for collectivization.

Monitoring as water citizenship

Rebecca Malby, co-founder of ICRG, revealed she 'felt let down on every level, as a consumer and as taxpayer', requiring the community take to the water itself to monitor quality levels. Prompted by the sight of raw sewage on the banks of the river, the community started to monitor CSO discharges, finding them releasing every time it rained, 201 times over 144 days in 2020 (Yorkshire Post, 2020). The group now organize seminars for other communities on how to effectively campaign for bathing-water status, with emphasis on 'citizen science testing', which promises to transform local campaigning on water quality. Local residents in Oxford established a community group in partnership with #EndSewagePollution to campaign for bathing-water status on a stretch of the Thames, collecting 5,000 signatures, which has led to the first and largest citizen science project analysing river bacteria levels, with samples sent to Thames Water for analysis. Initial results show that CSOs are increasing bacteria to unsafe levels, on average twice the recommended threshold during some months (Harris, 2021). There has been no routine monitoring of bacteria levels in rivers in England and, as stated previously, monitoring of CSOs, the primary source of bacteria, has been left to water companies since 2010, allowing for under-reporting. The EA has insisted 'we can't be sat on every outflow, we can't be monitoring

Figure 6.4: Penny Lane Grimesbottom combined sewer overflow, flowing into River Tame, Stockport, Greater Manchester

Note: The debris omitted from this CSO serves to screen the outfall, further hiding it from public view.

Source: Jamie Woodward

every pipe' (The Guardian, 2021c), which appears to be a defensive response to various reports of the regulator's faltering monitoring regime. CSOs are ubiquitous but they are also discrete, often difficult to locate let alone monitor (see Figure 6.4).

With the systematic neglect of monitoring and enforcement by the EA, community groups have sprung up across the country to monitor water quality instead, becoming stewards of a common in crisis. Angered by Southern Water's persistent use of CSOs, South Coast Sirens have successfully raised money through crowdfunding to purchase a mobile laboratory for water testing. The group also encourage local residents to report sewage spills to the EA and organize beach demonstrations such as the recent 'Sort your shit out'. Members are lobbying for more investment in the Victorian sewerage system and renationalization of the water sector to increase accountability. Hayling Sewage Watch, another group formed to monitor discharges, have offered guidance on monitoring and testing equipment. It was shocking drone footage of a 49-hour sewage discharge emanating from a 7 ft (2.1 m) outfall pipe into the protected coastal seas of Hampshire, captured by community activists from Hayling Sewage Watch, that provoked huge public outcry and ultimately forced the government into a policy U-turn on the environment bill amendment. The declared aims of the group are to safeguard the health of people through publication of sewage discharges, force a real-time SMS-based warning system on Southern Water, ensure accountability through lobbying, and to raise public awareness of pollution. Windrush Against Sewage Pollution (WASP), a group based in Oxfordshire, uses citizen science to collect and analyse date on water quality along the River Windrush, using pocket checkers and multi-parameter meters, which is used to lobby politicians and inform campaigns.

Without the monitoring being undertaken by its volunteers, the extent of the sewage pollution affecting the River Windrush would remain largely hidden, which has significantly impacted on the local ecology and wildlife. Over the last decade, a decade of austerity, the change in river ecology has been stark; the water greying, algal and fungal growth, weed decreasing, and invertebrate, fish and waterfowl population decline. They argue that a public inquiry is needed to investigate how state regulators have not only failed in their task but denied evidence of illegal discharges, which groups like WASP are exposing through monitoring, testing and public disclosing. Phil Hammond, a retired mathematics professor, has been a key member of WASP, using his expertize in machine learning to analyse data obtained through Environmental Information Requests (EIRs). Hammond led a team of citizen and professional scientists in an analysis of CSO discharges, finding that since water companies began to self-monitor in 2010, illegal sewage discharges are at least ten times greater than reported by the EA. In evidence submitted to an Environmental Audit Committee inquiry into sewage pollution, Hammond (2021) suggested the EA seemingly lacked the necessary computational expertize to analyse CSO discharges, as well as lacking staff capacity. This implies that a state regulator is less competent than a community group in testing water quality. Certainly, the EA's monitoring regime was described as 'absolutely dreadful … misleading, ineffective and a complete waste of money' by a former employee, relying on random spot sampling rather than continuous monitoring (Lloyd, 2021).

The final report by the Environmental Audit Committee (2022: 5) is highly critical of the monitoring being undertaken by the EA, both its technology and procedures, although it recognizes that funding cuts have significantly reduced its capacity to protect water quality: 'Getting a complete overview of the health of our rivers and the pollution affecting them is hampered by outdated, underfunded and inadequate monitoring regimes … rivers in England are in a mess'. Self-monitoring has allowed, indeed, encouraged, water companies to under-report, obfuscate and mislead, resulting in more frequent use of CSOs, even during periods of no rainfall. Incredibly, as the report acknowledges, it has fallen on community groups to reveal the extent of CSO usage and its consequences, monitoring more effectively and regularly, where both regulator and water companies, state and market, have failed in their role. The Environmental Audit Committee therefore suggests that 'water citizenship is growing across the country' (2022: 116), which should be cultivated by government to raise public awareness and buy-in. Yet water citizenship has proliferated despite and in opposition to government, precisely to address state retrenchment under austerity, prompted by the deterioration of the local water environment.

Conclusion

The sewage scandal demonstrates what often materializes when profit-seeking companies are unfettered from the 'red tape' of regulation. As commercial, shareholder-backed entities, water companies have sought to reduce costs and increase profits wherever possible, through increasing consumer bills, limiting capital expenditure on infrastructure, leveraging and growing debt, avoiding tax through overseas arrangements and, indeed, discharging sewage, legally and illegally, into public waters. The purpose of state regulators is to harness market forces, but under austerity the capacity to monitor and enforce has been severely diminished. Unable to fully execute its statutory duties, the EA has been forced to triage and even disregard pollution reports. The predictable outcome has been a declining water commons, as costs are socialized and benefits privatized. It was only due to community activism and public pressure that CSO reduction was included in the environment bill, which did not feature in the original draft. Brexit, driven to a significant extent by politicians seeking to deregulate the UK, further threatens existing protections. Former Brexit Opportunities Minister Jacob Rees-Mogg has pushed for all EU laws to be expired by 2026, including 330 relating to Defra, to remove what he considered unnecessary, burdensome red tape, not least the precautionary principle that he has publicly mocked. EU directives, transposed into domestic law, are already being questioned, with growing fear among NGOs that environmental standards will inevitably slide post-Brexit, with statements lacking legal duties and strong commitments.

This chapter has nonetheless sought to complicate the narrative by drawing attention to the infrastructural inheritance that came with privatization, where public authorities transferred a vast, dilapidating water network onto water companies' asset books. Sewerage has not received adequate investment during public or private management, leaving the Victorian-era system buckling under 21st-century pressures. Water quality levels improved initially under EU law after years of decline under public management, but the levels of investment required to maintain the infrastructure have not been forthcoming. With austerity, water companies have been emboldened to exploit regulatory gaps, using CSOs more frequently, and illegally, to reduce costs associated with treatment and maintenance. CSOs have been an integral, pervasive feature of the modern sewerage network since its inception, which not only facilitate and conceal the use of rivers as channels for sewage, but under private ownership they enable profiteering. Ofwat has encouraged water companies to sweat assets to keep customer bills down, leaving its sister regulator to deal with the environmental fallout. Indeed, Ofwat has recently been taken to court by environmental group Wild Justice on account of its alleged failure to monitor water companies and prevent sewage discharges under the Water Industry Act 1991, a legal claim supplemented by witness evidence from WASP and financed through crowdfunding. In June 2022, the Office for Environmental Protection (OEP), a new watchdog established under the Environment Act, also launched an investigation into Ofwat, EA and Defra for potentially failing in their statutory duties to enforce legislation, indicating a lack of responsiveness. Regulators, under growing pressure to enforce more effectively, have predictably dialled up their rhetoric, with the EA (2022) pushing for tougher fines and custodial sentences for chief executives: 'The water companies are behaving like this for a simple reason: because they can. We intend to make it too painful for them to continue as they are ... [they] exist to serve the public'. But even in the face of intense public anger, water companies continue to circumvent their legal responsibilities, enabled by hamstrung regulators and a government committed to cutting 'red tape' under austerity conditions.

With few options for resistance available in a disempowering regulatory framework, citizens have taken directly to rivers, reclaiming them physically – even putting their bodies at risk – through immersion, protest and monitoring. What makes urban commoning distinctive is the lack of a coherent political agenda and the ordinariness of its motives, grounded in immediate, local concerns. While this may appear limited politically, such actions can lead those involved to contemplate broader issues through initial engagement with everyday concerns. The challenges and affordances of different infrastructural systems for mobilization should be an agenda for urban commons and social movement studies, particularly in the era of austerity. As Lemanski (2020: 592) has argued, 'public infrastructure functions as a conduit for citizenship identities, practices, and expectations ... [it] is one of the key ways in which the state is made "visible"' (see also Shelton, 2017; Fredericks, 2018). Infrastructure provides a physical, concrete locus for recalibrating citizens' relationship with the state, particularly when it is overburdened or dilapidating, articulated in a biopolitical more than legal register. Infrastructural citizenship is a dynamic, unstable condition, which continues to evolve as providers change, markets fluctuate, materials decay and capacity drops. Here, disempowered water consumers, fragmented and pacified by the privatized infrastructural system, scaled up their claims from the household to the system as a whole, acting as citizens rather than customers.

It is important to remember the administrative capacity necessary for water and sewerage on an urban scale was integral to the rise of municipalism in the 19th and early 20th centuries, and with it ideas around the public realm and citizenship (Gandy, 2004; Moss, 2020). Municipal authorities assumed control from private companies that were unable or unwilling to provide universal supply, as infrastructure was capital-intensive and return of profit low, resulting in a fragmented, insufficient network. The provision of water and sewerage became a basic civic duty rather than source of profit, its infrastructural features assuming deep symbolic value, physically connecting citizens together within a unified, centralized system (Kaika, 2005). Indeed, in England and other industrialized countries, subsidized provision morphed into a basic entitlement of citizenship (Bakker, 2010). However, since the 1980s, with the rise of neoliberalism, the municipal ethos has largely dissipated as networked systems have been opened up to private interests and market logics, hastening the demise of the modern infrastructural ideal. As Gandy (2004: 371) contends, the decline of this ideal constitutes a 'weakening in the ostensible connection between urban infrastructure and the public realm'. Infrastructurally networked municipalism is a fragile thing, short-circuited historically not only by neoliberal capitalism but, as Moss (2020) reveals in his study of Berlin, fascism and socialism too.

However, across the world we have witnessed hundreds of cities begin to take water and sanitation services back into public hands under the banner of 'remunicipalization', after private water companies have failed to invest in infrastructure while increasing tariffs (McDonald, 2018). From Berlin, Paris and Budapest, to Accra, La Paz and Maputo, municipal authorities are assuming greater control of their water and sewerage, wresting control from private companies and national governments. This has not been simply about public ownership but the reassertion of civic purpose, where in addition to reported cost savings and increased investment, a renewed democratic culture has often flourished (Kishimoto et al, 2015). As Cumbers and Paul (2022: 202) attest, there is 'radical democratic potential' in water remunicipalization, which can enable more progressive coalitions and collective decision-making. There has been renewed interest in municipalism more generally as an antidote to neoliberalism and austerity, grounded in a civic politics of local service provision, drawing inspiration from commons thinking (Thompson, 2021). The 'new municipalism' seeks a public ethos that characterized urban government in the 19th century, where more equitable infrastructural service delivery can provide a practical basis for progressive political change, as witnessed in Preston and Salford, among many other places. Perhaps there is need yet again for municipal authorities to step in where private companies have failed, as happened 150 years ago, in England to also push back against the national government's agenda to shrink the state and deregulate. In the post-Brexit era, marked by weakening environmental regulation, underinvestment in services and an enfeebled local state at the hands of central government, municipalism offers an alternative vision at the juncture of the urban, infrastructural and political.

References

Alston, P. (2018) 'Statement on visit to the United Kingdom, by Professor Philip Alston, United Nations Special Rapporteur on extreme poverty and human rights', 16 November. Geneva: Office of the Commissioner for Human Rights. Available from: [Accessed 16 November 2022].

Amin, A. (2014) 'Lively infrastructure', *Theory, Culture & Society*, 31(7/8): 137–61.

Amin, A. and Howell, P. (eds) (2016) *Releasing the Commons: Rethinking the Futures of the Commons*, Abingdon: Routledge.

Anand, N. (2017) *Hydraulic City: Water and the Infrastructures of Citizenship in Mumbai*, Durham, NC: Duke University Press.

Apostolopoulou, E. and Kotsila, P. (2022) 'Community gardening in Hellinikon as a resistance struggle against neoliberal urbanism: spatial autogestion and the right to the city in post-crisis Athens, Greece', *Urban Geography*, 43(2): 293–319.

Bakker, K.J. (2000) 'Privatizing water, producing scarcity: the Yorkshire drought of 1995', *Economic Geography*, 76(1): 4–27.

Bakker, K.J. (2003) *An Uncooperative Commodity: Privatising Water in England and Wales*, Oxford: Oxford University Press.

Bakker, K.J. (2010) *Privatizing Water: Governance Failure and the World's Urban Water Crisis*, Ithaca, NY: Cornell University Press.

Benidickson, J. (2007) *The Culture of Flushing: A Social and Legal History of Sewage*, Vancouver: UBC Press.

Berlant, L. (2016) 'The commons: infrastructures for troubling times', *Environment and Planning D: Society and Space*, 34(3): 393–419.

Borch, C. and Kornberger, M. (eds) (2015) *Urban Commons: Rethinking the City*, Abingdon: Routledge.

Bresnihan, P. and Byrne, M. (2015) 'Escape into the city: everyday practices of commoning and the production of urban space in Dublin', *Antipode*, 47(1): 36–54.

Bunce, S. (2016) 'Pursuing urban commons: politics and alliances in community land trust activism in East London', *Antipode*, 48(1): 134–50.

Cumbers, A. and Paul, F. (2022) 'Remunicipalisation, mutating neoliberalism, and the conjuncture', *Antipode*, 54(1): 197–217.

Davies, M. (2021) 'Update – Environment Bill: sewage', Mims Davies MP Conservatives, 27 October. Available from: https://www.mimsdavies.org.uk/news/update-environment-bill-sewage [Accessed 8 March 2022].

Defra (Department for Environment, Food and Rural Affairs) (2020a) 'Designation of an area of the River Wharfe at Ilkley as a bathing water'. Available from: https://consult.defra.gov.uk/water/bathing-water-river-wharfe-ilkley/ [Accessed 16 November 2022].

Defra (Department for Environment, Food and Rural Affairs) (2020b) 'Consultation outcome: summary of responses and government response', 22 December. Available from: https://www.gov.uk/government/consul tations/bathing-waters-designation-of-an-area-of-the-river-wharfe-ilkley/ outcome/summary-of-responses-and-government-response [Accessed 16 November 2022].

EA (Environment Agency) (2001) 'Decade of clean-up brings best ever river and estuary quality results', press release, 5 November, Bristol: Environment Agency.

EA (Environment Agency) (2022) 'Water and sewerage companies in England: environmental performance report 2021', Bristol: Environment Agency. Available from: https://www.gov.uk/government/publications/ water-and-sewerage-companies-in-england-environmental-performance-report-2021 [Accessed 16 November 2022].

Eidelman, T.A. and Safransky, S. (2021) 'The urban commons: a keyword essay', *Urban Geography*, 42(6): 792–811.

Eizenberg, E. (2012) 'Actually existing commons: three moments of space of community gardens in New York City', *Antipode*, 44(3): 764–82.

Environmental Audit Committee (2022) *Water Quality in Rivers: Fourth Report of Session 2021–22*, HC 74, London: House of Commons. Available from: https://committees.parliament.uk/work/891/water-quality-in-riv ers/publications/ [Accessed 16 November 2022].

ENDS Report (Environmental Data Services) (2021a) 'This is the most polluted bathing site in England', 4 November. Available from: https:// www.endsreport.com/article/1732263/mapped-popular-bathing-spot-frontline-englands-sewage-problem] [Accessed 16 November 2022].

ENDS Report (Environmental Data Services) (2021b) '"The Only Thing We Can Do Is Withdraw Our Payments": Southern Water Bill Strike Gains Momentum, 12 November. Available from: https://www.endsreport.com/ article/1733053/the-thing-withdraw-payments-southern-water-bill-str ike-gains-momentum [Accessed 16 November 2022].

Federici, S. (2019) *Re-enchanting the World: Feminism and the Politics of the Commons*, Oakland, CA: PM Press.

Finewood, M.H. (2016) 'Green infrastructure, grey epistemologies, and the urban political ecology of Pittsburgh's water governance', *Antipode*, 48(4): 1000–21.

Foster, S. and Iaione, C. (2016) 'The city as a commons', *Yale Law and Policy Review*, 34(2): 281–349.

Fredericks, R. (2018) *Garbage Citizenship: Vital Infrastructures of Labor in Dakar, Senegal*, Durham, NC: Duke University Press.

Gandy, M. (2004) 'Rethinking urban metabolism: water, space and the modern city', *City*, 8(3): 363–79.

Gillespie, T., Hardy, K. and Watt, P. (2018) 'Austerity urbanism and Olympic counter-legacies: gendering, defending and expanding the urban commons in East London', *Environment and Planning D: Society and Space*, 36(5): 812–30.

Ginn, F. and Ascensão, E. (2018) 'Autonomy, erasure, and persistence in the urban gardening commons', *Antipode*, 50(4): 929–52.

Graham, S. and Marvin, S. (2001) *Splintering Urbanism: Networked Infrastructures, Technological Mobilities and the Urban Condition*, London: Routledge.

Graham, S. and Thrift, N. (2007) 'Out of order: understanding repair and maintenance', *Theory, Culture & Society*, 24(3): 1–25.

The Guardian (2013) 'David Cameron makes leaner state a permanent goal', The Guardian, 12 November. Available from: https://www.theguardian.com/politics/2013/nov/11/david-cameron-policy-shift-leaner-efficient-state [Accessed 16 November 2022].

The Guardian (2020a) 'Push for bathing water quality hailed as "game changer" for UK rivers', The Guardian, 6 February. Available from: https://www.theguardian.com/environment/2020/feb/06/push-for-bathing-water-quality-hailed-game-changer-uk-rivers [Accessed 16 November 2022].

The Guardian (2020b) 'One man's fight to get bathing water status for a stretch of river near Bath', The Guardian, 1 July. Available from: https://www.theguardian.com/environment/2020/jul/01/one-man-fight-bathing-water-status-bath-river-avon-johnny-palmer [Accessed 16 November 2022].

The Guardian (2021a) 'Water firms discharged raw sewage into English waters 400,000 times last year', The Guardian, 31 March. Available from: https://www.theguardian.com/environment/2021/mar/31/water-firms-discharged-raw-sewage-into-english-waters-400000-times-last-year [Accessed 16 November 2022].

The Guardian (2021b) 'Illegal sewage discharge in English rivers 10 times higher than official data suggests', The Guardian, 14 June. Available from: https://www.theguardian.com/environment/2021/jun/14/sewage-discharge-in-english-rivers-10-times-higher-than-official-data-suggests [Accessed 16 November 2022].

The Guardian (2021c) 'Swimming in sewage: how can we stop UK water firms dumping human waste in our rivers and seas?', The Guardian, 14 November. Available from: https://www.theguardian.com/environment/2021/nov/14/swimming-in-sewage-how-can-we-stop-uk-water-firms-dumping-human-waste-in-our-rivers-and-seas [Accessed 16 November 2022].

The Guardian (2022) 'Staff blow whistle on Environment Agency that "no longer deters polluters"', The Guardian, 20 January. Available from: https://www.theguardian.com/environment/2022/jan/20/environment-agency-cuts-staff-blow-whistle [Accessed 16 November 2022].

Hall, D. and Lobina, E. (2007) From a Private Past to a Public Future?, London: Public Services International Research Unit (PSIRU), Business School, University of Greenwich. Available from: https://gala.gre.ac.uk/id/eprint/2946/1/PSIRU_Report_9757_2008-02-W-UK.pdf [Accessed 16 November 2022].

Hammond, P. (2021) Written evidence submitted by Professor Peter Hammond BA MSc PhD MSc to the UK parliament. Available from: https://committees.parliament.uk/writtenevidence/22501/pdf/ [Accessed 16 November 2022].

Hansard (1995) Bathing water: Ecc Report, vol 564, 18 May. Available from: https://hansard.parliament.uk/Lords/1995-05-18/debates/38c36 5b6-e4cd-4078-92f1-7ae65fbe2f28/BathingWaterEccReport [Accessed 16 November 2022].

Hansard (2021) Environment Bill, vol 815, 26 October. Available from: https://hansard.parliament.uk/Lords/2021-10-26/debates/C4041 49A-D773-4E4B-BFD8-4757A09A05A7/EnvironmentBill [Accessed 16 November 2022].

Harris, T. (2021) A river fit for swimming Oxford: citizen science sampling interim report. Available from: https://www.thames21.org.uk/wp-content/uploads/2021/09/Oxford-interim-report.pdf [Accessed 16 November 2022].

Hassan, J. (1998) A History of Water in Modern England and Wales, Manchester: Manchester University Press.

Haughton, G. (1998) 'Private profits – public drought: the creation of a crisis in water management for West Yorkshire', Transactions of the Institute of British Geographers, 23(4): 419–33.

Huron, A. (2015) 'Working with strangers in saturated space: reclaiming and maintaining the urban commons', Antipode, 47(4): 963–79.

Jordan, A. and Greenway, J. (1998) 'Shifting agendas, changing regulatory structures and the "new" politics of environmental pollution: British coastal water policy, 1955–1995', Public Administration, 76(4): 669–94.

Kaika, M. (2005) City of Flows: Modernity, Nature, and the City, Abingdon: Routledge.

Kaika, M. and Swyngedouw, E. (2000) 'Fetishizing the modern city: the phantasmagoria of urban technological networks', International Journal of Urban and Regional Research, 24(1): 120–38.

Karvonen, A. (2011) Politics of Urban Runoff: Nature, Technology, and the Sustainable City, Cambridge, MA: MIT Press.

KentOnline (2021) 'Bob Geldof tells Southern Water to "**** off", and has his say on Boris Johnson, huge housing developments and the UK's biggest solar farm', 13 November. Available from: https://www.kentonl ine.co.uk/faversham/news/bob-geldof-tells-southern-water-to-f-off-257 355/ [Accessed 16 November 2022].

Kinnersley, D. (1994) *Coming Clean: The Politics of Water and the Environment*, London: Penguin.

Kishimoto, S., Lobina, E. and Petitjean, O. (eds) (2015) *Our Public Water Future: The Global Experience with Remunicipalisation*, Amsterdam: Transnational Institute.

Lemanski, C. (2020) 'Infrastructural citizenship: the everyday citizenships of adapting and/or destroying public infrastructure in Cape Town, South Africa', *Transactions of the Institute of British Geographers*, 45(3): 589–605.

Lloyd, P. (2021) Written evidence submitted by Peter Lloyd to the UK parliament. Available from: https://committees.parliament.uk/writtene vidence/22337/pdf/ [Accessed 17 November 2022].

Marvin, S. and Guy, S. (1997) 'Consuming water: evolving strategies of water management in Britain', *Journal of Urban Technology*, 4(3): 21–45.

McDonald, D.A. (2018) 'Remunicipalization: the future of water services?', *Geoforum*, 91: 47–56.

McFarlane, C. (2018) 'Fragment urbanism: politics at the margins of the city', *Environment and Planning D: Society and Space*, 36(6): 1007–25.

Melosi, M.V. (2000) *The Sanitary City: Urban Infrastructure in America from Colonial Times to the Present*, Baltimore, MD: Johns Hopkins University Press.

Morales, M. de C., Harris, L. and Öberg, G. (2014) 'Citizenshit: the right to flush and the urban sanitation imaginary', *Environment and Planning A: Economy and Space*, 46(12): 2816–33.

Moss, T. (2020) *Remaking Berlin: A History of the City Through Infrastructure, 1920–2020*, Cambridge, MA: MIT Press.

Outdoor Swimming Society (2021) 'Bathing water designation for local swim spots?', 8 February. Available from: https://www.outdoorswimming society.com/should-swimmers-seek-bathing-water-designation-for-local-swim-spots/ [Accessed 17 November 2022].

PMO (Prime Minister's Office) (2011) 'Letter from the Prime Minister on cutting red tape'. Available from: https://www.gov.uk/government/ news/letter-from-the-prime-minister-on-cutting-red-tape [Accessed 17 November 2022].

Rose, C. (1990) *The Dirty Man of Europe: The Great British Pollution Scandal*, London: Simon & Schuster.

Shelton, K. (2017) *Power Moves: Transportation, Politics, and Development in Houston*, Austin: University of Texas Press.

Star, S.L. (1999) 'The ethnography of infrastructure', *American Behavioral Scientist*, 43(3): 377–91.

Stavrides, S. (2016) *Common Space: The City as Commons*, London: Zed Books.

Swyngedouw, E. (2004) *Social Power and the Urbanization of Water: Flows of Power*, Oxford: Oxford University Press.

Thompson, M. (2021) 'What's so new about New Municipalism?', *Progress in Human Geography*, 45(2): 317–42.

Usher, M., Huck, J., Clay, G., Shuttleworth, E. and Astbury, J. (2021) 'Broaching the brook: daylighting, community and the "stickiness" of water', *Environment and Planning E: Nature and Space*, 4(4): 1487–514.

Ward, N. (1996) 'Surfers, sewage and the new politics of pollution', *Area*, 28(3): 331–8.

Williams, M.J. (2018) 'Urban commons are more-than-property', *Geographical Research*, 56(1): 16–25.

Woodward, J., Li, J., Rothwell, J. and Hurley, R. (2021) 'Acute riverine microplastic contamination due to avoidable releases of untreated wastewater', *Nature Sustainability*, 4: 793–802.

Yearwood, K. (2018) The privatised water industry in the UK: an ATM for investors, London: Public Services International Research Unit (PSIRU), Business School, University of Greenwich. Available from: https://gala.gre.ac.uk/21097/20/21097%20YEARWOOD_The_Privatised_Water_Industry_in_the_UK_2018.pdf [Accessed 17 November 2022].

Yorkshire Post (2020) 'Ilkley's bid to become UK's first river bathing spot steps forward as consultation closes after weighty debate', 3 October. Available from: https://www.yorkshirepost.co.uk/news/environment/ilkleys-bid-to-become-uks-first-river-bathing-spot-steps-forward-as-consultation-closes-after-weighty-debate-2991555 [Accessed 17 November 2022].

7

More than 'Where You Do Football': Reconceptualizing London's Urban Green Spaces through Green Infrastructure Planning

Meredith Whitten

Introduction

Lauded for their wide-ranging environmental, social and economic benefits, urban green spaces increasingly are presented as a 21st-century policy and planning panacea for addressing prominent global challenges, such as climate change mitigation (Mathey et al, 2011), public health (Kabisch et al, 2016), and biodiversity and habitat loss (Aronson et al, 2017). In particular, the multifaceted contributions green spaces make in densely developed and populated cities are recognized (Haaland and van den Bosch, 2015). Such contributions are magnified when green spaces are considered part of a broader network of natural and vegetated features, including street trees, vegetated roofs and walls, and verges (WHO, 2017; Massini and Smith, 2018).

However, in practice, urban green spaces rarely realize this full potential (Meerow, 2020). With a focus on London, this chapter argues that instead of being considered as critical, functional elements of a multifunctional, interconnected system of green infrastructure (GI), green spaces continue to be narrowly conceptualized as passive, aesthetic amenities, detached from the city around them (Reeder, 2006b). This is reinforced by planning processes that focus on individual spaces and by a fragmented GI-related governance. A gap between the policy ambitions of GI and practical implementation of

GI leads to missed opportunities to address (or at least mediate) the negative impacts of urbanization (Meerow and Newell, 2017; Meerow, 2020).

First, this chapter situates GI within a broader resurgence of infrastructural studies. It then discusses the evolution of GI as a framework and a practice. The case of London is laid out, providing context for the city's efforts to shift from a focus on traditional parks and conventional uses of these spaces, to a modern, inclusive approach that integrates a diversity of green features into the city's burgeoning footprint. The final sections discuss findings regarding the challenges cities like London face in trying to reach ambitious GI goals.

The chapter draws from qualitative research conducted from 2014 to 2019 in Inner London, which comprises the British capital's 13 most central boroughs. Inner London makes up 20 per cent of Greater London's geographical footprint, yet comprises 40 per cent of its population (GLA, 2017, 2018a). Specifically, the research was set in three boroughs: Islington, Tower Hamlets and Wandsworth. Each was one of the ten most densely populated boroughs in Greater London (GLA, 2018a), as well as among the five boroughs with the largest net gain in residential units (GLA, 2021b). As such, these three boroughs are dense and growing denser. This reflects London Plan policies calling for more compact development in Inner London (GLA, 2021a), and has ramifications for the boroughs' ability to supply green spaces to address the needs of their growing populations.

Primary data was collected through semi-structured interviews with participants whose work involves green space, including representatives from local and regional governments, charities and community groups, and developers, housing providers and landscape architects. Secondary research methods included site observation and archival work, which fleshed out details of issues – such as around heritage – that emerged from interviews.

A green-hued 'infrastructural turn'

Two decades ago, Graham and Marvin (2001) catapulted the study of infrastructure into the heart of urban studies. Their influential and inspirational work has led to a reconceptualization of infrastructure from mundane and predictable to dynamic and innovative (Wiig et al, Chapter 1, this volume). While this motivated the deeper study of 'the vital processes and politics of the cables, wires, pipes and roads that undergird urban development' (Wiig et al, 2022: 1), attention on a networked approach to the urban natural environment remained, much like green spaces themselves, somewhat of an afterthought. Indeed, discourse about infrastructure and nature usually hinged around well-trod conflicts between the built and natural environments (Campbell, 2016) and the resultant negative impacts, such as habitat fragmentation (Bekker and Iuell, 2003).

Yet, Graham and Marvin inspired a generation of scholars who have questioned the meaning of infrastructure, 'shifting ideas about what infrastructure actually *is*' (Wiig et al, 2022: 3, emphasis original). This has introduced the vision of infrastructure to urban landscape planning (Wiig et al, 2022), illustrating such a 'radical transformation' (Enright, 2022: 101) envisioned by Graham and Marvin. A green-hued 'infrastructural turn' fits well with the study of urban nature. For one, the natural environment is dynamic and constantly changing, as is infrastructure (Wiig et al, 2022). Cities and urban infrastructure exist 'within a constant state of flux' (McFarlane and Rutherford, 2008: 364). This makes an infrastructural approach to deeply embedded and rigid notions of green space instructive.

Further, with a global, urgent climate emergency and continuing environmental degradation, including in dense, urban environments, 'infrastructure is increasingly more than the concrete and the cabled. It is also the green and growing' (Gabrys, 2022: 14). Indeed, nature is infrastructural (Gabrys, 2022). GI, like other infrastructures, is thus critical in contesting and facilitating urban change (McFarlane and Rutherford, 2008). Yet, GI wrestles with a foundational fragmentation. Unlike other infrastructures, such as road or transport networks, GI did not originate from a strategic perspective. Rather, GI has the challenge of developing what has long been a localized and piecemeal approach to a city–nature coexistence – namely in the form of individual, local parks and green spaces – into a strategic, networked perspective. Conceptualizing these spaces on a citywide scale runs counter to well-entrenched and local approaches to planning. Also, green space has typically been considered as a 'cosmetic afterthought' (DOE, 1996: iii) at the end of development, rather than seen as essential and considered from the onset, as traditional infrastructures usually are. Further, given that infrastructure is inherently political (McFarlane and Rutherford, 2008), a shift to implementing GI remains a challenging work in progress.

Growing green infrastructure

In response to increasing urbanization and heightened global awareness of environmental crises – including the climate emergency, mass extinctions and irreversible degradation – modern, developed cities, such as London, have sought to expand the role of urban green space by connecting it with critical urban systems and services, including urban cooling, flood prevention and habitat restoration (Gill et al, 2007). As such, cities are positioning their green spaces as essential elements within a wider network of GI (Tzoulas et al, 2007). From this perspective, green space goes beyond public parks to include natural features, such as street trees, private gardens, housing amenity spaces, vegetated roofs and fencing, green walls, swales, verges, indoor gardens, and churchyards (Mell and Whitten, 2021).

Yet, more than just a definitional expansion, this shift extends to why and how green spaces are provided, what services these spaces are expected to deliver, and who plays a role in creating, managing and maintaining them. Further, this shift to GI is meant to portend a more strategic and less siloed approach to greening the urban environment, while holistically and simultaneously addressing climate change and ecological considerations, social development and economic valuation (Mell, 2015).

Benedict and McMahon provided an early, influential definition of GI as 'an interconnected network of green space that conserves natural ecosystem values and functions and provides associated benefits to human populations' (2002: 12). The concept's guiding principles include spatial connectivity, multifunctional landscapes, access to nature, and integrated policy and practice networks (Kambites and Owen, 2006; Wright, 2011; Lennon, 2015; Mell and Clement, 2019; Meerow, 2020). As such, GI refers to a range of green elements that are strategically planned, managed and connected at both a spatial and administrative scale (Matthews et al, 2015).

The term 'green infrastructure' burst on the scene, with its 'meteoric' (Lennon, 2015: 958) rise as a planning tool taken up by countries and cities, industries, and sectors largely occurring in the first 20 years of the 21st century (Mell et al, 2017). GI went 'from a reference in planning policy to the basis of emerging national policy' in just two years (2008–10) in England (Wright, 2011: 1005). Yet, of course, the concept and practice of GI did not 'come out of nowhere' (Thomas cited in Wright, 2011: 1004). Various explanations of its emergence exist (Wright, 2011; Mell, 2016). GI draws from landscape ecology (Roe and Mell, 2013; Lennon, 2015), conservation (Seiwert and Rößler, 2020), greenbelts (Amati and Taylor, 2010), greenways (Fábos, 2004) and garden cities (Howard, 1902), among others. GI's underlying principles of multifunctionality and interconnectivity are visible in the work of influential and prolific US landscape architect Frederick Law Olmsted and English urban planner Ebenezer Howard (Meerow, 2020).

GI notably diverges from traditional green space planning by equating urban greening with a city's other physical infrastructure (Mell, 2015). Planning for GI occurs at the beginning of development, concurrent with planning for grey infrastructure, such as transportation and utility networks (Eisenman, 2013). As such, GI can be seen as 'an organising framework for urban form and growth' (Eisenman, 2013: 288). And the use of the term infrastructure is deliberate (Lennon, 2015), as it is meant to overcome the idea that green spaces are solely 'a community amenity, an extra, even a frill' (McMahon, 2000: 4). Thus, GI 'represents a dramatic shift in the way local and state governments think about green space' (McMahon, 2000: 4), transforming green space from 'doing nothing to doing something' (Lennon, 2015: 964). The linking of green and grey infrastructure enables a broader network to be planned and designed more holistically (Benedict and McMahon, 2002; Davies and Lafortezza, 2017). Indeed, the strategic aspect of GI is fundamental and further departs from typical aesthetics-led green space planning (Amati and Taylor, 2010). Instead of considering each green space or green element as an independent, delineated site, GI focuses on how different elements function as a system to collectively provide a more beneficial, effective cumulative impact (McMahon, 2000; Mell, 2008).

While the simplicity of Benedict and McMahon's (2002) seminal definition has contributed to broad applicability and adoption of GI across varied disciplines, it also masks understanding of the 'variation in ecological, social and economic benefits that green space can provide' (Mell, 2019). Further, the broadness of the definition is seen as ambiguity that can lead to GI being a 'corruptible' (Wright, 2011: 1003) and 'nebulous' (Meerow, 2020) concept. Variations in defining GI across disciplines and geographies contribute to a definitional chaos, with Mell et al observing that 'there are currently as many interpretations of GI as there are people engaging with the concept' (2017: 335). Indeed, much of the GI literature remains preoccupied with defining the concept (Lennon, 2015; Whitten, 2023).

Definitional fragmentation reflects different geographical and disciplinary contexts (Mell and Clement, 2019; Matsler, et al, 2021). In North America, GI is rooted in stormwater management, while in the UK and Europe, GI planning is predominantly conceptualized around socio-economic functions of green space (Mell and Clement, 2019). In China, GI revolves around aesthetic improvement, real estate value and the promotion of 'sponge cities' to deliver the government's urban sustainability agenda (Matsler, et al, 2021). With discourse around GI becoming more localized rather than moving towards international consensus (Mell et al, 2017), GI's capacity for serving as a comprehensive and unifying framework that accommodates competing perspectives is uncertain (Whitten, 2023). Fragmented definitions and disjointed approaches to GI in practice limit its use and integration into wider service delivery efforts and make it more challenging to assess GI performance, establish standards and share knowledge (Matsler et al, 2021). Indeed, inherent trade-offs and conflicting priorities exist with planning for human–natural systems (Campbell, 2016), contributing to gaps between policy rhetoric about greening the urban environment and practical implementation of GI (Dempsey, 2020; Meerow, 2020).

Greening London

Envisioning a city with a broad range of green elements woven throughout its built environment would seem a natural extension of the story London tells about itself as both a global city and as a green city. London has a rich spatial legacy of parks, gardens, green squares and commons, reflecting the prominence access to nature has held throughout the city's post-industrial history (Garside, 2006). And, while many of the city's more than 3,000 existing parks and green spaces were inherited from previous eras, many are more recently established (Reeder, 2006a). This continuum of green spaces has been central to how London has evolved and developed (Reeder, 2006a, 2006b; Whitten and Massini, 2021). Indeed, from green wedges in Abercrombie's Greater London Plan 1944 (Lemes de Oliveira, 2014) to green roofs and walls in the London Plan 2021 (GLA, 2021a), green space in some form has been fundamental to the city's urban form.

London generally is considered 47 per cent green (GiGL, 2019). Variations in definitions and measurement impede cross-urban comparisons. Even within London, an exact amount of green space is difficult to pin down, as much of the data are provided by local authorities, who rely on varying definitions and methods of data collection, thus limiting pan-London comparability. Despite the prominence of well-known parks, such as Hyde Park, London's overall greenness comes from a range of green typologies, which fits with the concept of GI. For example, parks and gardens constitute just 5.83 per cent of London's total green space (GiGL, 2019). In recent years, London also has experienced a proliferation in green roofs, with 1.5 million square metres of green roofs in Greater London (including 291,598 sq m in Central London), an increase of nearly 39 per cent from the previous year (Grant and Gedge, 2019). Some 21 per cent of London lies under tree canopy, greater than the national average of 16 per cent (LUFP, 2020).

The Greater London Authority (GLA), the city's regional governance body, has adopted policies and strategies to enhance and increase GI in London (GLA, 2021a). First introduced in the 2008 London Plan – the Mayor of London's spatial development strategy – GI has evolved to feature prominently in a wide range of GLA policy and strategies (CRP, 2016), illustrated by Table 7.1.

Yet, while the GLA plays an influential role in steering policy and planning change, London's 33 local governments – 32 boroughs plus the City of London – have responsibility for interpreting that policy through local context and delivering GI in practice, giving the capital a fragmented governance structure (Travers, 2004) (see Figure 7.1). And, while the GLA was an enthusiastic early adopter of GI, this ambition has not been matched by all boroughs, as GI remains a relatively new concept to policy makers, planners and other practitioners (Mell, 2015; LGSC, 2020). While some local governments, like the City of London, have robust GI policies, others have adopted a weak policy, and half of London's boroughs do not have any GI strategy (LGSC, 2020). Although this variation allows for local priorities, it also presents challenges for developing a strategic and spatially and administratively connected GI approach beyond the local level.

Table 7.1: Select GLA-supported GI publications

Document	Publication date	Examples of GI-related provisions
London Plan	2021	Requires all major developments to include urban greening as a fundamental element of site and building design; introduces the use of an Urban Greening Factor to evaluate the quantity and quality of urban greening provided by a development proposal; sets out protections for London's greenbelt.
London Environment Strategy	2018	Sets out policies to increase the city's overall greenness to 50%; increase tree canopy cover by 10%; and to enhance biodiversity.
London Transport Strategy	2018	Puts increasing urban greening at the core of the Healthy Streets strategy; promotes increased urban greening to encourage walking and cycling.
London Urban Forest Plan	2020	Collaborative plan to protect, manage and enhance London's urban forest.
Grey-to-green guide	2020	Provides guidance for turning grey areas of impermeable surfacing to green.
London Sustainable Drainage Action Plan	2016	Promotes the awareness, and the retrofitting, of sustainable drainage systems.
Natural Capital Accounts for Public Green Space in London	2017	Demonstrated the economic value of health benefits to Londoners from the city's public green spaces.
All London Green Grid Supplementary Planning Guidance	2012	Guidance for policy framework to promote the design and delivery of green infrastructure across London.

London's green ambitions also run up against the realities of urban growth. Like other cities, such as Portland, Oregon (US), Düsseldorf (Germany) and Asahikawa (Japan), that have deliberately sought to curtail their sprawling footprint through urban containment policies, London faces barriers to expanding traditional green space (Haaland and van den Bosch, 2015; GLA, 2018b, 2021a). Between 2001 and 2011, London's population grew 11.6 per cent, more than any city/region in England (ONS, 2012). Today, London has a population of more than 9 million, the largest in its history. By 2041, population is projected to reach 10.8 million (GLA, 2021a). London also is significantly more densely populated than other English cities (ONS, 2012; GLA, 2018a). The city's population density has increased, in part, as the result of an emphasis on compact development to minimize sprawl

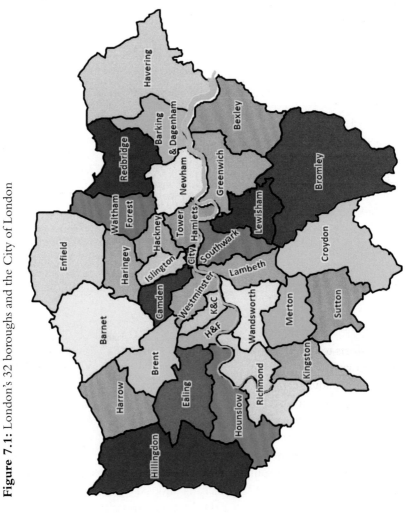

Figure 7.1: London's 32 boroughs and the City of London

Source: Greater London Authority. Contains Ordnance Survey data © Crown copyright and database rights

and its diseconomies (Scanlon et al, 2018; GLA, 2021a). An increase in infill and vertical development has led to more demand pressure on existing green space and constrained provision of new conventional green spaces (GLA, 2021a). This pressure is exacerbated by a critical housing shortage, with 66,000 new homes needed annually for 20 years to keep pace with demand (GLA, 2021a). As such, policies that call for compact development have implications for how green space is integrated into the changing urban environment.

Discussion

A network of GI comprising vegetated and natural elements, such as parks and gardens, green roofs, living walls, street trees, sustainable drainage systems (SuDS) and housing amenity spaces, can contribute to increasing and improving urban greening across cities, such as London, while simultaneously providing valuable health and ecological benefits (Hansen and Pauleit, 2014; Mell, 2019). Yet, the research discussed here found that a gap exists between the theoretical and policy discourses that equate green space with GI, and practical approaches to greening the urban environment. This is because of challenges shifting to a strategic, holistic perspective on urban greening from a deeply entrenched focus on conventional parks and gardens, as well as spatial disconnection and administrative fragmentation in GI delivery.

Conceptual embeddedness

Formal efforts to integrate nature into rapidly urbanizing places emerged in 19th-century Victorian England (Conway, 1991). Despite the innovation and economic advancement of industrializing English cities, the Victorians were decidedly anti-urban (Hulin, 1979). They considered the city dirty, corruptive and unhealthy (Malchow, 1985; Dempsey, 2009). This underscored their reverence for the countryside, which they viewed as pure, wholesome and restorative (Welch, 1991). Social reformers and others drew on this obsessive veneration for the pastoral idyll to address their concerns about overcrowding and the unhealthy and unsanitary urban environment in which the poor and working classes lived (Reeder, 2006b; Jones, 2018). This led to creation of public parks, a 'particularly Victorian solution' (Brück, 2013: 196) to address not only concerns about physical health, but also moral behaviour (Reeder, 2006b). With nature used as a counterpoint to population and development density, parks and green spaces from the outset were conceptualized as separate from the city, purposely detached from the rest of the urban environment (Gabriel, 2011). Indeed, for the Victorians, 'the "country-in-town" principle had almost become an obsession both with town-planners and social reformers' (Hulin, 1979: 17).

The theme of bringing the countryside into the city featured prominently in this research. For example, a council green space officer said the purpose of providing green space in London "is to encapsulate the countryside". Such comments tie directly to the Victorians' 'pastoral ideal' (Malchow, 1985: 97) and illustrate a path-dependency of urban green space as the antithesis of urban infrastructure. London's green spaces remain "frozen in time", as noted by a regional charity officer, by adherence to a traditional look and function that has become the accepted, or institutionalized, way of doing things. Contemporary green space planning practices are built on values and ideals about nature established centuries ago, 'with layers of values and understandings left from earlier times influencing new initiatives through institutional remembering and the strength of tradition and culture' (Clifford, 2016: 388).

Participants discussed urban green spaces as spaces 'other' to the city – as separate and disconnected from other urban features. A council green space officer described "complaints" that Wandsworth Council receives due to increasing and changing usage of green spaces, such as a proliferation of benches and sports pitches meant to attract visitors to local green spaces. Instead, the green space officer said, residents expect green spaces to be more representative of a space away from the bustle and noise of Inner London: "The number of people who don't recognise that [people in the park making noise] is a perfectly valid thing ... is unbelievable."

Similarly, a green space officer in Islington said residents expect the borough's green spaces to provide places for "quiet contemplation", despite Islington's long tenure as the densest borough in England, small parks and green spaces, and overall least amount of green space of London boroughs, except for the City of London, which is a statistical outlier (GLA, 2017). In Tower Hamlets – England's densest (ONS, 2021) and second-fastest-growing borough (ONS, 2018) – participants described urban green space as "space away from the density and the buildings" (council green space officer) and "quieter areas that people appreciate more" (council planner). Yet, given the increasing populations and infill and vertical development in these boroughs, they are unlikely to replicate the idealized peace and quiet of the countryside.

Figure 7.2, an advertisement that featured on London public transport, demonstrates how urban green space as technically in, but conceptually distant or fragmented from the city continues to be perpetuated. The advertisement connects one of London's newest urban green spaces, Queen Elizabeth Olympic Park – located in a heavily urbanized and intensively developing area in East London – with anti-urban thought (Malchow, 1985). Again, this underscores the Victorian belief that the city is a place

Figure 7.2: Advertisement for Queen Elizabeth Olympic Park

Source: Meredith Whitten

that needs escaping, and the countryside is a desirable place to escape to (Hulin, 1979; Brück, 2013).

Emphasis on the 'enduring strength of the imaginary of the "rural idyll"' (Harrison and Clifford, 2016: 602) remains central to English identity and cultural heritage (Lowenthal, 1991; Mischi, 2009) and 'fundamentally shapes how we [the English] design policy and make planning decisions' (Harrison and Clifford, 2016: 585). A deeply embedded cultural preference for the countryside has resulted in a 'powerful cultural institution' (Mace, 2018: 2) that contributes to an enduringly inflexible concept of green space. Indeed, a council planner observed that maintaining "the Victorian legacy" continues to influence green space planning today. This puts the approach to green space management increasingly at odds with a present-day, culturally diverse population, with more than one third of Londoners born outside of the UK (GLA, 2017).

Further, the firm grip of cultural heritage on the conceptualization of green space can conflict with principles of GI, which espouse modern and dynamic approaches to integrating nature into constantly changing cities (Thomas and Littlewood, 2010). Preserving urban green space for its connection to the past becomes a concern when it impedes the use of green space as a planning tool to address contemporary and urgent challenges, such as climate change. Indeed, an executive from a national planning organization commented that urban green spaces are "culturally very rich and very interesting, but they are looking back to the past, rather than looking forward to the future".

One way the powerful cultural institution of the countryside is embedded in planning policy is through the 27 statutory planning consultees (HM Government, 2015). Two consultees – Historic England and the Gardens Trust – approach urban green space from a heritage perspective. The 15 national park authorities comment on development that could affect land in national parks, none of which are urban. Despite the grassroots London National Park City Foundation successfully campaigning to recognize London as a 'national park city', this is not a land-use designation, and no national park authority for London will be established (NPCF, 2019).

Natural England, the government's advisor on the natural environment, is most aligned with urban green space interests, several participants said. The non-departmental body designed a 'Framework of Green Infrastructure Standards', which provides guidance to local authorities and other stakeholders about including GI in new residential developments, as well as greening existing public spaces (Natural England, 2020). However, participants said Natural England rarely comments on local issues – and almost all green space issues are addressed locally, most notably through local authority decision making. Thus, statutory champions exist for green spaces, but primarily related to heritage or non-urban spaces.

Funding also impedes adopting a GI planning approach. During a decade of austerity (Lowndes and Gardner, 2016), local authorities drastically cut their budgets for non-statutory services, including green space (Whitten, 2019). To fill the budget gap, they have turned to other funding sources, most notably the National Lottery Heritage Fund (NLHF), which has made substantial investment in UK parks (Clark, 2004; Eadson et al, 2020). Participants described efforts where local authorities prioritized heritage parks or heritage-related structures and uses over other types of GI because of the greater likelihood of receiving heritage funding than other grants. For example, a council green space officer questioned whether Tower Hamlets Council would have received a £5 million NLHF matching grant – a total £10 million investment – for restoring the borough's flagship Victoria Park in 2010 if the park did not have heritage value.

Limited options for large-scale investment beyond heritage-related funding further embeds a heritage focus, affecting the ability to manage urban green spaces as a modern system of GI. For example, Tower Hamlets Council's decision to apply for heritage funding had an impact on the types of improvements the council could make in Victoria Park. A council green space officer commented:

'Because it was a heritage fund we went for, we couldn't touch any of our sports facilities or anything. We couldn't spend any of the money on that. In some elements they [NLHF] wanted a lot of the Victorian designs brought back in … It all is very much to do with heritage and history.'

NLHF funding has further influence because its grants are matching grants and come with a requirement that a council maintain the improvements for up to ten years or lose the funding. Thus, local authorities' reduced green space budgets can go towards maintaining a heritage focus long term (Dempsey and Burton, 2012). A national charity manager addressed this:

'In some cases, they [the local authority] spent £6 million, £7 million, so that's going to be a challenge for an organisation. "How do I fund those two parks that have HLF investment from my parks budget if I have to maintain them because there's a real risk of that money being clawed back?" Does that happen at the expense of parks in the surrounding area?'

As such, heritage-oriented funding can divert a local authority's resources away from integrating green spaces into a network of GI. A national charity officer commented on this:

'There are a number of individual parks, which, largely thanks to the Heritage Lottery Fund, are now really nice, but they're little islands … Particularly thinking about climate change, public health, demographics – going forward, I think we need new sorts of green spaces that do an awful lot of different things at the same time … Every little space we've got is going to have to work a lot harder at providing a lot of different things.'

This is not to argue that heritage is not relevant to GI. Indeed, sociocultural aspects, such as heritage, are integral to the concept of GI, including community engagement and buy-in (Mell and Clement, 2019; Whitten, 2023). Rather, rigid adherence to a path-dependent fixation on a rural idyll impedes adoption of a more diverse and flexible range of green features that are strategically planned and maintained to address 21st-century challenges.

Spatial disconnection

An approach to parks as 'little islands' contributes to spatial fragmentation, contradicting GI's fundamental principle of interconnectivity (Kambites and Owen, 2006; Thomas and Littlewood, 2010). Many of London's urban green spaces are fenced, gated and locked at certain times, essentially disconnecting these public spaces from urban life (Figure 7.3).

Figure 7.3: Edwardian-era brick around South Park

Source: Meredith Whitten

The ornate and elaborate gates at many park and green space entrances bluntly differentiate these spaces from the city around them, 'marking as significant the transition from the chaos of the streets to spaces of calm and order' (Brück, 2013: 201) while protecting urban green space 'from the realities of its city surroundings' (Conway, 1991: 10). Passing through the gates powerfully signals visitors are leaving the city and stepping into the countryside (Rosenberg, 1996), indicating green spaces are 'literally and symbolically a world apart' from the city (Conway, 1991: 10). Within the fences, a green space's design, including horticultural choices and physical layout, deliberately contrasts to the city (Rosenberg, 1996). Although efforts such as rewilding, which seeks to reinstate natural landscape processes (Rewilding Britain, 2022), and 'no-mow' periods, when mowing is suspended to allow grass and wildflowers to grow and enhance biodiversity (Plantlife, 2022), are increasing in policy discourse and planning practice, a particular vision of 'conforming to an Arcadian ideal' (Malchow, 1985: 98) in which nature is 'organized and artfully displayed' (Pendlebury, 1997: 246) remains powerful.

Planning has been a leading sector in adopting GI, as GI's guiding principles fit well with planning's enthusiastic embrace of sustainability as a 'transcendental ideal' (Gunder, 2006: 209). Yet, at the same time that planning policy promotes GI, planning standards sustain spatial fragmentation. Most local authorities have adopted planning standards such as open space per capita, distance to open space and prevention of net loss of open space (Whitten, 2022), echoing wider trends in quantification as part of the turn towards new public management dating back to the 1990s (Dunleavy and Hood, 1994). Established at an arbitrary point in time, these standards do not reflect contemporary urban realities, including a denser, more vertical urban form. As such, they often are unrealistic and distract from a GI approach. For example, despite its standard of 1.2 ha of open space per 1,000 head of population, Tower Hamlets Council acknowledged that 'in the context of acute housing need in the Borough, such quantities [of green space] are not achievable' (2011: 19).

Such standards typically consider only conventional green spaces, not the broader network of green elements, such as vegetated roofs, increasingly required through planning processes to green the urban environment (Whitten, 2022). A prominent example is housing amenity space, which is not considered green space in planning terms even though these spaces are often green, can provide similar benefits as conventional parks and, in some cases, are larger than formally designated parks (Whitten, 2022). In some boroughs, including Islington, the amount of green space in housing estates and developments exceeds that in public parks (Whitten, 2022). In fact, 4.1 per cent of London comprises housing amenity space, not significantly less than the 5.8 per cent designated as parks and gardens (GiGL, 2019).

While vegetated roofs and green verges do not offer the same opportunities for recreation and sport that a public park does, these GI elements help address other policy and planning priorities, such as biodiversity gain and flood mitigation, in an increasingly crowded urban environment. Benefits from such non-conventional green elements could contribute to reducing health inequities, for example through air filtration, shading and cooling, and opportunities for quiet reflection (Tzoulas et al, 2007). Spatially connecting a range of GI elements does not supplant existing parks, but rather supplements them by expanding the benefits a network of urban greening can provide (Whitten and Massini, 2021).

Spatial fragmentation also impedes multifunctionality. Despite GI planning emphasizing the importance of factoring in multiple benefits to green spaces, 'decisions about where to site green infrastructure' are often opportunistic or based on one or a few benefits, rather than strategically focused on maximizing the full range of desired functions (Meerow, 2020: 3). Participants discussed limitations to multifunctionality given the pressure on Inner London green spaces for traditional uses, particularly sport and recreation. A regional green space charity executive called this "a fundamental challenge", adding that "green space ought to be seen as multifunctional, but too often it's not seen like that. It's seen as 'oh, this is where you do football'". Indeed, despite GI implying the ability to 'have it all' (Horwood, 2011: 971), a more limited focus perseveres in practice (Mell and Clement, 2019).

Administrative fragmentations

GI represents a shift from traditional approaches to planning that typically have addressed competing agendas through administrative and sectoral silos (Scott and Hislop, 2019), such as government departments working in isolation on issues like biodiversity or recreation (Rall et al, 2019). As an organizing framework, GI aims to overcome silos by reimagining parks, gardens, trees and other natural features as a strategic, multifunctional working landscape rather than as isolated elements, thus embedding a collaborative approach across once-fragmented teams and organizations (Kambites and Owen, 2006; Whitten, 2020).

Yet, local government organizational structures and funding processes can impede such collaborative ambitions. Typically, green space functions are organizationally structured with other non-statutory services (for example, leisure centres) or services seen as an amenity (such as libraries). Meanwhile, other departments or disciplinary teams have responsibilities for various aspects of GI. For example, Planning secures GI through negotiations and decisions around development. Highways oversees installation and management of SuDS and street trees; Health manages initiatives that promote use of green spaces for physical and mental health; and Housing manages amenity green spaces in housing estates (Figure 7.4). A regional charity executive said this fragmentation of green space management at the local level reflects disintegration at the national level:

> '[There are] silos within central government because parks are under the DCLG [Department for Communities and Local Government], but it's considered a cultural service by many. It doesn't come under the Department of Culture, Media and Sport. It's in a separate department. The two departments don't talk to each other. Then you extend that argument to, say, health or education and, again, no dialogue. All those silos have their funding schemes, as well. And, you have exactly the same in local authorities.'

This results in green space and other GI elements being both administratively and functionally separate, which 'can render the governance arrangements complex and fragmented' (Dempsey et al, 2016: 445). As such, "everybody is putting demand on the finite space", a council green space officer said. With GI spread among different departments and responsibilities, the benefits of administrative connectivity of GI are not realized. Internal fragmentation also affects council officers' interactions and negotiations with developers,

Figure 7.4: Housing amenity space

Source: Meredith Whitten

with a developer describing local authorities' GI activities as "a fragmented puzzle of opinions".

Green space's non-statutory status makes it vulnerable to budget cuts (Dempsey, 2020; Whitten, 2019). Indeed, despite green space being fundamental to a number of statutory services, investment in green space is 'precarious and disproportionately subject to tight fiscal pressures' (Dempsey and Burton, 2012: 13). While austerity measures introduced in England from 2010 affected all local government services, the deepest cuts occurred in discretionary functions (Brown and Wilson, 2015; Centre for London, 2018). Across the UK, 92 per cent of green space managers experienced cuts to their revenue budgets between 2013 and 2015 (NLHF, 2016). Spending on open space, which includes green spaces, by London councils decreased 18 per cent in four years, allowing for inflation (London Councils, 2015; LAEC, 2016).

As local governments' green space resources have been cut, they increasingly have turned to other partners, including developers, homebuilders and housing associations, charities and community organizations, to deliver, manage and maintain green spaces (Dempsey et al, 2016). This 'ongoing shift from (local) government green space management to a governance structure involving local non-governmental stakeholders' (Mathers et al, 2015: 126) has ramifications for implementing a holistic approach to urban greening.

In particular, increased reliance on community organizations in green space governance has occurred, with the number of 'friends' groups growing in London (Mathers et al, 2015; LAEC, 2017). Such community organizations often can devote more time and resources to local spaces than a local authority can (Mathers et al, 2015). As a result, community groups, such as the Friends of Luxmore Gardens in Lewisham, have transformed spaces neglected by local government into vibrant parts of the local community infrastructure (Whitten, 2019; FLG, 2022).

Yet, relying on community organizations and other partners presents challenges. These organizations often focus on an individual site, thus do not have a boroughwide or pan-London perspective (Whitten, 2019). A green space charity manager noted: "The penny hasn't dropped for a lot of [community groups] that, although local is important ... there's a bigger picture here, there's more at stake". Further, community organizations tend to take on management of smaller green spaces. This can lead these spaces to being managed solely for local use, thus ignoring the critical work smaller spaces contribute to a broad interconnected network of GI, including serving as strategic connectors between larger spaces (Van Herzele and Wiedemann, 2003).

A homogeneity in green space planning and management through a focus on amenity and recreation impedes the GI principle of multifunctionality. Certain functions, such as stormwater collection and climate change mitigation, are not a priority for some community organizations and local residents. This conflicts with policy discourse that increasingly presents multifunctional, spatially integrated and administratively connected GI simplistically as a panacea (Meerow, 2020; Whitten, 2022).

Conclusion

Urban green spaces increasingly are recognized for their wide-ranging contributions to human and ecological health. With crises such as the climate emergency, chronic health conditions and biodiversity loss commanding growing attention from policy makers and planners – as well as the public – urban policy increasingly is positioning green spaces not as an aesthetic amenity, but as critical infrastructure that can play a prominent role in addressing these global challenges. While consensus on a precise definition of GI remains elusive, the use of 'infrastructure' is deliberate, as it 'gives greater weight to the consideration of a broad spectrum of green space issues in planning policy formulation' (Lennon, 2015: 966).

Framing a range of green spaces, beyond the typical narrow focus on parks, as infrastructure 'implies something essential to city living' (Thomas and Littlewood, 2010: 210). This equates urban nature with traditional physical infrastructure, such as transport, utilities and communication, thus filling a gap in infrastructural discourse. Indeed, despite an 'infrastructural turn', urban studies largely overlooked green spaces as a networked system undergirding modern cities (Gabrys, 2022). Yet, as strategic, critical scaffolding (Eisenman, 2013), GI is recognized as dynamic, evolving and integral to the production of contemporary cities (Wiig et al, 2022).

However, if 'modern infrastructure is constructed by ideas and representations' (Enright, 2022: 102) as much as it is physical materials, shifting conceptualizations and approaches to integrating nature into the urban environment requires more than a change in terminology. Well-entrenched institutions and processes can perpetuate urban green spaces as detached from the city, both spatially and conceptually. Designing and managing a network of green elements to address current and future urban challenges, rather than simply reflecting their historic design and use, is a challenge, given the perseverance of administrative fragmentation, the embeddedness of institutional processes and the inherently political nature of infrastructure (McFarlane and Rutherford, 2008). Ultimately, GI, like other infrastructure, is 'intimately bound up with broader transformation in the geographies of cities and the experiences of urban life' (Graham and Marvin, 2022: 170). As such, GI must continue to evolve as the urban systems in which it exists continue to evolve, as well.

References

Amati, M. and Taylor, L. (2010) 'From green belts to green infrastructure', *Planning Practice & Research*, 25(2): 143–55.

Aronson, M., Lepczyk, C.A., Evans, K.L., Goddard, M.A., Lerman, S.B., MacIvor, J.S., et al (2017) 'Biodiversity in the city: key challenges for urban green space management', *Frontiers in Ecology and the Environment*, 15(4): 189–96.

Bekker, H. and Iuell, B. (2003) 'Habitat fragmentation due to infrastructure', Davis, CA: UC Davis, Road Ecology Center. Available from: https://escholarship.org/uc/item/9693w540 [Accessed 27 January 2022].

Benedict, M.A. and McMahon, E.T. (2002) 'Green infrastructure: smart conservation for the 21st century', *Renewable Resources Journal*, 20(3): 12–17.

Brown, R. and Wilson, B. (2015) Running on Fumes? London Council Services in Austerity, London: Centre for London. Available from: https://www.centreforlondon.org/wp-content/uploads/2016/08/CFL3888_Running-on-fumes_short_paper_12.11.15_WEB-1.pdf [Accessed 21 August 2021].

Brück, J. (2013) 'Landscapes of desire: parks, colonialism, and identity in Victorian and Edwardian Ireland', *International Journal of Historical Archaeology*, 17(1): 196–223.

Campbell, S. (2016) 'The planner's triangle revisited: sustainability and the evolution of a planning ideal that can't stand still', *Journal of the American Planning Association*, 82(4): 388–97.

Centre for London (2018) The London Intelligence, 4, London: Centre for London. Available from: https://www.centreforlondon.org/wp-content/uploads/2018/05/Issue-4-TLI.pdf [Accessed 21 August 2021].

Clark, K. (2004) 'Why fund heritage? The role of research in the Heritage Lottery Fund', *Cultural Trends*, 13(4): 65–85.

Clifford, B. (2016) '"Clock-watching and box-ticking": British local authority planners, professionalism and performance targets', *Planning Practice & Research*, 31(4): 383–401.

Conway, H. (1991) *People's Parks: The Design and Development of Victorian Parks in Britain*, Cambridge: Cambridge University Press.

CRP (Cross River Partnership) (2016) Green Capital: Green Infrastructure for a Future City. Available from: https://www.london.gov.uk/sites/default/files/green_capital.pdf [Accessed 3 February 2022].

Davies, C. and Lafortezza, R. (2017) 'Urban green infrastructure in Europe: is greenspace planning and policy compliant?', *Land Use Policy*, 69: 93–101.

Dempsey, N. (2009) 'Are good-quality environments socially cohesive? Measuring quality and cohesion in urban neighbourhoods', *Town Planning Review*, 80(3): 315–45.

Dempsey, N. (2020) 'Measuring the gap between rhetoric and practice: examining urban green space interventions post-implementation', in N. Dempsey and J. Dobson (eds) *Naturally Challenged: Contested Perceptions and Practices in Urban Green Spaces*, Cham: Springer, pp 167–87.

Dempsey, N. and Burton, M. (2012) 'Defining place-keeping: the long-term management of public spaces', *Urban Forestry & Urban Greening*, 11(1): 11–20.

Dempsey, N., Burton, M. and Selin, J. (2016) 'Contracting out parks and roads maintenance in England', *International Journal of Public Sector Management*, 29(5): 441–56.

DOE (Department of the Environment) (1996) *Greening the City: A Guide to Good Practice*, London: HMSO.

Dunleavy, P. and Hood, C. (1994) 'From old public administration to new public management', *Public Money and Management*, 14(3): 9–16.

Eadson, W., Harris, C., Parkes, S., Speake, B., Dobson, J. and Dempsey, N. (2020) Why Should We Invest in Parks? Evidence from the Parks for People Programme. Available from: https://www.heritagefund.org.uk/sites/default/files/media/attachments/Parks%20for%20People%20report.pdf [Accessed 21 September 2021].

Eisenman, T.S. (2013) 'Frederick Law Olmsted, green infrastructure, and the evolving city', *Journal of Planning History*, 12(4): 287–311.

Enright, T. (2022) 'The infrastructural imagination', *Journal of Urban Technology*, 29(1): 101–7.

Fábos, J.G. (2004) 'Greenway planning in the United States: its origins and recent case studies', *Landscape and Urban Planning*, 68(2/3): 321–42.

FLG (Friends of Luxmore Gardens) (2022) 'About'. Available from: http://www.loveluxmore.co.uk/?page_id=25 [Accessed 27 January 2022].

Gabriel, N. (2011) 'The work that parks do: towards an urban environmentality', *Social & Cultural Geography*, 12(2): 123–41.

Gabrys, J. (2022) 'Programming nature as infrastructure in the smart forest city', *Journal of Urban Technology*, 29(1): 13–19.

Garside, P.L. (2006) 'Politics, ideology and the issue of open space in London, 1939–2000', in P. Clark (ed) *The European City and Green Space: London, Stockholm, Helsinki and St Petersburg, 1850–2000*, Aldershot: Ashgate, pp 92–122.

GiGL (Greenspace Information for Greater London CIC) (2019) 'Key London figures'. Available from: https://www.gigl.org.uk/keyfigures/ [Accessed 12 September 2021].

Gill, S.E., Handley, J.F., Ennos, A.R. and Pauleit, S. (2007) 'Adapting cities for climate change: the role of the green infrastructure', *Built Environment*, 33(1): 115–33.

GLA (Greater London Authority) (2017) 'London borough profiles'. Available from: https://web.archive.org/web/20210511083051/https://data.london.gov.uk/dataset/london-borough-profiles [Accessed 18 August 2021].

GLA (Greater London Authority) (2018a) 'Land area and population density, ward and borough'. Available from: https://data.london.gov.uk/dataset/land-area-and-population-density-ward-and-borough [Accessed 8 May 2021].

GLA (Greater London Authority) (2018b) *London Environment Strategy*, London: GLA. Available from: https://www.london.gov.uk/sites/default/files/london_environment_strategy_0.pdf [Accessed 20 July 2021].

GLA (Greater London Authority) (2021a) *The London Plan: The Spatial Development Strategy for Greater London*, London: GLA. Available from: https://www.london.gov.uk/sites/default/files/the_london_plan_2021.pdf [Accessed 14 June 2021].

GLA (Greater London Authority) (2021b) 'Planning London datahub: residential completion dashboard'. Available from: https://data.london.gov.uk/dataset/planning-london-datahub [Accessed 14 June 2021].

Graham, S. and Marvin, S. (2001) *Splintered Urbanism: Networked Infrastructures, Technological Mobilities and the Urban Condition*, New York: Routledge.

Graham, S. and Marvin, S. (2022) '*Splintering Urbanism* at 20 and the "infrastructural turn"', *Journal of Urban Technology*, 29(1): 169–75.

Grant, G. and Gedge, D. (2019) *Living Roofs and Walls: From Policy to Practice*. London: European Federation of Green Roof and Green Wall Associations and Livingroofs.org. Available from: https://livingroofs.org/london-2019-green-roof-report/ [Accessed 14 October 2021].

Gunder, M. (2006) 'Sustainability: planning's saving grace or road to perdition?', *Journal of Planning Education and Research*, 26(2): 208–21.

Haaland, C. and van den Bosch, C.K. (2015) 'Challenges and strategies for urban green-space planning in cities undergoing densification: a review', *Urban Forestry & Urban Greening*, 14(4): 760–71.

Hansen, R. and Pauleit, S. (2014) 'From multifunctionality to multiple ecosystem services? A conceptual framework for multifunctionality in green infrastructure planning for urban areas', *AMBIO*, 43(4): 516–29.

Harrison, G. and Clifford, B. (2016) '"The field of grain is gone; It's now a Tesco Superstore": representations of "urban" and "rural" within historical and contemporary discourses opposing urban expansion in England', *Planning Perspectives*, 31(4): 585–609.

HM Government (2015) Town and Country Planning (TCP) Act (Development Management Procedure) (England) Order 2015 (schedule 4): consultations before the grant of permission. Available from: http://www.legislation.gov.uk/uksi/2015/595/schedule/4/made [Accessed 16 November 2021].

Horwood, K. (2011) 'Green infrastructure: reconciling urban green space and regional economic development – lessons learnt from experience in England's north-west region', *Local Environment*, 16(10): 963–75.

Howard, E. (1902) *Garden Cities of To-morrow*, London: Swan Sonnenschein. Available from: http://www.gutenberg.org/files/46134/46134-h/46134-h.htm [Accessed 22 August 2021].

Hulin, J.-P. (1979) '"Rus in urbe": a key to Victorian anti-urbanism?', in J.-P. Hulin and P. Coustillas (eds) *Victorian Writers and the City*, Lille: Publications de l'Université de Lille III, pp 11–40.

Jones, K.R. (2018) '"The lungs of the city": green space, public health and bodily metaphor in the landscape of urban park history', *Environment and History*, 24(1): 39–58.

Kabisch, N., Strohbach, M., Haase, D. and Kronenberg, J. (2016) 'Urban green space availability in European cities', *Ecological Indicators*, 70: 586–96.

Kambites, C. and Owen, S. (2006) 'Renewed prospects for green infrastructure planning in the UK', *Planning Practice & Research*, 21(4): 483–96.

LAEC (London Assembly Environment Committee) (2016) 'Scoping note: Green Spaces, Appendix 1'. Available from: https://www.london.gov.uk/about-us/londonassembly/meetings/documents/s60651/05a%20Appendix%201%20-%20Green%20Spaces%20Scope.pdf [Accessed 22 May 2021].

LAEC (London Assembly Environment Committee) (2017) *Park Life: Ensuring Green Spaces Remain a Hit with Londoners*. Available from: https://www.london.gov.uk/sites/default/files/environment_committee_-_park_life_report.pdf [Accessed 22 May 2021].

Lemes de Oliveira, F. (2014) 'Green wedges: origins and development in Britain', *Planning Perspectives*, 29(3): 357–79.

Lennon, M. (2015) 'Green infrastructure and planning policy: a critical assessment', *Local Environment*, 20(8): 957–80.

LGSC (London Green Spaces Commission) (2020) London Green Spaces Commission Report. Available from: https://www.london.gov.uk/sites/default/files/4244_-_gla_-_london_green_spaces_commission_report_v 7_0.pdf [Accessed 22 August 2021].

London Councils (2015) *Spending Review 2015: London Councils' Submission to HM Treasury*. Available from: https://www.londoncouncils.gov.uk/sites/default/files/Policy%20themes/Local%20government%20finance/LC_Spe nding_Review01d.pdf [Accessed 15 October 2021].

Lowenthal, D. (1991) 'British national identity and the English landscape', *Rural History*, 2(2): 205–30.

Lowndes, V. and Gardner, A. (2016) 'Local governance under the Conservatives: super-austerity, devolution and the "smarter state"', *Local Government Studies*, 42(3): 357–75.

LUFP (London Urban Forest Partnership) (2020) London Urban Forest Plan. Available from: https://www.london.gov.uk/sites/default/files/lond onurbanforestplan_final.pdf [Accessed 11 November 2021].

Mace, A. (2018) 'The Metropolitan Green Belt, changing an institution', *Progress in Planning*, 121: 1–28.

Malchow, H.L. (1985) 'Public gardens and social action in late Victorian London', *Victorian Studies*, 29(1): 97–124.

Massini, P. and Smith, H. (2018) *PERFECT Expert Paper 2: Planning for Green Infrastructure – the Green Space Factor and Learning from Europe*. Available from: https://www.interregeurope.eu/fileadmin/user_upload/tx_tevproje cts/library/file_1551105810.pdf [Accessed 2 February 2022].

Mathers, A., Dempsey, N. and Molin, J.F. (2015) 'Place-keeping in action: evaluating the capacity of green space partnerships in England', *Landscape and Urban Planning*, 139: 126–36.

Mathey, J., Rößler, S., Lehmann, I. and Bräuer, A. (2011) 'Urban green spaces: potentials and constraints for urban adaptation to climate change', in K. Otto-Zimmermann (ed) *Resilient Cities: Cities and Adaptation to Climate Change – Proceedings of the Global Forum 2010*, Dordrecht: Springer, pp 479–85.

Matsler, A.M., Meerow, S., Mell, I.C. and Pavao-Zuckerman, M.A. (2021) 'A "green" chameleon: exploring the many disciplinary definitions, goals, and forms of "green infrastructure"', *Landscape and Urban Planning*, 214: art 104145, https://doi.org/10.1016/j.landurbplan.2021.104145.

Matthews, T., Lo, A.Y. and Byrne, J.A. (2015) 'Reconceptualizing green infrastructure for climate change adaptation: barriers to adoption and drivers for uptake by spatial planners', *Landscape and Urban Planning*, 138: 155–63.

McFarlane, C. and Rutherford, J. (2008) 'Political infrastructures: governing and experiencing the fabric of the city', *International Journal of Urban and Regional Research*, 32(2): 363–74.

McMahon, E.T. (2000) 'Green infrastructure', *Planning Commissioners Journal*, 37: 4–7.

Meerow, S. (2020) 'The politics of multifunctional green infrastructure planning in New York City', *Cities*, 100: art 102621. Available from: https://doi.org/10.1016/j.cities.2020.102621 [Accessed 20 November 2022].

Meerow, S. and Newell, J.P. (2017) 'Spatial planning for multifunctional green infrastructure: growing resilience in Detroit', *Landscape and Urban Planning*, 159: 62–75.

Mell, I. (2008) 'Green infrastructure: concepts and planning', *FORUM*, 8: 69–80.

Mell, I. (2015) 'Green infrastructure planning: policy and objectives', in D. Sinnett, N. Smith and S. Burgess (eds) *Handbook on Green Infrastructure: Planning, Design and Implementation*, Cheltenham: Edward Elgar, pp 105–23.

Mell, I. (2016) *Global Green Infrastructure: Lessons for Successful Policy-Making, Investment and Management*, Abingdon: Routledge.

Mell, I. (2019) *Green Infrastructure Planning: Reintegrating Landscape in Urban Planning*, London: Lund Humphries.

Mell, I. and Clement, S. (2019) 'Progressing green infrastructure planning: understanding its scalar, temporal, geo-spatial and disciplinary evolution', *Impact Assessment and Project Appraisal*, 38(6): 449–63.

Mell, I. and Whitten, M. (2021) 'Access to nature in a post Covid-19 world: opportunities for green infrastructure financing, distribution and equitability in urban planning', *International Journal of Environmental Research and Public Health*, 18(4): art 1527. Available from: https://doi.org/10.3390/ijerph18041527 [Accessed 20 November 2022].

Mell, I., Allin, S., Reimer, M. and Wilker, J. (2017) 'Strategic green infrastructure planning in Germany and the UK: a transnational evaluation of the evolution of urban greening policy and practice', *International Planning Studies*, 22(4): 333–49.

Mischi, J. (2009) 'Englishness and the countryside: how British rural studies address the issue of national identity', in F. Reviron-Piégay (ed) *Englishness Revisited*, Newcastle upon Tyne: Cambridge Scholars, pp 109–24.

Natural England (2020) A Rapid Scoping Review of Health and Wellbeing Evidence for the Framework of Green Infrastructure Standards. Available from: http://publications.naturalengland.org.uk/file/5992890930298880 [Accessed 12 October 2021].

NLHF (National Lottery Heritage Fund) (2016) State of UK Public Parks. Available from: https://www.heritagefund.org.uk/sites/defa ult/files/media/attachments/state_of_uk_public_parks_2016_fi nal_for_web%281%29.pdf [Accessed 19 August 2021].

NPCF (National Park City Foundation) (2019) 'Frequently asked questions'. Available from: https://www.nationalparkcity.london/faq [Accessed 12 February 2022].

ONS (Office for National Statistics) (2012) 2011 census: population and household estimates for England and Wales, March 2011. Available from: www.ons.gov.uk/ons/dcp171778_270487.pdf [Accessed 30 November 2021].

ONS (Office for National Statistics) (2018) 'Subnational population projections for England: 2018-based'. Available from: https://www.ons. gov.uk/peoplepopulationandcommunity/populationandmigration/popula tionprojections/bulletins/subnationalpopulationprojectionsforengland/ 2018based [accessed 25 September 2021].

ONS (Office for National Statistics) (2021) Estimates of the population for the UK, England and Wales, Scotland and Northern Ireland, mid-2020: 2021 local authority boundaries. Available from: https://www.ons. gov.uk/file?uri=/peoplepopulationandcommunity/populationandmigrat ion/populationestimates/datasets/populationestimatesforukenglandandw alesscotlandandnorthernireland/mid2020/ukpopestimatesmid2020on20 21geography.xls [Accessed 28 June 2021].

Pendlebury, J. (1997) 'The statutory protection of historic parks and gardens: an exploration and analysis of "structure", "decoration" and "character"', *Journal of Urban Design*, 2(3): 241–58.

Plantlife (2022) 'No Mow May'. Available from: https://www.plantlife. org.uk/uk/discover-wild-plants-nature/no-mow-may [Accessed 15 February 2022].

Rall, E., Hansen, R. and Pauleit, S. (2019) 'The added value of public participation GIS (PPGIS) for urban green infrastructure planning', *Urban Forestry & Urban Greening*, 40: 264–74.

Reeder, D. (2006a) 'London and green space, 1850–2000: an introduction', in P. Clark (ed) *The European City and Green Space: London, Stockholm, Helsinki and St Petersburg, 1850–2000*, Aldershot: Ashgate, pp 54–64.

Reeder, D. (2006b) 'The social construction of green space in London prior to the Second World War', in P. Clark (ed) *The European City and Green Space: London, Stockholm, Helsinki and St Petersburg, 1850–2000*, Aldershot: Ashgate, pp 65–91.

Rewilding Britain (2022) 'Defining rewilding'. Available from: https:// www.rewildingbritain.org.uk/explore-rewilding/what-is-rewilding/defin ing-rewilding [Accessed 15 February 2022].

Roe, M. and Mell, I. (2013) 'Negotiating value and priorities: evaluating the demands of green infrastructure development', *Journal of Environmental Planning and Management*, 56(5): 650–73.

Rosenberg, E. (1996) 'Public works and public space: Rethinking the urban park', *Journal of Architectural Education*, 50(2): 89–103.

Scanlon, K., Whitehead, C. and Blanc, F. (2018) *A Sustainable Increase in London's Housing Supply?* London: London School of Economics and Political Science. Available from: https://www.lse.ac.uk/geography-and-environment/research/lse-london/documents/Reports/REPORT-LSE-KEI-digital.pdf [Accessed 25 September 2021].

Scott, A. and Hislop, M. (2019) 'What does good GI policy look like?', *Town & Country Planning*, 88(5): 177–84.

Seiwert, A. and Rößler, S. (2020) 'Understanding the term *green infrastructure*: origins, rationales, semantic content and purposes as well as its relevance for application in spatial planning', *Land Use Policy*, 97: art 104785. Available from: https://doi.org/10.1016/j.landusepol.2020.104785 [Accessed 20 November 2022].

Thomas, K. and Littlewood, S. (2010) 'From green belts to green infrastructure? The evolution of a new concept in the emerging soft governance of spatial strategies', *Planning Practice & Research*, 25(2): 203–22.

Tower Hamlets Council (2011) *An Open Spaces Strategy for the London Borough of Tower Hamlets, 2006–2016, Mid-point Update*. Available from: http://www.queenelizabetholympicpark.co.uk/-/media/lldc/local-plan/local-plan-examination-documents/other-strategy-papers/s17-tower-hamlets-open-space-strategy-mid-point-update.ashx?la=en [Accessed 8 July 2021].

Travers, T. (2004) *The Politics of London: Governing an Ungovernable City*, Basingstoke: Palgrave Macmillan.

Tzoulas, K., Korpela, K., Venn, S., Yli-Pelkonen, V., Kaźmierczak, A., Niemela, J. and James, P. (2007) 'Promoting ecosystem and human health in urban areas using green infrastructure: a literature review', *Landscape and Urban Planning*, 81(3): 167–78.

Van Herzele, A. and Wiedemann, T. (2003) 'A monitoring tool for the provision of accessible and attractive urban green spaces', *Landscape and Urban Planning*, 63(2): 109–26.

Welch, D. (1991) *The Management of Urban Parks*, Harlow: Longman.

Whitten, M. (2019) 'Blame it on austerity? Examining the impetus behind London's changing green space governance', *People, Place and Policy*, 12(3): 204–24.

Whitten, M. (2020) 'Contesting longstanding conceptualisations of urban green space', in N. Dempsey and J. Dobson, (eds) *Naturally Challenged: Contested Perceptions and Practices in Urban Green Spaces*, Cham: Springer, pp 87–116.

Whitten, M. (2022) 'Planning past parks: overcoming restrictive green space narratives in contemporary compact cities', *Town Planning Review*, 93(5): 469–93.

Whitten, M. (2023) 'Engaging resilience: integrating sociocultural dimensions into green infrastructure planning', in C.G. Sant'Anna, I. Mell and L.B. Schenk (eds) *Planning with Landscape: Green Infrastructure to Build Climate-Adapted Cities*, Springer Nature.

Whitten, M. and Massini, P. (2021) 'How can inequalities in access to green space be addressed in a post-pandemic world? Lessons from London', in R. Van Melik, P. Filion and B. Doucet (eds) *Global Reflections on COVID-19 and Urban Inequalities, Volume 3: Public Space and Mobility*, Bristol: Bristol University Press, pp 87–96.

WHO (World Health Organization) (2017) *Urban Green Spaces: A Brief for Action*, Copenhagen: WHO. Available from: https://apps.who.int/iris/rest/bitstreams/1363607/retrieve [Accessed 22 September 2021].

Wiig, A., Karvonen, A., McFarlane, C. and Rutherford, J. (2022) '*Splintering Urbanism* at 20: mapping trajectories of research on urban infrastructures', *Journal of Urban Technology*, 29(1): 1–11.

Wright, H. (2011) 'Understanding green infrastructure: the development of a contested concept in England', *Local Environment*, 16(10): 1003–19.

8

Global Infrastructure and Urban Futures: London's Transforming Royal Albert Dock

Jonathan Silver and Alan Wiig

Introduction

The Royal Albert Dock in London was transformed – not without controversy – from an abandoned industrial waterfront into a node for Chinese multinational business, creating a hub of 'Silk Road urbanism' in the UK's capital (ABP, 2017). The Royal Docks, inclusive of the Royal Albert Dock, have been a global infrastructure space since the 19th century, first as the maritime 'heart of empire' in imperial London, as a point for the 'import and export of people' and goods (Driver and Gilbert, 1998: 21). This repurposing of a globalized space is an exemplar of the epochal shifts in infrastructure that drive the urbanization process. After shutting in the 1960s due to ports shifting to standardized shipping containers, the Royal Docks sat derelict and as at the 2010s remained a large undeveloped parcel in the centre of London, showing all the hallmarks of urban and economic misalignment and obdurate infrastructure. The attention paid to the prospect of turning long-standing derelict land into a node of Chinese business highlighted the UK's ambitions to reorder trade patterns towards Asia after the post-war decline of North Atlantic, industrial capitalism (Wallerstein, 1979) and more recently the geopolitical disruption of Brexit (Peters, 2018). The Royal Albert Dock may one day transform into a prominent node for global firms, but it still sits alongside working–class neighbourhoods where, 'despite their sometimes spectacular physical impacts (as in London Docklands), [large-scale redevelopment has] had at best only modest success in raising the economic and social well-being of deprived local populations' (Watt, 2013: 103). Consequently, this redevelopment operates within the broader context of the surrounding city, where the infrastructural inheritances from 19th century and earlier define the borough's relationship to the Thames River as well as to the unevenness of economic opportunity more generally. Before we turn to considering the urban dimensions of global infrastructure, some background on China's Belt and Road Initiative in London.

In May 2017, a new cargo land-route opened between China and the UK when a train travelled 7,456 miles from Yiwu City, Zhejiang Province to Barking Rail Terminal, East London (Kentish, 2017), about six kilometres (four miles) north of the Royal Albert Dock. This was a small if distinguishable part of the Chinese-led Belt and Road Initiative (hereafter BRI), a reimaging of the Silk Road trade routes for the 21st century with the aim of reshaping the world economy (Summers, 2016; Sidaway and Woon, 2017) and, in so doing, transforming global urban geographies. Given the operations of the new cargo route and the transforming Royal Albert Dock it is evident that the BRI is now attempting to restructure urban space thousands of miles away from China (see Apostolopoulou, 2021; Zheng et al, 2021). The arrival in western Europe of a transcontinental transport infrastructure from the 'East' makes clear the technological and territorial reordering of global capitalism's connections, relations and circulations of people, goods and capital (Roberts, 2011). Deploying this rail line required significant cooperation on spatial, technological and regulatory planning across nine nation states including China, Kazakhstan and Poland. Infrastructurally, it also demanded compatible train track gauges and track gauge switching, synchronization of monitoring systems, border controls and new visa regimes, regularized packaging, new lifting technologies and new workforce organization (Chen, 2018). All this in turn emphasizes the imperative to standardize economic circulations across multiple heterogenous infrastructure systems, operations and globalized urban spaces. This process of deploying global infrastructure speaks to the contradictory, often competing logics of capitalist standardization (Easterling, 2014; Schindler and Marvin, 2018) that inherently underpin cities and the connections between them in the world economy.

Global infrastructure is those systems, networks and spaces that facilitate the daily operations of multinational capitalism, an economic form that is organized through offices, warehouses and other operational nodes within cities and urban regions (Sassen, 2011). This category of infrastructure sits alongside, and indeed often requires connection to municipal utilities and local transport networks but is centred on international airports (Kasarda and Lindsay, 2011), ports and logistics clusters (Cowen, 2014; Carse and Lewis, 2017), rail and road transportation corridors, data centres and telecommunications (Pickren, 2018), to fuel pipelines and energy transmission systems (Bouzarovski et al, 2015). Assembled together, global infrastructure standardizes and prioritizes connections to the far-away and is the vessels through which capitalist circulations of people, goods and information enter into and reconfigure cities. In doing so they play a prominent role in reinforcing or enabling the splintered, inequitable dynamics that shape the urban experience (Graham and Marvin, 2001). Of course, this vision of the city as a static, predetermined object of economic exchange ignores the significant geographical differentiation inherent in a city's infrastructural legacy, built and natural environment, and lived experience, all of which interferes with the ambitions to standardize and connect.

Identifying investment in global infrastructure has become crucial for understanding how contemporary capitalism attempts to accumulate profit out of social and economic uncertainty and upheaval. A report by CounterBalance, a European coalition of NGOs that draws attention to public finance of megaprojects, has documented hundreds of global infrastructure projects, and whether in planning, under construction or in use, these projects are indicative of 'an age of what might be termed extreme infrastructure' (Hilyard and Sol, 2017: 1). Private, multinational professional services firms like KPMG popularize global infrastructure for its capacity to navigate 'disruption, confusion and uncertainty' with the ability to then address some of the most significant challenges of the 21st century (KPMG, 2018: 2, 19). In turn, urban researchers have examined the new geographies of this global infrastructure. Kanai and Schindler (2018: 303) note the 'planetary proliferation of cross-border infrastructure networks being built in the context of multipolar, competitive capitalist globalization'. As the Global South continues its rapid urbanization, and as cities in the Global North go about repurposing deindustrialized areas' obdurate, sometimes shattered infrastructures, examining how, where and for whom global infrastructure deploys between, across and within cities is analytically necessary to comprehend urban futures.

With this chapter, we set out four generative concepts – speculation, delineation, alignment, pivoting – to convey the stages through which global infrastructure deployment proceeds, incorporating but also exceeding standardization. After presenting these concepts, we discuss the redevelopment of London's Royal Albert Dock by a Chinese real estate concern to show, first, the ways in which global infrastructure is upending historical trade and power relations through new configurations, operations and investments and, second, to highlight the ways global infrastructure unfolds in variegated and contingent ways across urban space, producing particular, capitalist urban futures and consequently limiting the possibility of alternate visions for the city to take hold.

An urban perspective on global infrastructure

Debates in urban studies have centred on the linkages between economic globalization and urbanization (Brenner and Schmidt, 2015; McNeill, 2017).

The potential of using infrastructure to understand these joined processes is significant and forms a growing body of literature (Schindler and Kanai, 2021). Transcontinental and/or ocean-going infrastructure first standardized the modern world economy for North Atlantic capitalism (Williams, 1993; Linebaugh and Rediker, 2013; Beckert, 2015). In a global era of uncertainty, 'multipolarity' and 'new world (dis)order' (Roberts, 2011), or even the emergence of a 'New Cold War' between China and the US (Schindler et al, 2022), global infrastructure is the material mechanism for cities to maintain existing ties or forge new political-economic relations. While much of this scholarly critique (and even this chapter) highlight China's BRI as a counter-hegemonic geography of US-dominated global capitalism (Chen, 2018; Martin et al, 2018), global infrastructure more generally reorders the technologies and territories of the capitalist world system, ushering in diverse, potentially unanticipated futures and pointing away from the anchor of the North Atlantic's economies. New geographies are forged out of these processes spanning, for instance, the Indian Ocean between east Africa and south Asia in which the colonial metropole no longer figures as a primary interloper.

Standardization relies on technological, territorial and jurisdictional control, which in turn is managed through procedures and regulations determined by global governance regimes originating in Europe or North America, such as the International Organization for Standardization (ISO) (Barry, 2006; compare Easterling, 2014). As argued by Timmermans and Epstein (2010: 82), these standards extend 'the infrastructural power of the modern state: its capacity, for good or ill, to penetrate its territories and co-ordinate social life'. This process of making goods, information and business practices, and the built environment consistent across diverse locations is not separate from urbanization.

Recognizing standardization as an urban process enables scholars to ground the political economy of global capitalism in space and place. Whether via the extraction of oil or the provision of electricity, the logic of standardization facilitates capitalist operations including those that reorder or utterly transform urban space (Brewster, 2017; Danyluk, 2018). Standardization requires what Schindler and Marvin (2018: 299) term a 'regime of urban control that rests on an epistemology that understands cities as a multitude of people and things with comprehensible and instrumental relationships that can be known and mapped'. This process of control in turn produces urban spaces where 'differences between technical practices, procedures or forms have been reduced, or common standards have been established' (Barry 2006: 239). This logic of standardized control is facilitated through the 'centres of calculation' (McNeill 2017: 97–123): the nodes within cities that command and control global capitalism (Sassen, 2011), where global infrastructure's integration into urban space is foundational to the space's economic utility. For instance, this process is evident in the direct, high-speed transport linkage between an international airport and a financial district such as those provided between London's Heathrow Airport and the city centre by an express train line that does not serve adjacent neighbourhoods.

Standardization's logic is to find agreement between multiple and otherwise different networks, configurations and circulations of infrastructure (Timmermans and Epstein, 2010), and without standardization, the 'vast, complex, and dynamic infrastructures that support modern societies and economies' would not unite (Carse and Lewis, 2017: 13). Infrastructural standardization includes the plans, codes, rules and regulations cultivating the growth of cities in the Global South (Datta and Shaban, 2016), extending into the 'fantasies' of smart city districts (Watson, 2014; compare De Boeck, 2011; Datta, 2015), in addition to the redevelopment of deindustrialized areas within cities of the Global North, revitalizing their usefulness to a new era of capitalist enterprise (Wiig, 2016). Understanding the urbanization of global infrastructure thus requires identifying the commonalities found across diverse technologies, patterns of service, and megaprojects, but also recognizing the multiple temporalities, rhythms and spatialities of city life that always inherently intersect, intercede and weave into capitalist standardization itself.

Conceptualizations of the infrastructure of capitalist globalization have primarily identified two standardized forms: the node and the corridor. These structures bring order to patterns of circulation and flow, integrating a city's economy into wider networks of international trade (Easterling, 2014; Schindler and Marvin, 2018). However, this chapter argues that focusing on the standardization itself does not account for the dynamic, unstable and often contested geographies associated with infrastructural deployment within and beyond any individual city's boundaries. The standardization of economic or logistical connections for some cities can result in disconnection and political marginalization for others. We utilize concepts emanating out of urban and infrastructure studies centred on cities of the Global South to recognize there are tools that consider the shifting, contested and unpredictable geographies of everyday, informal urbanization (Simone, 2004, 2016; compare Rao, 2014; McFarlane and Silver, 2017) and its attendant disruption and interruption of networked utilities (Graham, 2010). Next, we turn to discussion of these standardized forms of urbanization.

Corridor and node: the standardized forms of urbanization

Corridors move people, goods and information (Harvey and Knox, 2015), and nodes concentrate and organize what corridors circulate. Corridors include trade, transportation and logistics networks (Cowen, 2014), as well as telecommunications cabling and energy pipelines (Bouzarovski et al, 2015). Air and sea corridors are expressed through their land-based nodal points: airports and oceanic ports (Neilson et al, 2018). Worldwide, urbanization proceeds alongside corridors and within or adjacent to nodes, replicating standardized built forms of housing, work and education, consumption and cultural exchange, and recreation (Harris, 2013; Easterling, 2014). In 2017, the Global Infrastructure Connectivity Initiative, a project of the G20, identified 30 newly established or in-planning cross-border trade and transport corridors (not including energy systems) on or between six continents (GICA, 2017). Hence, the infrastructural corridor is also understood as the spatial, forward-looking vision of cities, nation states and regional trading blocs to integrate into specific accumulation regimes, historical conditions and geographical contexts.

Nodes bring infrastructure networks together, joining logistics and distribution hubs with advanced business services in central business districts and peripheral, back-office locations. Nodes are the material form of a 'technological zone' (Barry, 2006) that translates between disparate transnational flows, bringing these flows together in specific spaces. Without global connection, nodes cannot operate (Chalfin, 2010). They rely on world-spanning networks as well as premium technological services that typically exclude and thus fragment the surrounding urban spaces (Graham and Marvin, 2001). Cities' and nation states' ambitions for cultivating or expanding ties into global capitalism have often led to the state ceding control of the planning, development and governance of these nodes to the corporations locating within, regardless of the anti-democratic implications of this turnover (Wiig, 2019; Apostolopoulou, 2021). Corridors and nodes embody global capitalism's desire for 'frictionless' circulations (Enright, 2016) and, as we will discuss later with regard to London, despite the emphasis within the literature on standardization, from an urban perspective these spaces must be understood as much through what is absent, excluded and outside, as by what is included in the standardization (Silver, 2021).

Deploying global infrastructure often reinforces the fragmentation of a city into spaces for a global elite and local 'others' through the rollout of premium networks privileging capitalist profits over local needs (Coutard, 2002). The standardized technologies directly involved in economic exchange within and between corridor and node also incorporate widespread securitization and privatization of urban space beyond the generic area. Indeed, maintaining 'frictionless' trade requires controlling the city at large. In Southern megacities such as Karachi, the node becomes an ordered and stable enclave, apart from the perceived danger and violence of the 'other' city (Kaker, 2014: 93). In declining, formerly industrial Northern cities such Camden, New Jersey, central neighbourhoods next to the globalized node are deemed hostile and unsafe, requiring algorithmic surveillance and militaristic policing (Wiig,

2018). The urban resident deemed surplus to the economy is excluded from the node to secure the space for global capitalism (Zeiderman, 2016).

Deploying global infrastructure: speculation, delineation, alignment and pivoting

Here we offer a mode of analysis for understanding the deployment of global infrastructure as uneven and contingent amid a transforming global economy. We turn to strands of infrastructure studies scholarship that look at infrastructure-as-process, recognizing Easterling's point that '[s]ome of the most radical changes to the globalizing world are being written, not in the language of law and diplomacy, but in these spatial, infrastructural technologies' (Easterling, 2014: 15). Considering infrastructure both as noun and verb (as in the title of this book) recognizes the active and transformative agency of infrastructure to drive urban change. This framing emphasizes infrastructural urbanization as open-ended and broader than the logic of standardization alone. We theorize global infrastructure deployment across urban space as an ongoing process of spatial and temporal transformation involving four stages: (1) speculation, (2) delineation, (3) alignment and (4) pivoting.

While the stages of deployment can proceed non-linearly, where an existing project is adapted to new or perceived opportunities, speculation typically occurs first and underscores how urban, national and international intermediaries imagine that economic growth, technology and cities are brought together through global infrastructure. National, regional and local states propose multiple and often competing infrastructure visions and plans with the goal of engineering urban space for global capitalism. These are developed as spatial strategies to withstand geopolitical turbulence and shift towards new trade routes and potential new markets and sources of investment (like the Yiwu City–London train route *could* offer for both the UK, China and points in between). Speculation then becomes a way for cities to attempt to manoeuvre through urban uncertainty (Zeiderman et al, 2015). As Rao (2014: 39-58) asserts: 'infrastructure becomes visible as a reformulation that feeds back specific ideas about the future into an urban imaginary' although the assumption as to whose future is included in this imaginary is often left unsaid. Speculation can involve multiple, competing visions of high-tech, globally integrated urban futures (Watson, 2014; Datta, 2015), but the importance of the node and corridor (whether these specific terms are employed or not) remain unchallenged.

Efforts to ensure particular urban futures through deployment belie the inherently risky nature of investment in nodes and corridors. Urban histories show how geopolitical turbulence and technological innovation have led to economic and associated infrastructural collapse, most visibly in industrial cities (Hall, 2002), such as through the closure of London's Royal Docks due to the containerization of oceanic trade (Campling and Colás, 2021). Speculation focuses analysis on the ways in which infrastructure constructs urban futures as a negotiation and navigation through the shifting conditions of global capitalism, but also of everyday life for residents who may or may not be included in these visions.

Delineation calls attention to the process of making legible the speculative visions of global infrastructure deployment. By inscribing global infrastructure into material form, a city reorders itself to facilitate connection into established or nascent capitalist circulations and operations. Delineation expresses the methods through which particular sites and populations become integrated into or isolated from global capitalism through various forms of planning, zoning and urban transformation. The goal of delineation is to remake of urban space so multinational firms and industries can synchronize inputs and outputs. This city transforms itself around global infrastructure, prioritizing these spaces over those proverbially or literally left outside, proximate but disconnected from global capitalism and occupying a divergent city. Even so, to delineate space into global infrastructure requires engaging with the informal spaces and obdurate uses of the city. Delineation as a process remains tentative and at risk of demolition, collapse or malfunction (Simone, 2004, 2016). The term highlights the spatial division that infrastructural deployment initiates. The space outside or apart from the delineation offers a counter-vision of an urban future, one separate from the standardization of global capitalism. Much like the other three stages of deployment, delineation requires constant negotiation and reworking the plan as attempts to securitize and standardize are reliant on external actors, like foreign corporations or trade agreements that can falter regardless of the ambition of any one city to connect to and profit from global capitalism.

Alignment emphasizes the stage of deployment where different networked technologies, buildings and operational procedures are assembled alongside the communicative, regulatory and financial components of a node in order to position the entire space towards global capitalism. This stage highlights the multiplicity of processes required to 'fit' urban spaces into the standardization that the world economy requires. Alignment recognizes the sometimes-contradictory methods required to integrate discrete infrastructural components into the collective, logical and standardized 'whole' that pivots the city into new economic opportunities. This stage of deployment encapsulates the counter-notion, to misalign. As Simone (2012) warns, 'there are no predetermined reasons why things or events should necessarily connect'. No matter how well planned out, it is always possible that projected trade relations fail and that desired futures do not materialize. Whether because of diplomatic breakdown, a global pandemic, the climate crisis, the rise of new industrial clusters, or technological advances like automation and robotics, global infrastructure investments can fail to connect with the desired profitable economic circulations, a point we will return to later with regard to the ultimate failure of the Royal Albert Dock's Chinese redevelopment.

Pivoting describes the combinatory stage of deployment, where multiple alignments converge to transition or shift the fundamental relations between a city and global capitalism. Pivoting recognizes the ways infrastructure networks facilitate global trade and capitalist urbanization, both in the past as well as in the current era's geopolitical, ecological and viral turbulence. As Gupta (2015) argues, 'infrastructures are often long-term investments. They tell us a great deal about aspirations, anticipations, and imaginations of the future, both for cities and nations'. The variegated deployment of global infrastructure emphasizes that many cities hold ambitions to establish new economic ties through transforming infrastructurally mediated, transnational relationships. And yet, pivoting may not always succeed. Just as localized, municipal services can remain disconnected, global infrastructure networks may also remain incomplete, as Prince Guma expands on in his Afterword (see also Guma, 2020). Nation states, regions and cities may miscalculate or face contestation and conflict from the deployment of global infrastructure, leaving them on the periphery of new power, circulation and exchange. Conceptually, pivoting analyses global infrastructure in the process of making, maintenance and of repair; a similar process as those describes in the chapter by Bigger and Millington, as well as that by Sheller. It does so by locating cities, nation states, and their joined economic desires into the layers of connectivity (or disconnection) that tie nodes and corridors together over international borders and oceans.

These four concepts draw attention to the variegated and diverse urban futures being forged through the deployment of global infrastructure. This approach recognizes the standardization of space that occurs but also emphasizes the fragile and contingent ways global infrastructure materializes. In so doing, we centre the (re)making of various technologies, networks and systems as they shift urban and national government policy efforts and planning agendas, particularly those focused on trade, connection and financial circulation.

Silk Road urbanism through global infrastructure

China's strategic rollout of the BRI demonstrates how the rapid, ongoing transformation of the world economy is leaving cities to navigate uncertain futures as the North Atlantic hegemony of global capitalism is challenged. What constitutes worthy investment for the BRI is indicative of China's aspirations to become dominant in the technologies of global capitalism

(Sidaway and Woon, 2017) via joining into overseas financial markets (Töpfer and Hall, 2018), infrastructure investment (Schulhof et al, 2021) and new types of infrastructural standardization (Hui and Cargill, 2017). China's influence on infrastructure-led development is felt around the world, whether in major finance and banking centres like London, peripheral but ancient cities like Athens or postcolonial regional hubs like Colombo (Apostolopoulou, 2021). For example, as Apostolopoulou notes, Athens's port may sit at the far edge of Mediterranean Europe, but it is the 'head of the dragon' for Chinese maritime trade through the Suez Canal (Apostolopoulou, 2021: 9). This spatial reordering is significant as formerly disparate cities converge into new transnational points for business exchange and logistical circulation. Chinese futures envision a global order altered around speculative spatial demarcations where infrastructures are deployed to 'make territory' (Bouzarovski et al, 2015: 217). These corridors and nodes imprint new purpose onto established regions and construct new cities alongside new trade routes, and in combination these investments highlight the infrastructural power behind narratives of 'Rise of China' or the 'Asian Century' (Walton and Kavalski, 2016).

Global infrastructure is what propels the territorial integration of cities and nation states with China: the BRI's economic vision rests on two distinct if related projects. The 'New Silk Road' (Fallon, 2015; Sidaway and Woon, 2017) is the transcontinental unification of Central Asian, African and European economies into the Chinese territory via six recently assembled rail and road corridors (Summers, 2016; Eder, 2018; Chen, 2021). Then, the 21st Century Maritime Silk Road targets 'the maritime regions of Southeast Asia, South Asia, the Middle East, East Africa, and the Mediterranean' (Arase 2015: 24), through the construction or expansion of ports. Adjacent to these developments are amplified urbanization processes (Lu et al, 2017; Bunnell, 2021; Zheng et al, 2021) in addition to speculation on the part of both cities and their respective nations to China's infrastructural deployment (Barisitz and Radzyner, 2017). China has offered an 'infrastructure-led approach to [an alternative] globalization' that is primarily aimed at the Global South (Chen, 2018: 36), but also stretches into the Global North such as with the Yiwu City–London train route and the redevelopment of the Royal Albert Dock. With regard to urban and infrastructural futures, pivoting to China is largely a variation on the capitalist theme: drawing in Chinese investment and solidifying strategic corporate partnerships that look beyond Europe and North America. While the next section is focused on London, we want to stress two points: that this process of deployment is occurring throughout cities around the world, and to highlight the need to better interrogate the meeting of the extraordinary infrastructural power of the BRI with particular combinations of urban conditions, histories and relations.

The redevelopment of London's Royal Albert Dock

East London's Thames River waterfront was for centuries a place of capitalist exchange, commodity circulation and labour, of the loading and unloading of maritime goods transported between colonial periphery and the metropole (Linebaugh, 2006). The entire area, including the enclosed waterway of the Royal Docks built from the 1800s onwards, suffered through decades of post-industrial and postcolonial abandonment and decline through the latter half of the 20th century, similar to other cities across the Global North. Beginning in the 1980s, the waterfront was reimagined as multinational corporate nodes, especially financial enterprise (Hall, 2002). As jobs and employment opportunity shifted to the information, creative and finance sectors (Massey, 2007), the diverse but poor neighbourhoods that border the waterfront remain proximate to but largely unable to access the social and economic opportunities found in these nodes of global capitalism themselves (Watt, 2013). Over the first two decades of this century, the disinvested districts of East London have sat alongside gentrification, global finance, remnant sites of the 2012 Olympics, and transit-oriented, shopping centre retail. The waterfront itself has seen attempts at spatial regeneration since the 1970s (Brill, 2018) that have flowed east from the City of London, first into Docklands–Canary Wharf and more recently toward the Royal Docks and their surrounding borough of Newham. This recent redevelopment of the Royal Albert Dock into a node of the BRI can help illustrate how variegated and contingent the deployment of global infrastructure can be.

Plans for the Royal Albert Dock's revitalization were announced by then-London mayor, Boris Johnson in 2013, four years before the opening of the Yiwu City–London rail route. In this period, China was establishing a presence in banking and overseas financial markets including those in the City of London as well as Canary Wharf (Töpfer and Hall, 2018). While the contract to redevelop the Dock was signed prior to the 2016 vote to separate from the EU, the post-Brexit imperative to attract non-European businesses to the UK intensified. At the time, the UK and China were celebrating a 'Golden Era' for the two countries economic relations (see for instance Lidington, 2018). Part of solidifying these UK–China relations occurred through awarding the contract to develop the site to Advanced Business Parks (ABP), a China-based developer who had never worked in the UK (Pickford and Hammond, 2013a). See Figure 8.1 for a preconstruction photograph of the node.

At the project unveiling, the Royal Albert Dock was envisioned to become a 3.5 million square foot 'Asian Business Port' for Asian businesses to expand into the UK and European markets (Pickford and Hammond, 2013a, 2013b). Upon projected completion in the mid-2020s, this speculative plan intended to transform an unused, publicly owned post-industrial site into a

Figure 8.1: The site that would become the Royal Albert Dock, 2017

Note: Construction had not yet started, and the waterfront path was closed to the public. Written on the building site fencing is text that celebrates the potential of the location to become 'London's next business district', 'Breathing life in to a world famous dock' and operating 'At the heart of London's future'.

Source: Alan Wiig

standardized, globalized node with the potential to increase London's share of Asian financial firms. This vision privileged the far over the near to turn what was empty docklands for the London metropole into a space where Chinese enterprise could interface with London, close to London City Airport's business class flights to Europe, and a 20-minute journey on light rail to the cluster of banks and financial firms in Docklands–Canary Wharf. Hyperbolic language in the plan promoted the intent 'to run [the zone] as a 24-hour mini-city to accommodate the needs of Asian businesses focused on Beijing time, which is eight hours ahead of London' (Pickford and Hammond, 2013a), a notable temporal break of clock time away from Greenwich Mean Time. While this proposal was never put into practice, the idea that this would be of value for potential tenants emphasizes the intentional, temporal separation of the node from the surrounding neighbourhoods.

ABP's selection as developer was unexpected. The 2011 statement of invitation for development proposals did not name them as a potential bidder (Madison Brook, 2011). The UK's Channel 4 television news found a significant lack of transparency tending towards what opposition politicians criticized as low-level corruption in the handling of the bidding process (Crick, 2014). This investigation uncovered that, in 2010–11, no less than £162,000 in donations to Johnson's Conservative political party originated from the Anglo-Chinese wife of a Conservative politician with ties to ABP's leader (Crick, 2014). Regardless of these revelations, ABP's bid for the site was approved. This lack of transparency and accountability continued at the local level. With ABP's design partners and contractors, Newham Borough Council – whose offices sit next to the site – began planning the redevelopment largely without soliciting community input (Kennard, 2016), even though there was a long history of community engagement around revitalizing East London's waterfront, including a comprehensive plan drafted in 1988 (Brownill, 1988). The lack of community involvement in land-use planning around the delineation of large-scale redevelopment is reflective of what Apostolopoulou terms 'authoritarian neoliberal urbanism' (2021: 831) and is common in these sorts of projects. This redevelopment process highlights how global infrastructure, even in countries with democratic, elected governments like the UK, operate for the most part outside local oversight. In London and elsewhere, the formation of public–private partnerships to oversee capitalist development reinforce democratic deficits as they inevitably favour profit for industry over any other metric of success, such as local job creation (see Wiig, 2019 for further analysis of this phenomenon).

Aligning the Royal Albert Dock's 35 acres with the BRI entailed turning over control of one of the largest intact land parcels in central London to a Chinese real estate firm with no previous experience in the UK. The Dock's future rested on the delineation of the area into a privileged zone with priority connection achieved through convenient location, transportation linkages, high-quality office spaces and culturally relevant amenities for workers. Much of what makes the Dock attractive as a globalized node contributed to its fragmentation from Newham's surrounding residential neighbourhoods. When jobs on the working waterfront disappeared, the rationale for spatially integrating the area into the community diminished. Sandwiching a Docklands Light Rail transit line, the Royal Albert Way's four lanes of traffic separate the communities of Newham from the Dock, and little has been done to materially or symbolically join the node to the borough itself. Public open space is lacking as the borough does not have a large urban park to promote recreation, health, nor everyday well-being (Dines et al, 2006: 5). At 37 per cent of the population, Newham faces the second-highest poverty levels in London (Tison et al, 2017). Unemployment is high, and among those with jobs, 32 per cent of workers are employed in low-paying ones (Tison et al, 2017). Even so, like the entirety of Greater London, housing costs are among the highest in the UK and the borough has the greatest incidence of homelessness in the city. These sorts of statistics draw attention to the contrast between global infrastructure nodes and the surrounding city, and how the logic of capitalist standardization produces urban spaces that are better integrated into transnational circulations than the needs of those city residents in the vicinity.

This appraisal is not meant to insinuate that the Dock's redevelopment inherently foreclosed opportunities for the local community. Newham provided oversight of the redevelopment, and the government encouraged ABP to hire workers from nearby (ABP, 2017: 4). Even so, the project was approved without making a distinct effort to involve residents, community groups and service sector organizations in planning the design and use of the district. Without insisting on accountable provisions for local economic development or workforce education, Newham and London's respective levels of government gave precedence to unsecured, potential investment from afar over addressing known needs. To this critique, those working in Newham's government offices, which incidentally bordered the Dock redevelopment, would argue that the very fact that investment flowed into the borough reflects positive transformation and a net increase in opportunities for the greater area. However, and echoing the issues facing large-scale redevelopments since the 1980s (Swyngedouw et al, 2002) this neoliberal logic rests on assumptions for future economic growth that may or may not occur given the ongoing turbulence of the world economy.

The transformation of vacant waterfront into the Royal Albert Dock further emphasized a vision for the city that is privatized, securitized and designed to attract speculative business opportunity over meeting known community needs like affordable housing (Minton, 2017; see also Shenker, 2015). While this political process proceeded similarly to the entrepreneurial planning (Hall, 2002) that led to the corporate success of Docklands–Canary Wharf in the 1980s and 1990s, 21st-century London is a vastly different city than it was in that era of post-industrial decline and economic uncertainty. Ultimately, in what Atkinson (2020) terms Alpha City London, the Dock intended to fulfil ambitions to remain at the top of the global hierarchy by strategically tying this large-scale urban redevelopment into China's vision for the world economy.

The £1.7 billion first stage of building and utilities construction was completed in 2018 and funded by four Chinese banks and one Thai development fund (Parker et al, 2016). Figure 8.2 shows the finished, but still vacant, construction as at September 2019. This use of international financing is notable in that it reflects the transnational nature of global infrastructure financing. This initial set of five buildings consisted of 21 commercial units, approximately 700,000 square feet of office space in total. The node's master plan called for '3.7 million square feet of high-quality work, retail and leisure space, including 2.5 million square feet of offices' intended to cultivate 'a rich mix of both Asian and indigenous businesses to develop and thrive' (Farrells, 2019); however, the full buildout was never completed. The node's design referenced the historic industrial waterfront's warehouses, with five storey, box-like volumes of tan brick and mirrored windows grouped close together with narrow, alley-like pavements closed

Figure 8.2: Looking towards London's Docklands–Canary Wharf from the Royal Albert Dock, 2019

Source: Alan Wiig

to traffic, and most parking clustered on the perimeter. Ground-floor units were intended for cafes and shopping for workers and passers-by, with offices on the upper floors and no residential lodging nor hotels.

After completion of the initial office buildings, ABP saw little success in securing tenants. Initial statements from 2013 noted ten Chinese firms had pledged to take office space (HM Government, 2013), but absent those companies, ABP promoted the Dock as a 'high-tech hub' (Royal Docks, 2019). The first occupant was announced in December 2019, and instead of an Asian financial institution, it was the UK offices of Advantech, a Taiwanese Internet-of-Things firm (Royal Docks, 2019). Over this same period, the 'Golden Era' of China–UK geopolitical relations faded due to the UK's 2020 prohibition of 5G cellular infrastructure from the Chinese telecommunications firm Huawei, as well as support of Hong Kong's protests over Chinese rule in 2021. The economic uncertainty arising out of the COVID-19 public health pandemic and its resulting restrictions on in-country and international travel as well as the complications this has created for multinational businesses also affected the Royal Albert Dock's ability to secure tenants (Ford and Hughes, 2020).

In summer 2022, the Greater London Authority removed the developer for not meeting the schedule for completion of construction. Existing buildings sat empty, a £99 million loan was unpaid, plans for the construction of further buildings remained on hold, the accounting firm Deloitte was overseeing receivership of the developer and the entire node was put up for sale (Ungoed-Thomas, 2022; Wainwright, 2022). The global ambitions for the Royal Albert Dock were reduced to the mundane reality of commercial real estate vacancy and unpaid bills. Under new ownership, the Dock could ostensibly attract tenants in the coming years and achieve a degree of economic success. However, the initial plan for a full buildout by the middle 2020s will not be met.

What is clear regarding London's future is that plans involving global infrastructure can fall through, that the jobs for nearby residents may not materialize, perhaps other than as security guards for the project. Recognizing the failure of the project to revitalize the area, a member of the London Assembly representing east London said, 'This was meant to be a jewel in the crown for east London, and it's now a ghost town' (quoted in Ungoed-Thomas, 2022). ABP and its Chinese partners invested £300 million, but for further development to move forward required approval from the Chinese government itself (Sidders, 2020), which was not forthcoming. Recognizing the economic uncertainty facing London due to Brexit, the unevenness of recovery from the COVID-19 pandemic, and the continuing elevation of the city into an elite, exclusive space (Atkinson, 2020), the Royal Albert Dock appears to be an example of infrastructural misalignment. Ultimately, the urbanization of global infrastructure, in the form of the Royal Albert Dock, was a Chinese decision, out of the hands of those in London. No matter the ambitions described in announcing the project, the node has so far sat disconnected from both local and international markets.

Conclusion

Twenty-first century capitalist urban futures rely on global infrastructure's connective potential. The rapid increase in global infrastructure projects is an indication of the importance of techno-territorial reconfiguration as a calculated attempt to chart unsettled urban futures, made even more uncertain by the ongoing climate emergency and COVID-19 public health crisis. In this chapter, we focused on the world-spanning ambitions of China and its BRI as it arrived in London, a long-standing centre of economic and political power. We demonstrated the ways these deployments of global infrastructure transformed – or failed to transform – the Royal Albert Dock in contingent and uneven ways. To better understand this transformation in relation to urban futures, we synthesized disparate scholarly debates attendant to the rise of global infrastructure as urbanization within and beyond individual cities. Infrastructural standardization has been a primary way that researchers are examining global infrastructure as urbanization.

With this chapter, we contend that this focus on standardization is indicative of the uniform, replicable and generic spaces of global capitalism.

However, we suggested that the attention to capitalist standardization of cities does not adequately recognize the dynamic and volatile urban geographies in which these infrastructures are embedded. Existing modes of analysis of the deployment of global infrastructure into cities too often overlook how all infrastructure, including global infrastructure, depends on the correct prediction of what inevitably are uncertain futures. Moving forward, research on urban futures must centre on this uncertainty among geopolitical, climatic and public health turbulence. Assuming that uniform urban and economic flows, maintained through transcontinental infrastructural circulations, will continue to function as planned is no longer the case (if it ever truly was the case). Urban spaces of global infrastructure will always remain incomplete and open to change.

This chapter has explored the power of global infrastructure in determining particular capitalist visions for the urban future. Our case study situates the Royal Albert Dock as part of the broader configuration of the BRI and the role that new global infrastructure space plays in what the editors of this book term the 'the uneven and contradictory logics of contemporary capitalist accumulation'. The logic behind standardized global infrastructural deployment is to connect, but doing so is never straightforward. It is subject to factors most often outside the control of any single city, even one as prominent as London, demonstrating how infrastructuring urbanization is very much a global process.

Acknowledgements

This paper draws on the authors' jointly written paper: A. Wiig and J. Silver (2019) 'Turbulent presents, precarious futures: urbanization and the deployment of global infrastructure', *Regional Studies*, 53(6): 912–23 as well as: A. Wiig (2022) 'Inside the zone, outside the commons: London's waterfront redevelopment as enclosure', *New Geographies 12: Commons*, Cambridge, MA: Harvard Graduate School of Design, pp 177–86.

References

ABP (2017) ABP Royal Albert Dock London: Quarterly Review. Formerly available from: http://www.abp-london.co.uk/assets/Brochures/Quarte rly-Review/ABP-Quarterly-Review-01-October-2017.pdf [Accessed 11 January 2018].

Apostolopoulou, E. (2021) 'Tracing the Links between Infrastructure-Led Development, Urban Transformation, and Inequality in China's Belt and Road Initiative', *Antipode,* 53(3): 831–858.

Arase, D. (2015) 'What to make of the Asian Infrastructure Investment Bank', The Asian Forum, 26 June. Available from: http://www.theasanfo rum.org/what-to-make-of-the-asian-infrastructure-investment-bank/ [Accessed 24 July 2018].

Atkinson, R. (2020) *Alpha City: How London Was Captured by the Super-Rich*, London: Verso.

Barisitz, S. and Radzyner, A. (2017) 'The New Silk Road, part I: a stocktaking and economic assessment', *Focus on European Economic Integration*, 3: 8–30.

Barry, A. (2006) 'Technological zones', *European Journal of Social Theory*, 9(2): 239–53.

Beckert, S. (2015) *Empire of Cotton: A Global History*, New York: Knopf.

Bouzarovski, S., Bradshaw, M. and Wochnik, A. (2015) 'Making territory through infrastructure: the governance of natural gas transit in Europe', *Geoforum*, 64: 217–28.

Brenner, N. and Schmid, C. (2015) 'Towards a new epistemology of the urban?', *City*, 19(2/3): 151–82.

Brewster, D. (2017) 'Silk Roads and strings of pearls: the strategic geography of China's new pathways in the Indian Ocean', *Geopolitics*, 22(2): 269–91.

Brill, F. (2018) 'Playing the game: a comparison of international actors in real estate development in Modderfontein, Johannesburg and London's Royal Docks', *Geoforum*, 134: 197–204.

Brownill, S. (1988) 'The people's plan for the Royal Docks: some contradictions in popular planning', *Planning Practice & Research*, 2(4): 15–21.

Bunnell, T. (2021) 'BRI and beyond: comparative possibilities of extended Chinese urbanisation', *Asia Pacific Viewpoint*, 62(3): 270–3.

Campling, L. and Colás, A. (2021) *Capitalism and the Sea: The Maritime Factor in the Making of the Modern World*, London: Verso.

Carse, A. and Lewis, J. (2017) 'Toward a political ecology of infrastructure standards: or, how to think about ships, waterways, sediment, and communities together', *Environment and Planning A: Economy and Space*, 49(1): 9–28.

Chalfin, B. (2010) *Neoliberal Frontiers: An Ethnography of Sovereignty in West Africa*, Chicago: University of Chicago Press.

Chen, X. (2018) 'Globalisation redux: can China's inside-out strategy catalyse economic development and integration across its Asian borderlands and beyond?', *Cambridge Journal of Regions, Economy, and Society*, 11(1): 35–58.

Chen, X. (2021) 'Reconnecting Eurasia: a new logistics state, the China–Europe freight train, and the resurging ancient city of Xi'an', *Eurasian Geography and Economics*, ahead of print. Available from: https://doi.org/10.1080/15387216.2021.1980075.

Coutard, O. (2002) '"Premium network spaces": a comment', *International Journal of Urban and Regional Research*, 26(1): 166–74.

Cowen, D. (2014) *The Deadly Life of Logistics: Mapping Violence in Global Trade*, Minneapolis: University of Minnesota Press.

Crick, M. (2014) 'Big questions for Boris over billion dollar property deal', Channel 4 News, 13 November. Available from: https://www.chann el4.com/news/boris-johnson-london-propery-deal-china-albert-dock [Accessed 10 March 2020].

Danyluk, M. (2018) 'Capital's logistical fix: accumulation, globalization, and the survival of capitalism', *Environment and Planning D: Society and Space*, 36(4): 630–47.

Datta, A. (2015) 'New urban utopias of postcolonial India: "entrepreneurial urbanization" in Dholera smart city, Gujarat', *Dialogues in Human Geography*, 5(1): 3–22.

Datta, A. and Shaban, A. (eds) (2016) *Mega-Urbanization in the Global South: Fast Cities and New Urban Utopias of the Postcolonial State*, Abingdon: Routledge.

De Boeck, F. (2011) 'Inhabiting ocular ground: Kinshasa's future in the light of Congo's spectral urban politics', *Cultural Anthropology*, 26(2): 263–86.

Dines, N., Cattell, V. Gesler, W. and Curtis, S. (2006) *Public Spaces, Social Relations and Well-Being in East London*, Bristol: Policy Press, for the Joseph Rowntree Foundation.

Driver, F. and Gilbert, D. (1998) 'Heart of empire? Landscape, space and performance in imperial London', *Environment and Planning D: Society and Space*, 16(1): 11–28.

Easterling, K. (2014) *Extrastatecraft: The Power of Infrastructure Space*, London: Verso.

Eder, T. (2018) 'Mapping the Belt and Road initiative: this is where we stand', Mercator Institute for China Studies, 7 June. Available from: https://www.merics.org/index.php/en/bri-tracker/mapping-the-belt-and-road-initiative [Accessed 14 June 2018].

Enright, T. (2016) *The Making of Grand Paris: Metropolitan Urbanism in the Twenty-First Century*, Cambridge, MA: MIT Press.

Fallon, T. (2015) 'The New Silk Road: Xi Jinping's grand strategy for Eurasia', *American Foreign Policy Interests*, 37(3): 140–7.

Farrells (2019) 'Projects: Royal Albert Dock'. Available from: https://farre lls.com/project/royal-albert-dock [Accessed 3 March 2020].

Ford, J. and Hughes, L. (2020) 'UK–China relations: from "golden era" to the deep freeze', Financial Times, 13 July. Available from: http://www.ft.com/content/804175d0-8b47-4427-9853-2aded76f48e4 [Accessed 30 July 2020].

GICA (Global Infrastructure Connectivity Initiative) (2017) *G20 Global Infrastructure Connectivity Alliance: 2017 Work Plan*, Singapore: G20. Available from: https://www.bundesfinanzministerium.de/Content/EN/Standard artikel/Topics/world/G7-G20/G20-Documents/GICA-2017-work-plan. pdf?__blob=publicationFile&v=3 [Accessed 17 July 2018].

Graham, S. (ed) (2010) *Disrupted Cities: When Infrastructure Fails*, Abingdon: Routledge.

Graham, S. and Marvin, S. (2001) *Splintering Urbanism: Networked Infrastructures, Technological Mobilities and the Urban Condition*, New York: Routledge.

Guma, P.K. (2020) 'Incompleteness of urban infrastructures in transition: scenarios from the mobile age in Nairobi', *Social Studies of Science*, 50(5): 728–50.

Gupta, A. (2015) 'Theorizing the contemporary: suspension', Society for Cultural Anthropology, 24 September. Available from: https://culanth.org/fieldsights/suspension [Accessed 22 August 2018].

Hall, P. (2002) *Urban and Regional Planning*, 4th edn, Abingdon: Routledge.

Harris, A. (2013) 'Concrete geographies: assembling global Mumbai through transport infrastructure', *City*, 17(3): 343–60.

Harvey, P. and Knox, H. (2015) *Roads: An Anthropology of Infrastructure and Expertise*, London: Cornell University Press.

Hilyard, N and Sol, X. (2017) *How Infrastructure Is Shaping the World: A Critical Introduction to Infrastructure Mega-Corridors*, Brussels: CounterBalance. Available from: https://counter-balance.org/publications/how-infrastructure-is-shaping-the-world [Accessed 14 January 2018].

HM Government (2013) 'London Mayor announces 10 Chinese businesses to the Royal Docks Enterprise Zone', HM Government, 18 October. Available from: https://enterprisezones.communities.gov.uk/london-mayor-announces-10-chinese-businesses-royal-docks-enterprise-zone/ [Accessed 3 March 2020].

Hui, L. and Cargill, C.F. (2017) *Setting Standards for Industry: Comparing the Emerging Chinese Standardization System and the Current US System*, Honolulu, HI: East-West Center.

Kaker, S.A. (2014) 'Enclaves, insecurity and violence in Karachi', *South Asian History and Culture*, 5(1): 93–107.

Kanai, J.M. and Schindler, S. (2019) 'Peri-urban promises of connectivity: Linking project-led polycentrism to the infrastructure scramble', *Environment and Planning A: Economy and Space*, 51(2): 302–322.

Kasarda, J.D. and Lindsay, G. (2011) *Aerotropolis: The Way We'll Live Next*, New York: Farrar, Straus and Giroux.

Kennard, M. (2016) 'Selling the silverware: how London's historic dock was sold to the Chinese', Pulitzer Center, 7 June. Available from: http://pulitzercenter.org/reporting/selling-silverware-how-londons-historic-dock-was-sold-chinese [Accessed 9 January 2018].

Kentish, B. (2017) 'First direct train service from China to the UK arrives in London', The Independent, 18 January. Available from: https://www.independent.co.uk/news/uk/home-news/first-direct-train-china-to-uk-arrives-east-london-yiwu-city-barking-channel-tunnel-a7533726.html [Accessed 15 January 2018].

KPMG (2018) *Emerging Trends in Infrastructure*. Available from: https://ass ets.kpmg/content/dam/kpmg/xx/pdf/2018/02/emerging-trends-in-inf rastructure.pdf [Accessed 24 July 2018].

Lidington, D. (2018) 'Writing a new chapter in the global era', speech to the UK–China Senior Leadership Forum in Beijing, GOV.UK, 11 April. Available from: https://www.gov.uk/government/speeches/writing-a-new-chapter-in-the-global-era [Accessed 19 July 2018].

Linebaugh, P. (2006) *The London Hanged: Crime and Civil Society in the Eighteenth Century*, 2nd edn, London: Verso.

Linebaugh, P. and Rediker, M. (2013) *The Many-Headed Hydra: Sailors, Slaves, Commoners, and the Hidden History of the Revolutionary* Atlantic, 2nd edn, Boston, MA: Beacon Press.

Lu, L., Guo, H. and Pesaresi, M. (2017) 'Remote sensing of urbanization dynamics along the Belt and Road', *Bulletin of Chinese Academy of Sciences*, 32(1): 74–81.

Madison Brook (2011) 'Top developers aim to build new Royal Albert Docks', Madison Brook International, 8 December. Available from: http://madisonbrook.com/Article/Top-developers-aim-to-build-new-Royal-Alb ert-Docks/76.html [Accessed 7 February 2022]. (See also: https://www.london.gov.uk/sites/default/files/mgla201219-9261-_attachment_redac ted.pdf)

Martin, R., Tyler, P., Storper, M., Evenhuis, E. and Glasmeier, A. (2018) 'Globalization at a critical conjuncture?', *Cambridge Journal of Region, Economy, Society*, 11(1): 3–16.

Massey, D. (2007) *World City*, Malden, MA: Polity Press.

McFarlane, C. and Silver, J. (2017) 'Navigating the city: dialectics of everyday urbanism', *Transactions of the Institute of British Geographers*, 42(3): 458–71.

McNeill, D. (2017) *Global Cities and Urban Theory*, Thousand Oaks, CA: Sage.

Minton, A. (2017) *Big Capital: Who Is London For?*, London: Penguin.

Neilson, B., Rossiter, N. and Samaddar, R. (eds) (2018) *Logistical Asia: The Labour of Making a World Region*, Singapore: Palgrave Macmillan.

Parker, G., Evans, J. and Hornby, L. (2016) 'Theresa May welcomes £1.7bn Chinese project in London's Docklands', Financial Times, 10 November. Available from: https://www.ft.com/content/23372450-a693-11e6-8898-79a99e2a4de6 [Accessed 3 March 2020].

Peters, M. (2018) 'The end of neoliberal globalisation and the rise of authoritarian populism', Educational Philosophy and Theory, 50(4): 323–5.

Pickford, J. and Hammond, E. (2013a). 'Boris Johnson to seal £1bn docks deal with Chinese developer', Financial Times, 28 May. https://www.ft.com/content/f7b5599c-c7b0-11e2-9c52-00144feab7de [Accessed 11 January 2018].

Pickford, J. and Hammond, E. (2013b) 'China investor waits to tie up at quays of old British empire', Financial Times, 10 May. Available from: https://www.ft.com/content/138bb0fa-b99a-11e2-bc57-00144feabdc0 [Accessed 21 January 2018].

Pickren, G. (2018) '"The global assemblage of digital flow": critical data studies and the infrastructures of computing', Progress in Human Geography, 42(2): 225–43.

Rao, V. (2014) 'Infra-city: speculations on flux and history in infrastructure-making', in S. Graham and C. McFarlane (eds) Infrastructural Lives: Urban Infrastructure in Context, Abingdon: Routledge, pp 53–72.

Roberts, J.T. (2011) 'Multipolarity and the new world (dis) order: US hegemonic decline and the fragmentation of the global climate regime', Global Environmental Change, 21(3): 776–84.

Royal Docks (2019) 'The first tenant in the new Royal Docks business district has been revealed', Royal Docks, 10 December. Available from: https://web.archive.org/web/20200814115307/https://www.royaldocks.london/articles/first-tenant-in-royal-albert-docks [Accessed 8 February 2022].

Sassen, S. (2011) Cities in a World Economy, 4th edn, London: Sage.

Schindler, S. and Kanai, J.M. (2021) 'Getting the territory right: infrastructure-led development and the re-emergence of spatial planning strategies', Regional Studies, 55(1): 40–51.

Schindler, S. and Marvin, S. (2018) 'Constructing a universal logic of urban control? International standards for city data, management, and interoperability', City, 22(2): 298–307.

Schindler, S., DiCarlo, J. and Paudel, D. (2022) 'The New Cold War and the rise of the 21st century infrastructure state', Transactions of the Institute of British Geographers, 47(2): 331–46.

Schulhof, V., van Vuuren, D. and Kirchherr, J. (2021) 'The Belt and Road Initiative (BRI): what will it look like in the future?', Technological Forecasting and Social Change, 175: art 121306. Available from: https://doi.org/10.1016/j.techfore.2021.121306 [Accessed 21 November 2022].

Shenker, J. (2015) 'Privatised London: the Thames Path walk that resembles a prison corridor', The Guardian, 24 February. Available from: https://www.theguardian.com/cities/2015/feb/24/private-london-exposed-thames-path-riverside-walking-route [Accessed 12 June 2020].

Sidaway, J.D. and Woon, C.Y. (2017) 'Chinese narratives on "One Belt, One Road" (一带一路) in geopolitical and imperial contexts', The Professional Geographer, 69(4): 591–613.

Sidders, J. (2020) 'London's newest ghost town was financed by China', Bloomberg Magazine, 30 July. Available from: https://www.bloomberg.com/news/articles/2020-07-30/he-built-it-but-no-one-came-china-chills-the-next-canary-wharf [Accessed 11 December 2021].

Silver, J. (2021) 'Corridor urbanism', in M. Lancione and C. McFarlane (eds) *Global Urbanism: Knowledge, Power and the City*, New York: Routledge, pp 251–8.

Simone, A. (2004) 'People as infrastructure: intersecting fragments in Johannesburg', *Public Culture*, 16(3): 407–29.

Simone, A. (2012) 'Infrastructure: commentary', Cultural Anthropology. https://journal.culanth.org/index.php/ca/infrastructure-abdoumaliq-simone [Accessed 19 July 2018].

Simone, A. (2016) 'Passing things along: (in)completing infrastructure', *New Diversities*, 17(2): 151–62.

Summers, T. (2016) 'China's "New Silk Roads": sub-national regions and networks of global political economy', *Third World Quarterly*, 37(9): 1628–43.

Swyngedouw, E., Moulaert, F. and Rodriguez, A. (2002) 'Neoliberal urbanization in Europe: large-scale urban development projects and the new urban policy', *Antipode*, 34(3): 542–77.

Timmermans, S. and Epstein, S. (2010) 'A world of standards but not a standard world: toward a sociology of standards and standardization', *Annual Review of Sociology*, 36: 69–89.

Tison, A., Ayrton, C., Barker, K., Barry-Born, T. and Long, O. (2017) *London's Poverty Profile*, London: Trust for London. Available from: https://www.trustforlondon.org.uk/data/ [Accessed 22 February 2020].

Töpfer, L.-M. and Hall, S. (2018) 'London's rise as an offshore RMB financial centre: state–finance relations and selective institutional adaptation', *Regional Studies*, 52(8): 1053–64.

Ungoed-Thomas, J. (2022) 'Boris Johnson's flagship London dock scheme on brink of collapse', The Guardian, 5 February. Available from: https://www.theguardian.com/business/2022/feb/05/boris-johnsons-flagship-london-dock-scheme-on-brink-of-collapse [Accessed 7 February 2022].

Wainwright, O. (2022) '"It's been a disaster": how Boris Johnson's docklands business hub turned into a ghost town', The Guardian, 20 July. Available from: https://www.theguardian.com/artanddesign/2022/jul/20/empty-promise-the-fantasy-city-within-a-city-that-turned-into-a-ghost-town [Accessed 2 August 2022].

Wallerstein, I. (1979) *The Capitalist World-Economy*, Cambridge: Cambridge University Press.

Walton, D. and Kavalski, E. (eds) (2016) *Power Transition in Asia*, Abingdon: Routledge.

Watson, V. (2014) 'African urban fantasies: dreams or nightmares?', *Environment and Urbanization*, 26(1): 215–31.

Watt, P. (2013) '"It's not for us"', *City*, 17(1): 99–118.

Wiig, A. (2016) 'The empty rhetoric of the smart city: from digital inclusion to economic promotion in Philadelphia', *Urban Geography*, 37(4): 535–53.

Wiig, A. (2018) 'Secure the city, revitalize the zone: Smart urbanization in Camden, New Jersey', *Environment and Planning C: Politics and Space*, 36(3): 403–22.

Wiig, A. (2019) 'Incentivized urbanization in Philadelphia: the local politics of globalized zones', *Journal of Urban Technology*, 26(3): 111–29.

Williams, R. (1993) 'Cultural origins and environmental implications of large technological systems', *Science in Context*, 6(2): 377–403.

Zeiderman, A. (2016) 'Submergence: precarious politics in Colombia's future port-city', *Antipode*, 48(3): 809–31.

Zeiderman, A., Kaker, S.A., Silver, J. and Wood, A. (2015) 'Uncertainty and urban life', *Public Culture*, 27(2): 281–304.

Zheng, H.W., Bouzarovski, S., Knuth, S. Panteli, M., Schindler, S., Ward, K and Williams, J. (2021) 'Interrogating China's global urban presence', *Geopolitics*. Available from: https://doi.org/10.1080/14650 045.2021.1901084.

AFTERWORD 1

On Fetishes, Fragments and Futures: Regionalizing Infrastructural Lives

Michael Glass, Jen Nelles and Jean-Paul Addie

To research infrastructural networks is to wrestle with the foundations of future worlds. Decisions about the provision or dismantling of infrastructures (often seen through processes of investment or disinvestment and use or neglect) critically structure the ever-emergent landscapes of both urban and rural areas (Gansauer and Haggerty, 2021). Whereas the very term 'infrastructure' can connote geographically expansive investments in networks including highways, sewerage systems or broadband, the chapters of this book clearly recognize that urban futures are constituted through intimate and embodied encounters between technical systems and individuals. Our own work approaches the problematic of infrastructuring future worlds through a complementary but distinct research agenda; one that centres on dual tasks of applying a regional perspective to the infrastructure turn (thinking about infrastructure through regions) and engaging infrastructure as empirical and conceptual objects of analysis to interrogate regional processes (thinking about regions through infrastructure) (Glass et al, 2019; Addie et al, 2020). As a scale, the region resides somewhere between the global scope of the Chinese Belt and Road project and the intimate origins of sanitary waste. Regions, in this sense, form a type of 'plastic space' that is shaped by the iterative interaction of territorialized and relational processes (Harrison, 2013; Jones, 2022). They continue to matter for geographic and infrastructural research because they are consequential spaces that capture and control social equality, environmental impact and economic development. We introduced the concept of 'infrastructural regionalism', in part, to help identify how infrastructure systems – their production, governance and maintenance – can influence the formation of new spatial imaginaries and political subjectivities (Addie et al, 2020). In this afterword we build on this idea to put forward three ways that infrastructuring urban futures might be recontextualized when perceived from a slightly different (scalar and analytical) perspective: that of the region. By focusing on fetishes, fragments and futures we highlight how the distributed agency and possibilities embedded in infrastructures come to shape regional lives.

Navigating spatial fetishes: scalar dialogues and missed connections

In any investigation, researchers must make choices about what to focus on – which questions, which actors and at what scales – in a process that is imperilled by several 'traps'. Despite our best efforts, our approaches are in part shaped by comfortable frames, proximity (intellectual, relational, physical) and perspectives. These and other factors can result in blind spots or fetishism, a problem that presents itself as 'a form of distortion where the attributes and powers, the essence, of the person or social relation appear as natural, intrinsic, attributes of powers of the "thing"' (Allman, 2007: 37). In infrastructural research, the 'local trap' focuses our thinking on the most primary, localized elements of systems – the subway network, the water treatment plant, the highway interchange – and consequently what is considered local becomes reified, rather than understood as a place-based expression of processes and relations that shift in time and space (Carpenter, 2015). Crucially, this local fetish does not exclude acknowledging extra-local factors, but may consider these as functionally remote, exerting only limited (although potentially significant) influence through interfaces identified and bounded by the topic of study. The fetishist is dominated from this conceptual position by a disciplining focus on local outcomes and definitions of what is local, categorized in more intimate (albeit possibly invisible) embraces. Depending on the positionality of the researcher, escape from this conceptual bondage may require more than a scalar safe word. However, adopting a regional lens can encourage different interpretations and understandings (see Figure AW1.1).

One interesting feature of contemporary infrastructure research, exemplified by many of the contributions in this volume, is the explicit drive to transcend the local and understand how infrastructure systems are embedded in and affected by broader forces, particularly through the logics of connections and flows, financialization and other vectors of neoliberal internationalism. This emerges explicitly in chapters such as Sheller's work on the Greater Antilles. It is here that the inventiveness of locals in exploiting loopholes created by infrastructures and technologies of global capitalism

Figure AW1.1: Westphalian energy landscapes – local patterns, infrastructural regionalisms

Source: Michael Glass

enables the extraction and repatriation of profits even as their spaces continue to be exploited, in turn, by simultaneously globally connected and institutionally exempt crypto-predators. Global markets both finance and extract rents from the New York City subway system and privatized water authorities in the UK. Chinese interests and logics of standardization are shaping urban redevelopment in London and access to it, just as the city declares itself the world's first 'national parks city' presumably to position itself at the forefront of the liveable city movement.

These contributions explicitly juxtapose and link the local to the *international*, demonstrating the influence of global networks and how localities submit to, struggle against and exploit these interfaces. Less well acknowledged, however, is the role of the *regional*. It is a perfectly acceptable oversight for scholars facing the boundedness of both word limits and the rationality of actors. However, these choices result in stories told, and understood, from specific vantage points. The Royal Albert Dock redevelopment has not significantly raised the fortunes of neighbouring areas of deprivation. But then, why would it? Labour and housing markets operate at much broader scales and while local(ized) infrastructure development can have substantial influences, these are just one a sea of other competing and complementary feedback loops (themselves, it should be noted, operating at myriad intersecting scales). Usher's damning description of the dereliction of water companies following the fragmentation and privatization of the sector refers to these regional entities but does not challenge how those constructed, extra-local, infrastructural territories and governance structures also shape and constrain their actions. How water district boundaries were established, and what consequences they had for their inheritors, remains unclear. Even the water fouling is regarded in some ways as localized to one definable jurisdiction, when the effects must flow downstream across numerous boundaries, and out and into the ecosystem through streams, springs and other outflows. In other contributions, broader infrastructural lives are acknowledged, but are still relatively implicit. Poughkeepsie was forced to respond to shifts in regional transportation flows and, in turn, its infrastructural decisions altered these flows and, with them, regional patterns of settlement and economic development. Bristol's peripherality to the regional power grid, and the institutional distance implied, created spaces for experimentation. In a more pointed exploration of the roles of the regional past, we learn that the historical development of New York City's transport infrastructure arrested the commuting flows of communities of colour, privileging the mobility of the largely White suburban population, remaking the racial landscape of the city. These patterns, born of localized responses to evolving infrastructural regionalisms (themselves occurring in at a specific and not locally bounded sociopolitical moment), consolidated the uneven map of vulnerability, access and injustice that persists – patterns that also created feedback loops and enduring regional spatial legacies.

As we acknowledged earlier, scalar traps may be impossible to elude, and a rich literature has emerged aiming to connect as many aspects of the complex systems of infrastructure as possible to problematize and explain localized outcomes. This volume contains many examples of this practice. Here, we merely observe the opportunities inherent in bringing a regional scale into the mix and how shifting frames reveals different questions and alternative readings of infrastructural configurations.

Infrastructural fragments in a regional world

The preceding chapters have brought an impressive array of such configurations into dialogue. Drawing on the provocative recent work of Colin McFarlane (2021), we can read each as an assemblage of infrastructural 'fragments'. Such fragments resonate most immediately in 'hard' infrastructural terms, reflecting both the visceral materiality of the concrete, cables and containers that – however incomplete (Guma, 2020) – provide the conditions that make distinct ways of life possible, while also rendering visible the 'political, economic, and cultural inequities of the city' that interpolate such artefacts as objects of political contestation (McFarlane, 2021: 5). The infrastructural configurations we encounter in this volume, then, do not simply appear as material artefacts that constitute, and affect, the city in differing ways. The process of infrastructuring urban futures discloses 'multiple stories proposing how things got to be the way they are, of how different aspects of urban regions are articulated, while at the same time generating differentiation in the very operations of that narrative' (Simone, 2022: 80). Heterodox ways of knowing infrastructure – which McFarlane frames as 'knowledge fragments'; 'provocations that demand recognition that the world is more than simply plural' (2021: 7) – are collocated in messy and overlapping ways in time and space. Fragments may be concentrated in urban space as forces of globalization touch down in discrete places – a Bristol household, a London Park, a toilet in Ilkley – where they interface viscerally with the private sphere of urban inhabitation. But at the same time, 'disjunct fragments' are also projected outwards into the operational hinterlands and reticulated geographies of planetary capitalist urbanization, often at great speed (Lefebvre, 2003: 14).

Thinking with McFarlane's reading of the fragmented city, our contention here is that the region, as an empirical object and analytical lens, can bring together disparate fragments and infrastructural moments in ways that recontextualize narratives of infrastructuring. This is not to suggest city and region are mutually exclusive (or superior) spatial frames or preferable arenas to organize collective provision (Schafran et al, 2020). Rather, shifting our analytical lens from the urban to the regional can generatively reframe the central questions animating this collection and in doing so, proffer alternative readings – sometimes complementary, sometimes challenging – of how the future is infrastructured materially, discursively and politically.

In proposing the value of regionalizing infrastructural futures, we are interested in understanding 'the relations between infrastructure and regions (each broadly conceived) and their capacity to effect new spatial imaginaries and political subjectivities' within a broader and relationally constituted scalar architecture (Addie et al, 2020: 12). Infrastructure's regionality foregrounds modalities of boundedness, territoriality and a certain form of political pragmatism. Yet with this, infrastructural regionalism animates what Swati Chattopadhyay (2012: xxiii) terms 'conjunctural spaces' whose contingencies, contradictions and dynamism prompt us to re-evaluate our understanding of both the materiality of the city (per se) and how infrastructural subjects themselves are interpolated and act. In this context, we would like to not only address the provocative question of 'what kind of people live in Poughkeepsie, anyway?' but – by thinking regionally – unpack the territorial inclusions/exclusions that normatively frame claims to, and allocations of, 'infrastructural citizenship' (Lemanski, 2019) and what this means for understanding who has the right to produce infrastructural futures, and at what scale.

We are drawn to this question, and to the region as an analytical lens, because infrastructures are both shaped by and produce distinct regional formations: be they networked, administrative, ecological, lived or otherwise. Importantly, as Bigger and Millington's and Sheller's contributions pointedly demonstrate, the ability to inhabit, appropriate and produce such infrastructural spaces and infrastructural futures is timed, placed and raced. Clearly, we do not view the region as a problematically 'fuzzy' concept (Markusen, 2003). Infrastructural regions are not pregiven, immutable containers for social activity but they are defined by their temporary coalescence into partially cohesive territorial, functional and political spaces (Jones, 2022). As such, we draw attention to relational perspectives on infrastructure by noting how elements including microgrids, intermodal yards and social movements can gain context and clarity by elevating these fragments into a position where their *raison d'être* is couched in less idiographic and more situated terms. What we mean by this is that by recognizing the conceptual coherence of multiple scales, researchers can attend to knowing infrastructure – and its associated political claims – in ways that illuminate the partiality of individual urban infrastructural fragments.

A relational regional posture toward infrastructure may therefore expose blind fields and elevate silenced voices in ways that contextualize how ostensibly localized processes are plugged into multiscalar fields that converge around, and confound, the operation of infrastructure. Issues of governance come to the fore here as Enright and Ward argue, both 'due to variations in institutional, legal, and regulatory contexts (the governance of infrastructure) [and] the unevenness of infrastructure networks themselves (the governance by infrastructure)' (2021: 1026). Engaging specific infrastructures' material and knowledge fragments through a regional lens gives a foundation to conceptualize and empirically explore the drive towards collective agency and action that galvanize around infrastructure as medium and message (Filion, 2013) and the multiple, divergent narratives and epistemic frames that refract the everyday experience of infrastructural lives.

Infrastructural lives, infrastructural futures

What matters most for us, then, is pursuing a regional perspective to understand better the promises that infrastructural networks make for constituent communities, and the geographic extent of infrastructural systems that these promises imply. The ethnographic work of Anand et al (2018) has opened new lines of discussion about the promises of infrastructure, revealing questions about the roles that infrastructure plays for people who clamour for its provision. Their research showed how the design, allocation and maintenance of water systems, road networks, electrical grids and telecommunication webs created new opportunities for the people who grow to rely upon them. There is occasionally an emancipatory potential to this promise, as Judith Butler (2015: 127) writes when describing the demand for infrastructure as the 'demand for a certain kind of inhabitable ground' that can create the catalyst for social action or change.

The manifold promises made by infrastructure function simultaneously at different scales, from the personal hope that drinkable water will emerge from the tap whenever a lever is turned, to the more communal promise that an airport or highway will foster greater connectivity. Throughout this book we see other instances of this promise: the business owners of Poughkeepsie who anticipated infrastructure's role in maintaining the regional relevance of a decaying secondary city, the advocates for sustainable urbanism in Bristol who imagine a better future through datafied energy infrastructure, or the promises of global connectivity hoped for by the redevelopment of the Royal Albert Dock. The promises made by these instances of infrastructure development are fundamentally promises made to the future, as funding is allocated to infrastructural projects (whether new or maintained) with the anticipation that these investments will be worthwhile, creating positive benefits beyond the immediate period and into a gauzy time yet to come.

Although the promise of infrastructure, as Kregg Hetherington (2017) observes, is one made in the future perfect tense, the parameters of our infrastructural futures are themselves profoundly conditioned by the temporal modalities shaping our infrastructural imaginaries, whether locked into linear narratives of modernity and progress or disrupted by non-teleological indigenous and postcolonial understandings of time (Hoefsloot et al, 2022). Following Rob Kitchin (2019), we can ask whether urban futures are projected through the lens of the 'present future', with likely developments forecast on the basis of current circumstances and assumptions of how urban and infrastructural systems function? Or do they disclose a 'future present' modality that backcasts from idealized future scenarios to illuminate possible pathways towards desired transformation? Or perhaps infrastructure's temporality itself captures us in a perpetual 'present-present', with smart technologies aspiring to control the city in real time and precarious infrastructural lives becoming existentially bound by the need to secure what is required to make it through the day.

Recognizing the promises made by infrastructure is therefore a necessary yet insufficient condition for understanding the construction of infrastructural lives; especially those lived in an ongoing state of suspension, waiting in the shadows of unfinished future (Carse and Kneas, 2019). Activating the promise of infrastructure requires tools that can justify the investments needed to turn a promise into practice, and to materialize an imagined urban future. The construction of an urban future is predicated upon tools that create new regional spaces – for example, cost–benefit analyses and municipal bonds. Cost–benefit analysis is a common technique used in planning and engineering to evaluate the prospective return on investment for a proposed development, such as a road or building. This form of accounting practice allocates value on both sides of the ledger: for instance, the benefits of a new highway might be conceived of as the reduction of congestion, the heightened access to new markets, and the jobs created during the construction period (leaving open the question of to whom these benefits accrue). On the negative side, the costs of displacement, raw materials, and the necropolitics of roads (actuarial quantification of the fatalities caused by higher speed limits and larger roads) are summed and assessed to see whether the risks are outweighed by the rewards. Overlooked as a modifiable parameter within cost–benefit calculations are the roles of geography and time (Addie et al, forthcoming); the benefits of infrastructure may be diminished if the project is represented as having a solely local benefit over a short time horizon, whereas the benefits will appear magnified if a sufficiently large regional catchment and a longer time horizon is used to determine the multiplier effects of a new road or electrical grid. A similar role is performed by regional spaces for the municipal bonds used to finance new infrastructure. As the risks of infrastructure financing is reduced with the construction of different spatial envelopes, the justification for new infrastructures can be hastened by expanding the number of investors or underwriters who will vouch for the creditworthiness of a new investment (see Figure AW1.2). The regional scale of risk mitigation reflected by the modern tools of infrastructure financing therefore brings about new communities to share in the risks and potential rewards of infrastructures.

It is in these ways that infrastructural lives are shaped by the imagined spaces required of infrastructural investment and their attendant temporal modalities. Looking beyond the local scale and bringing together infrastructural fragments are both necessary for understanding how the promises of infrastructure are maintained, and to understand what the consequences of new imaginaries will be, based on the technical means used by the developers.

To think about infrastructures regionally is therefore to recognize how the contingent and mutating shape of regional spaces are conditioned by the provision and experience of converging infrastructural networks. Recognizing urban infrastructural futures is a necessary step towards a more grounded and flexible explanation for how technical systems cohere to construct new spatial imaginaries and regional subjects. We have argued in this afterword that the infrastructural turn must embrace a plurality of scalar perspectives, since a singular scalar/territorial lens can only provide a partial accounting for the lives created through and by infrastructural systems. Similarly, infrastructures in and of themselves should be recognized as partial and fragmentary. Individual infrastructural networks obviously collide and confuse, hence a heterodox accounting of the different infrastructural stories that emerge in given places and times should be recognized in and across

Figure AW1.2: New highway construction in Casablanca: how will the promises of infrastructure be justified?

Photo credit: Edouard Tamba. Source: https://unsplash.com/photos/J-hYMYa2jY8

our analyses. Finally, the future as shaped by infrastructural time and regional definition requires continued attention. The promises made to the future by infrastructural investment are predicated on the calculations and rhetorical appeals made to relevance at multiple scales over an indeterminate timescale. Taken together then, the fetishes, fragments and futures of infrastructures call for analytical approaches that transcend rigid spatial and temporal conceptualization and that instead reflect the territorialized and relational character of seemingly fixed infrastructure systems.

References

Addie, J.-P.D., Glass, M.R. and Nelles, J. (2020) 'Regionalizing the infrastructure turn: a research agenda', *Regional Studies, Regional Science*, 7(1): 10–26.

Addie, J.-P.D., Glass, M.R. and Nelles, J. (Forthcoming) *Infrastructural Times: Temporality and the Making of Global Urban Worlds*, Bristol: Bristol University Press.

Allman, P. (2007) *On Marx: An introduction to the revolutionary intellect of Karl Marx*, Rotterdam: Sense.

Anand, N., Gupta, A. and Appel, H. (2018) *The Promise of Infrastructure*, Durham, NC: Duke University Press.

Butler, J. (2014) 'Rethinking vulnerability and resistance', in J. Butler, Z. Gambetti, and L. Sabsay (eds) *Vulnerability in Resistance*, Durham, NC: Duke University Press, pp 12–27.

Butler, J. (2015) *Notes Toward a Performative Theory of Assemblage*, Cambridge, MA: Harvard University Press.

Carpenter, S. (2015) 'The "local" fetish as reproductive praxis in democratic learning', *Discourse: Studies in the Cultural Politics of Education*, 36(1): 133–43.

Carse, A. and Kneas, D. (2019) 'Unbuilt and unfinished: the temporalities of infrastructure', *Environment and Society*, 10(1): 9–28.

Chattopadhyay, S. (2012) *Unlearning the City: Infrastructure in a New Optical Field*, Minneapolis: University of Minnesota Press.

Enright, T. and Ward, K. (2021) 'Governing urban infrastructure under pandemic conditions: some thoughts', *Urban Geography*, 42(7): 1023–32.

Filion, P. (2013) 'The infrastructure is the message: Shaping suburban morphology and lifestyle' in R. Keil (eds) *Suburban constellations: Governance, land and infrastructure in the 21st century*, Berlin: Jovis, pp 39–45.

Gansauer, G. and Haggerty, J. (2021) 'Beyond city limits: infrastructural regionalism in rural Montana, USA', *Territory, Politics, Governance*, ahead of print. Available from: https://doi.org/10.1080/21622671.2021.1980428.

Glass, M.R., Addie, J.-P.D. and Nelles, J. (2019) 'Regional infrastructures, infrastructural regionalism', *Regional Studies*, 53(12): 1651–6.

Guma, P.K. (2020) 'Incompleteness of urban infrastructures in transition: scenarios from the mobile age in Nairobi', *Social Studies of Science*, 50(5): 728–50.

Harrison, J. (2013) 'Configuring the new "regional world": on being caught between territory and networks', *Regional Studies*, 47(1): 55–74.

Hetherington, K. (2017) 'Surveying the future perfect: anthropology, development and the promise of infrastructure', in P. Harvey, C.B. Jensen and A. Morita (eds) *Infrastructures and Social Complexity: A Companion*, Abingdon: Routledge, pp 40–50.

Hoefsloot, F.I., Martínez, J. and Pfeffer, K. (2022) 'An emerging knowledge system for future water governance: sowing water for Lima', Territory, Politics, Governance, ahead of print. Available from: https://doi.org/10.1080/21622671.2021.2023365.

Jones, M. (2022) 'For a "new new regional geography": plastic regions and more-than-relational regionality', *Geografiska Annaler: Series B, Human Geography*, 104(1): 43–58.

Kitchin, R. (2019) 'The timescape of smart cities', *Annals of the American Association of Geographers*, 109(3): 775–90.

Lefebvre, H. (2003) *The Urban Revolution*, Minneapolis: University of Minnesota Press.

Lemanski, C. (ed) (2019) *Citizenship and Infrastructure: Practices and Identities of Citizens and the State*, Abingdon: Routledge.

Markusen, A. (2003) 'Fuzzy concepts, scanty evidence, policy distance: the case for rigor and policy relevance in critical regional studies', *Regional Studies*, 37(6/7): 701–17.

McFarlane, C. (2021) *Fragments of the City: Making and Remaking Urban Worlds*, Oakland: University of California Press.

Schafran, A., Smith, M.N. and Hall, S. (2020) *The Spatial Contract: A New Politics of Provision for an Urbanized Planet*, Manchester: University of Manchester Press.

Simone, A. (2022) 'Splintering, specificity, unsettlement: a commentary on Splintering Urbanism', Journal of Urban Technology, 29(1): 79–85.

AFTERWORD 2

Incomplete Futures of Urban Infrastructure

Prince Guma

Urban infrastructure is continuously constructed, and is always susceptible to incremental and continual redefinition. Upon their establishment, infrastructures constitute different temporal configurations of unfinishedness (Carse and Kneas, 2019) and in their evolvement, they endure an ever-present incompleteness (Simone, 2016; Guma, 2020, 2022b) with their uses never being fixed but drawing from varied social, political, economic and technical negotiations (Larkin, 2013; Anand et al, 2018) – both trivial and significant, mundane and strange (Star, 1999). The question that becomes imperative in our understanding of urban infrastructures in transition is – how does incompleteness reframe the way we think about and theorize urban infrastructural futures?

This afterword addresses this question by examining urban infrastructure through its incomplete futures. I offer a conception that highlights partial, provisional and contingent processes and practices that go into making and shifting infrastructures, and one that foregrounds situated and temporal engagements, negotiations and relations. In so doing, I demystify infrastructural ambivalence and ambiguity, counteract normative proposals that disparage infrastructural processes which do not yield or conform to standards, and explicate situated processes of development that diverge from certain norms and ideals of completeness.

I demonstrate that rather than reproaching unfamiliar and strange infrastructural progressions or development processes, it is important to disentangle them and better understand them as reflective of infrastructure's incomplete futures. In so doing, I argue that this means considering infrastructural futures beyond essentialist and judgemental overtones towards an expanded view of canons, knowledge and ways of

Figure AW2.1: With the current urge to realize new urban futures, increased infrastructure developments and upgrade, including flyovers, highlight an image of Southern cities as incomplete sites constantly under construction.

Source: Prince Guma

knowing. I make the case for the need to go beyond the language of the normative, to consider context and non-linear trajectories. I contend that this is imperative for purposes of transcending a priori and teleological conceptions of infrastructure development and investments. Accordingly, I contribute to chapters that comprised this book, which, in varied ways, reflect inscriptions to incomplete futures of urban infrastructures – whether viewed through their networked disposition, uneven and contradictory logics, or varying urban locations in the Global South or Global North or both.

Infrastructural incompleteness

Policy makers, planners and related experts remain limited in their understanding and addressing of extensive urban infrastructures. Infrastructures still remain highly construed as closed, stable and banal constructions that are non-contestable, with the ultimate goal of their design construed as achieving universality, seamless functioning and completeness. Here, infrastructures tend to be viewed through unidimensional, utopian– dystopian, and transformative–incrementalist approaches. Within these tendencies, portrayals of deviation and nonconformity are often mobilized to validate some infrastructures as defective, divergent or failed simply because they significantly differ from the desired ideal (see Figure AW2.2). Such portrayals demonstrate a general urge and desire to read infrastructure futures through the lens of globally sanctioned trademarks of what a modern infrastructure, and thus modern city, should look like, feel like and operate as. Consequently then, enigmatic, ambivalent and ambiguous unknowns are often identified as 'other' through maintaining the homogenizing, essentialist and reductionist descriptions of how urban infrastructures should actually look like or function.

Empowered to find solutions to often cited divergences, discrepancies and absences of nonconforming infrastructure, most policy makers, practitioners and experts barely look beyond neoliberal level precarity and compliance, where profit margins and capitalistic visions delimit what infrastructure can be. Thus, occurrences of infrastructural failure and shortfall become used as a fundamental validation for calls and rationalities that align with the general principle that for infrastructure systems to function 'properly' (see Figure AW2.2), they require constant attention and periodic updating from those with technical capacity. Within this frame of thought, infrastructural deviations become blamed on the incompetence and short-sightedness of political elites, engineers, technicians and planners. In so doing, some experts and elites suggest, as a solution, extensive recommendations for substitution of state with non-state actors, or top-down with bottom-up approaches. Sometimes they suggest mechanisms of repair, renovation, or demolition and replacement (see Figure AW2.1) as solutions to purported deficiencies, failures and inadequacies. Other times, they suggest proposals for furthering and enhancing investment, financing, planning, governance and regulatory reform. But always, what constitutes urban infrastructure and what sort of populations decide on the infrastructure needs of a city remains contained with these experts.

At the epitome of these dispositions is the subtle expectation that urban infrastructures must evolve either in the same way as their counterparts elsewhere, or in a linear trajectory from less complete to more complete arrangements. While the rationale behind such calls cannot exclusively be disparaged, such dispositions for infrastructural connection and control not only fall short regarding what exactly constitutes failure, deficiency and incompleteness, they barely provide conclusive positions regarding infrastructural futures and the transitions necessary to build more inclusive, just and sustainable cities. As such, they tend to neglect the fact that different infrastructures within their particular contexts will always tend to function in a multiplicity of ways, occasionally materializing in ways that diverge from so-called norms and ideals (see, for example, Figure AW2.3; Guma, 2022a). While well-structured and engineered instruments and institutional controls do indeed curtail ubiquitous and complex infrastructural failures and breakdowns everywhere, and may sometimes act to achieve seamless

Figure AW2.2: A new market constructed by the Ugandan government in Lukaya city

Note: The market cost US$474,621 and, while operational since May 2021, has only attracted about two or three vendors as of June 2021. Over 700 roadside vendors whom the government initially targeted still operate from their old makeshift stalls and markets adjacent to the new market, reflecting contradictory urban futures and logics of infrastructure development.

Source: Prince Guma

ordering, smooth-functioning and completion of regimes; the idea that ambiguities and ambivalences of nonconforming infrastructure systems explain infrastructural failure rather than inherent incompleteness appears to be somewhat exaggerated.

Contradictory logics

Infrastructure projects are not always future-proof or universally explicable, nor completely disciplined to conform to the logics of neoliberalism and apolitical and business-as-usual trajectories (see, for example, Larkin, 2013; Anand et al, 2018). Rather, they are negotiated and translated by different actors and stakeholders, each of whom may possess different interests and gains in the actual process of infrastructure deployment. These may include wealthy global investment funds attempting to shift urban trajectories and expand their own portfolios; private entrepreneurs seeking to create new markets and expand existing ones; corporate elites creating niche opportunities for accumulating wealth through rent seeking and negotiating lucrative deals; local small-scale sojourners eyeing an opportunity to profit on price escalations; strategic politicians eager to reframe and realign their own political agendas; practitioners seeking to realize urban redevelopment, upgrading, renewal and formal service provision; preference-outliers seeking

Figure AW2.3: Material practices of urban life and livelihood

Note: These practices highlight an awareness among residents that to inhabit and navigate cities and infrastructure as incomplete sites is to assert one's right to and claim over the city in profoundly different ways. This is seen here, for example, where residents may use movable, makeshift and incremental technologies like an umbrella, a kiosk or motor vehicle.

Source: Prince Guma

to advance their resistance and specialist claims-making towards new projects; community leaders, representatives and vanguards of social order seeking to play a gatekeeping function; and dissenters reminiscent of the destabilizing effects of the modes of extraction exercised by big corporations upon rather than by and through the citizens.

Yet beyond these actors and stakeholders, it is also important to consider the role of urban populations in shaping the eventual development of urban infrastructure. Urban populations might insert themselves, or they may be conscripted at various points as an outcome of the involvement of various publics by 'experts' along the way. They are thus not to be perceived as passive recipients at the receiving end, but rather active participants and citizens constantly making claims and from within themselves, seeking solutions to the flawed, the imprecise, the imperfect and the inadequate by seeing them simply as half built, incomplete, open-ended, and therefore to be improved, improvised, repaired, repurposed and adapted (see Figures AW2.1, AW2.2 and AW2.3). Thus, they open infrastructures up to different passages and possibilities, revealing infrastructures to be neither static, immobile nor closed-ended, but as domains that are subject to residents' inclination for keeping things incomplete. In their unscripted ways, they lead infrastructure to attain new meanings (Simone, 2004, 2016). They employ tactics that derive from their own situated and ordinary ways of life. Here, urban populations fashion infrastructures in ways that may appear to sidestep the precincts of hegemonic processes of city making (see, for example, Guma, 2021). They open up urban infrastructures through modifications, so much so that their growth and development may appear to deviate from the official and institutionalized modes dominated by technical experts and professionals.

Therefore, different actors and stakeholders, through their strategic interests and speculations, undergird the interface of global networks as Silver and Wiig indicate in their chapter. Such processes may demonstrate how urban infrastructures become deliberate projects of actors and institutions seeking to ensure financial and structural dependencies on projects that are not quite finished. Here, processes of design, deployment and consumption or use easily become deliberate and continuous processes for those involved over time to ensure ongoing financial and structural dependencies from the project's incompleteness. Such articulations reveal infrastructures as sociotechnical constellations supported by different actors, stakeholders and their varied agendas that in due course become the reason that infrastructures become and remain incomplete. They reflect how different junctures and dynamics of infrastructure design, deployment and appropriation demonstrate non-linear trajectories and multiple temporalities of infrastructure development.

Contradicting logics explain the reality in which infrastructure projects become sites of constant remaking, in which the different actors and stakeholders themselves in one way or another may actively contribute to keeping a project in a continuously incomplete and unfinished state (Carse and Kneas, 2019; Guma, 2022b). Take, for example, system developers who may build technologies not from scratch but from indications and technologies of what already exists, deliberately keeping the technology in a sustained form of incompleteness; under constant maintenance and repair – not because it is broken or ineffective, but because it is acknowledged by them as incomplete. Here, technology developers may create and maintain continuous materialities of incompleteness, where a technology is not necessarily viewed as an end goal or its design an ultimate standard, but rather as one constantly in the making (Guma, 2020); where its incompleteness is in fact a normal, acceptable and even inevitable condition of its materiality.

Ultimately, these articulations serve as a reminder that despite their linear motives, urban infrastructures are not always future-proof or universally explicable. In other words, they are not completely disciplined to conform to the logics of neoliberalism's purportedly apolitical and business-as-usual trajectories. Rather, they are negotiated and translated by situated actors and citizens, some of whom pursue alternative forms of inclusion, participation and engagement. Incomplete infrastructures persist at the interstices or in suspended form of constant maintenance, caretaking and repair not because they are viewed as broken or ineffective, but because they are ultimately acknowledged by their users and developers alike as incomplete.

Incomplete futures

Infrastructure domains are constant works in progress (Guma, 2022b). They are neither static, closed nor foreclosed systems. For instance, some may last only a short time before yielding to ephemerality – albeit not disappearing completely, but rather creating possibilities and leading to different forms by providing life to new and emergent regimes of urban life. Some infrastructures may be contingent on surroundings that open infrastructure up to new possibilities, reflecting the nature in which infrastructures are constantly shifting, mutating and always in transition (Guma, 2022b). In this instance, infrastructures are not to be defined by imposed or inflicted voids in light of inevitable risks but rather by their persistence and perseverance – as the chapters by Bigger and Millington and Usher might demonstrate. In other words, infrastructures are to be defined through their continuous development and progression – that is, where their continuity becomes indicative of a refusal to actually stop. It is this refusal that aptly defines infrastructure systems in transition. Where they may be incomplete not because of what is 'missing' or 'lacking' but because in reality, they are always and constantly in the making.

Furthermore, it is important to note that infrastructure domains everywhere are not only always bound to acquire accretions and surface irregularities, but also bound to be sabotaged, destroyed and may become worn. They may rust, leak, crack and corrode with time. And sometimes they may diverge or break down. The point here is that all infrastructures require continual maintenance, repair and reconstruction given their incomplete futures – especially as there is no material or certain endpoint to them as they are never fully completed. However, it is at the same time imperative to transcend the tendency to explicitly disparage infrastructures that fail to yield or conform to the singularity, dominancy and universality of this frame as failed, broken or lying outside of the norm (that is, Figure AW2.3). Infrastructure domains in different places are inherently different, incomplete and contested since as Sheller argues in Chapter 5, they do not enter people's lives as a 'black box' and 'neutral set', but are affected by a wide array of social, economic and political actors and stakeholders.

Considering infrastructural incompleteness is therefore important for comprehending infrastructure developments beyond monolithic, dualistic and negativist frames and predispositions that render infrastructures as 'incomplete' only when they (or their services) fail to keep up with the changing demands and needs. It is conceptually innovative in attempting to counter completist pursuits in the study of infrastructure, as well as to question the privileging and dominancy of singular accounts, and the universality of networked infrastructure. As such, incompleteness recognizes that different infrastructures within their different contexts will always tend to function in different and multifarious ways, sometimes diverging from so-called norms and ideals.

Seeing through infrastructure's incomplete futures provides a productive reading of infrastructure as relational, and infrastructure development as a process that is not affected solely by neoliberal interventions, but also by situated socio-material practices. This lens offers an invitation for us to go beyond analyses that view institutional, well-structured and distinct prescriptions and instruments as the driving force of urbanization and technology development. Thus, it opens up further room for novel ways of seeing infrastructure in cities beyond conventional and completist frames. In so doing, this lens invites us to draw direct attention to realities in which the growth and development of urban infrastructure may not always be clearly neat but often uncertain, entailing complex, contingent and heterogeneous elements and effects. It allows a proper grasp of contingent and place-based articulations of urban infrastructures whose growth and development, while banal, ordinary, deviant and divergent, are not to be read as synonymous with failure, incompetence, incoherence and inadequacy.

In summation, acknowledgement of infrastructural futures as incomplete is important as it highlights the constantly shifting and mutating nature of domains across time and space. It highlights the true nature of infrastructure domains as always in the making, requiring constant repair and maintenance. It draws us to continuous processes through which technology users and developers alike are constantly patching things up, piece by piece, through incremental innovation and modification. Acknowledgement of infrastructural futures highlights the nature in which technological infrastructures are transient, evolving and contingent, which invites us to focus attention away from the failures and limits of infrastructures, towards a less teleological approach to the study of infrastructure development. It is integral for provoking critical engagement with broader infrastructure debates (see, for example, Star, 2002; Larkin, 2013; Simone, 2016; Anand et al, 2018; Carse and Kneas, 2019; Guma, 2020).

In dealing with urban infrastructures, it is important to revisit the qualifiers of 'the ideal', recognizing that it might be pointless to strive for a singular modality. All infrastructures in their varied forms as highlighted in the chapters of this book are most likely to evolve in non-linear and complex, or even messy and dispersive ways, counter to the prevailing neoliberally informed norms and standards. Infrastructures ought not to be understood through static and techno-utopian and deterministic descriptions, but through more critical conceptions that problematize infrastructures as paradigms open to interpretation beyond stereotypically top-down, neoliberal and repressive models of infrastructure towards more located, dynamic and inclusive models.

Theoretically, this calls for the need to consider incomplete futures of urban infrastructure in transition. It calls for the provincializing of urban and infrastructure studies beyond pejorative, utopian and teleological framings, pursuits and fixations, and to transcend old classifications, categories and schemas by which to understand urban complexity and elusive infrastructural progressions. It calls for a more concerted effort to better understand evolving and variegated articulations of infrastructure arrangements. This focus is imperative as it sets us back to the foundational question of teleology within infrastructure studies, particularly concerning what it means for an infrastructure in transition to be 'complete' (see, for example, Guma, 2020, 2022b).

Infrastructure systems are best comprehended through their numerous and ever-changing natures. They ought not to be rendered as 'incomplete' only when they (or their services) fail to keep up with the changing demands and needs. They are best understood when one moves beyond minimalist accounts and acknowledges infrastructure futures as incomplete, where infrastructure and the future are intricately interwoven, coexistent and co-constituted within the web of incompleteness. Thus, there ought not be artificial distinctions construed between infrastructure and the future but, rather, whatever future is being prefigured and made more likely is in part shaped by the infrastructure that emerges, and how it emerges and evolves.

Hence, further research needs to advance appropriate vocabularies that seek a more nuanced understanding of urban and infrastructural temporalities and dynamics that shape city lives and realities within situated settings. Starting points for future work would be to employ different optics that transcend one-size-fits-all frameworks and methodologies to those that attend to idiosyncrasies and context-specificities of new infrastructures; to produce knowledge within the wider collective wheel of knowledge production that speaks to everyday-lived realities; and that consider incomplete infrastructures in and of themselves as knowledge reservoirs with the ability to provoke a revisiting and expansion of our understanding of urban infrastructural futures and imaginaries.

Methodologically, it is important to critique the stereotypically top-down and technocratic infrastructure development projects within the urban environments in which they are deployed and shaped by varied, 'ordinary' facets and routinized place-based practices. This requires urban scholars to be more propositional. It requires them to be more open to other forms of articulation, and in so doing recognize the molecular details of everyday life. Moreover, it calls for developing unexpected comparisons that problematize how urban change and the possibilities of infrastructure futures have, of late, been conceived within the flows of ideas in urban studies in a postcolonial world; employing a mode of theorization that pays analytical attention to the infrastructural geographies of 'ordinary cities' thinking cities through elsewhere (rather than the paradigmatic cities of urban studies); and employing a relational approach to urbanization to understand, via grounded, participatory and embedded methods that incorporate everyday, unequal experiences and urbanisms of infrastructure. In so doing, scholars can open up space for alternative conceptions that illuminate how cities produce novel forms of urbanism and infrastructure futures that exceed what might tend to be – at any given time – the most dominant and hegemonic forms and articulations.

References

Anand, N., Gupta, A. and Appel, H. (eds) (2018) *The Promise of Infrastructure*, Durham, NC: Duke University Press.

Carse, A. and Kneas, D. (2019) 'Unbuilt and unfinished: the temporalities of infrastructure', *Environment and Society*, 10(1): 9–28.

Guma, P.K. (2020) 'Incompleteness of urban infrastructures in transition: scenarios from the mobile age in Nairobi', *Social Studies of Science*, 50(5): 728–50.

Guma, P.K. (2021) *Rethinking Smart Urbanism: City-Making and the Spread of Digital Infrastructures in Nairobi*, Utrecht: Eburon Academic.

Guma, P.K. (2022a) 'On tackling infrastructure: the need to learn from marginal cities and populations in the Global South', *Journal of the British Academy*, 10: 29–37.

Guma, P.K. (2022b) 'The temporal incompleteness of infrastructure and the urban', *Journal of Urban Technology*, 29(1): 59–67.

Larkin, B. (2013) 'The politics and poetics of infrastructure', *Annual Review of Anthropology*, 42(1): 327–43.

Simone, A. (2004) 'People as infrastructure: intersecting fragments in Johannesburg', *Public Culture*, 16(3): 407–29.

Simone, A. (2016) 'Passing things along: (in)completing infrastructure', *New Diversities*, 17(2): 151–62.

Star, S.L. (1999) 'The ethnography of infrastructure', *American behavioral scientist*, 43(3): 377–391.

Star, S.L. (2002) 'Infrastructure and ethnographic practice: working on the fringes', *Scandinavian Journal of Information Systems*, 14(2): art 6. Available from: https://aisel.aisnet.org/sjis/vol14/iss2/6/.

Index

References to figures appear in *italic* type; those in **bold** type refer to tables.

209

INFRASTRUCTURING URBAN FUTURES

water management devices (WMDs) 55–8, *56*
water quality *see* sewerage systems
water remunicipalization 130–1
water shortages 43, 44, 52–4, 57, 124
water supply/access
  Cape Town, South Africa 52–8, *53–4, 56–7*
  cost of 53–5, 56–8, 92–3
  green bonds 55–8
  and inequalities 52–9
  non-payment of bills 124–5
  patchwork concept 89
  post-earthquake Haiti *92*, 92–3
  regionalizing infrastructural lives 190–1
  remunicipalization of 130–1
  shortages 43, 44, 52–4, 57, 124
  water management devices (WMDs 55–8, *56*
  see also sewerage systems

Watt, P. 164
Western Power 72, 74, 75
White, D.F. 69, 71
White flight 5
Whitstable Bluetits 123
Wiig, A. 138, 139
Wilbert, C. 69, 71
Wild Justice 129
wild swimming 122–4
Windrush Against Sewage Pollution (WASP) 127, 129
World Smart Cities Award 3–4
Wright, H. 140, 141

Y

Yates, J.S. 56, 57
Yorkshire Water 122